POSTMODERNISM—
PHILOSOPHY AND
THE ARTS

CONTINENTAL PHILOSOPHY III

POSTMODERNISM— PHILOSOPHY AND THE ARTS

Edited by Hugh J. Silverman

ROUTLEDGE
NEW YORK AND LONDON

Published in 1990 by

Routledge
an imprint of Routledge, Chapman and Hall, Inc.
29 West 35th Street
New York, NY 10001

Published in Great Britain by

Routledge
11 New Fetter Lane
London EC4P 4EE

Library of Congress Cataloging in Publication Data

Postmodernism: philosophy and the arts / edited by Hugh J. Silverman.
    p.   cm.—(Continental philosophy; 3)
  Bibliography: p.
  ISBN 0-415-90193-6; ISBN 0-415-90194-4 (pbk.)
  1. Postmodernism. 2. Arts—Philosophy. I. Silverman, Hugh J.
II. Series.
B831.2.P68 1989
700'.1—dc20   89-8745

British Library Cataloguing in Publication Data also available

CONTENTS

CONTENTS

Notes

Bibliography

POSTMODERNISM
Hélène Volat-Shapiro

Notes on Contributors

INTRODUCTION:
THE PHILOSOPHY OF
POSTMODERNISM

Hugh J. Silverman

Postmodernism has no special place of origin. The meaning and function of postmodernism is to operate at places of closure, at the limits of modernist productions and practices, at the margins of what proclaims itself to be new and a break with tradition, and at the multiple edges of these claims to self-consciousness and auto-reflection. Postmodernism is not as such a new style of creating artworks, of synthesizing novel self-expressions, and of justifying theoretically its aesthetic practices. Postmodernism does not open up a new field of artistic, philosophical, cultural, or even institutional activities. Its very significance is to marginalize, delimit, disseminate, and decenter the primary (and often secondary) works of modernist and premodernist cultural inscriptions.

Postmodernist thinking offers to re-read the very texts and traditions that have made premodernist and modernist writing possible—but above all it offers a reinscription of those very texts and traditions by examining the respects in which they set limits to their own enterprises, in which they incorporate other texts and traditions in a juxtapositional and intertextual relation to themselves. Postmodernist thinking involves rethinking—finding the places of difference within texts and institutions, examining the inscriptions of indecidability, noting the dispersal of signification, identity, and centered unity across a plurivalent texture of epistemological and metaphysical knowledge production.

Postmodernism brings the modernist hegemony to closure. It examines the ends, goals, hopes of modernist activity, situating it in its context of premodernist frameworks. However, just as the post-impressionism of Van Gogh and Cézanne was not an *attack upon and rejection of* the impressionism of Monet, Renoir, Manet, Degas, and Pissarro, so too postmodernism is not a simple refusal to accept modernist principles and perspectives. Rather postmodernism extends but also brings to a close the fundamental tenets and activities of a modernist outlook. This means that the lines of demarcation between modernism and postmodernism are not well-defined. A region of indeterminateness prevails such that although the Joyce of *Portrait of the Artist as a Young Man* and *Ulysses*, along with Virginia Woolf's *Mrs. Dalloway* and *To the Lighthouse*, Proust's *Remembrance of Things Past*, and Kafka's *The Trial*, are major documents of modernist literary production, Joyce's *Finnegans Wake* along with Robbe-Grillet's *Jealousy*, Beckett's *Malone Dies* and *The Unnameable*, and Borges's *Fictions* take on features of a postmodern textual practice. Indeed to be able to identify particular literary works as postmodernist as opposed to modernist is itself the kind of enterprise invoked by the modernist critic seeking to distinguish modernism from romanticism (just as romantics were set off against—and set themselves off against—those of the classical style). But postmodernism in fiction, for instance, is not the successor to modernism—rather it is modernism taken to its extremes. Postmodernism signals the end of what has become commonplace and ordinary in the modernist outlook. Postmodernist literary practice operates at the edge of the modernist manner.

To be modern is to break with tradition, to interrupt the endless reiteration of classical themes, topics, and myths, to become self-consciously new, to attend to the *modes* of the times, to offer a critique of the conditions of one's own culture and society, to represent reality—not as it is—objectively and devoid of evaluation, but rather as it is *experienced*—subjectively and with the transcendental or critical consciousness available especially to the artist. To be modern is to "break with the past" and to "search for new self-conscious expressive forms." Whether the "new self-expressive forms" are abstract like those of Kandinsky and Pollock, or geometrical like those of Mondrian and Josef Albers, or alienated like those of Edvard Munch and Max Beckmann, or fanciful like those of Giacometti and Paul Klee, they all give shape to the concept of modern art. The modern artist claims to take a privileged view of the social and psychological concerns of the day. Modern man and modern woman are plagued with uncertainties, despair, bureaucratization, and mechanization. Their concern is how to cope with such solidifications and preoccupations of modern times—the Charlie Chaplin film whose title gave a name to Sartre's new journal in 1945 is but a caricature of the modern condition. And the modern artist has an interior consciousness that knows how to express the realities of industrial society. Critics and professors of art or literature extol the virtues of the modern artist; they praise his or her abilities to perceive better than the rest of us; and they look to the artist for guidance as to how to articulate (if not diagnose or cure) the modern predicament. But the *postmodern* artist has no such privileged status. The postmodern artist is on the margins of things in such a way that it is not the artist who counts but rather the paintings and inscriptions themselves. And these texts and performances achieve their significance and value in their intertextual relations with other texts and performances. The postmodernist text *is* by its difference from other productions—including critical writings and alternate aesthetic or cultural genres.

The modern music of Schönberg, Bartok, Weber, and, in a different way, Stravinsky, offers a radical break with the classical styles of Bach, Beethoven, and Brahms. Where the romantic expressions of Berlioz and Mahler gave something other than the prior classical styles, they nevertheless could not be considered sufficiently radical, sufficiently modern, to be "a true break" with tradition. When Wagner introduced his music dramas, he brought together many different art forms. Although the medieval *Nibelungenlied* was the basis for his Ring cycle, just as the Romantic poets latched onto Macpherson's (imaginary and mythical sixth-century) Ossian for their inspiration, Wagner created what was hailed by Verlaine and others as *definitely* modern. Certainly he was not providing the sort of operatic work that Rossini, Mozart, Puccini, or even Verdi offered. Here was something solidly new, unquestionably modern, very much *à la mode*, praised not only by the *Revue Wagnerienne* but also by Nietzsche's 1872 *The Birth of Tragedy out of the Spirit of Music*. Nietzsche's disappointment—as elaborated later in *The Case of Wagner* (1888)—was indicative of the self-delimitation of Wagnerian modernism. But Nietzsche—identified by Michel Foucault in

3

1966 as a threshold figure, along with Mallarmé—was himself a spokesman for the postmodernism that had come too early, before its time, *avant la lettre*. Nietzsche's ultimate turn—away from Wagner, his view that Wagnerism was not, after all, the proper work of *his* "philosopher" Dionysus—was an early inscription of modernism's self-circumscription. But postmodernism has no place of origin—it can inscribe itself in different places, at various limit points—and Nietzsche's rereading of Wagner is only one such locus.

But what is *postmodernist thinking*? Philosophers are wont to cite Bacon and Galileo, Descartes and Malebranche, as the beginnings of modern thought. The idea that man can be an "interpreter of nature" (Bacon) or an observer of the universe through an instrument such as the telescope (Galileo), that one can reshape and control the world through science—inaugurates the "modern" world view. Descartes's further specification of the self or subject as able to distrust bodies and extended substances, as a thinking substance whose existence can be affirmed by a clear and distinct idea of its own activity, as offering a set of rules for directing the mind—these are all proclaimed to be distinctively "modern." Although not engaged *as such* in the *querelle des anciens et des modernes* (which Boileau and other seventeenth-century critics ascribed to their new writers), Descartes nevertheless asserted his rejection of the scholastic style of philosophizing. Thus while literary debates of the seventeenth and eighteenth centuries—in France for instance—focused on the dispute between the ancients and the moderns, philosophers set the so-called modernist views of rationalism and empiricism into motion. The dichotomy between the philosophical claim that Descartes, Hume, and Kant are modern philosophers while literary scholars proclaim Joyce, Woolf, Proust, and Kafka as modern is only one indication of the effects of discipline segregation. But that Molière, La Rochefoucauld, and Fontenelle are sometimes called "modern" suggests that even among literary disciplines the extent of cooperation in naming is not very significant. Similarly, modern *art* is clearly post-romantic or more definitively post-post-impressionist, namely futurist, fauvist, abstract expressionist, cubist, surrealist, dadaist, and so forth.

While the arts do not correspond with respect to what counts as modern, where philosophy interprets itself as modern since

4

the late Renaissance, what is to be said of nineteenth-century philosophy? Surely Hegel, Marx, Mill, and Comte are also modern—but they are modern with a twist, or several twists. Dialectic, the utilitarian principle, and positivism give a new look to the Kantian critical philosophy. So if rationalism, empiricism, critical philosophy, dialecticism, utilitarianism, Marxism, and Comtean positivism are all "modern" philosophies, then what sense does modernist thinking have? And in what respect can it be said that modernist thinking—when self-delimited—establishes the condition for a postmodernist position? If it can be said—as I shall here—that postmodernist thinking *enframes, circumscribes*, and *delimits* modernist thinking, then where are the places in which modernism in philosophy comes to an end? This closure occurs in many places and in many different ways. Postmodernism enframes modernism without identity or unity. It is fragmented, discontinuous, multiple, and dispersed. Where modernism asserts centering, focusing, continuity—once the break with tradition has already occurred—postmodernism decenters, enframes, discontinues, and fragments the prevalence of modernist ideals. But this self-delimitation does not occur all at once. Indeed, the coordinate philosophical practices of the early twentieth century reaffirm, reconstruct, and then set the stage for their own self-circumscription. The determination of the ends of metaphysics and the paths of thinking is also the framework for the closure of modernism.

Concomitant with—and perhaps even antecedent to—the reign of twentieth-century modernist writers like Joyce, Woolf, Proust, and Kafka, certain philosophies of consciousness achieve dominance in a variety of different contexts. In concert with William James's characterization of lived time as a "stream of consciousness," and Husserl's "phenomenology of internal time-consciousness," Freud developed a view of the psychic realm which is comprised both of consciousness and of unconscious fields. Each of these philosophies of consciousness is also a theory of self-consciousness and self-reflection. The Kierkegaardian call to individual subjectivity is defined by James, Bergson, Husserl, and Freud as a field available for scrutiny, investigation, and detailed inventory. One can examine one's own field of consciousness and describe, both temporally and spatially, the flow of conscious experience as distinct from the objective, em-

5

pirical data of the external world. But not that many philosophers of the twentieth century were favorably disposed to the idea of a "ghost in the machine" (as Ryle, in 1949, called it). Wittgenstein (in his earlier incarnation) wanted to remain silent about such matters. And Sartre (1936) discovered that the transcendental ego, which Husserl so steadfastly maintained (phenomenologically) at the heart of conscious life, could not be found—at least not *in* consciousness. For Sartre the ego was an object of consciousness, out there in the world, available for investigation just like any other thing. Consciousness, for Sartre (1943), was at best not anything at all, only pure freedom without any content. So along with the development of a modernist theory of self-consciousness, there are also the very seeds of its demise—in Ryle, in Sartre, and in Heidegger.

Heidegger does not provide the closure that the postmodernist will want to call for. Lacan and Derrida—to name some notable signatures—take the circumscription to its further stages of development. Heidegger's way is to call for the end of philosophy (1961, 1966). Once philosophy sets its own limits, rereads its traditions from the time of the Greeks, it can demarcate what it would be for philosophy to accomplish the tasks it sets out for itself. If philosophy could achieve, through its acts of interpretation, an understanding of philosophical writers who sought to account for the essence of truth, the disclosure of truth, the uncovering of what has remained hidden over the centuries, then the path of thinking might become evident. Hegel had proclaimed that one could bring about the end of philosophy. Philosophy could bring its own activity to absolute knowledge— the full and complete synthesis would thereby be achieved. The *telos* or goal of philosophy would be the finalization of the movement toward the place where all knowledge is encompassed by its own activity. Heidegger sought to find the place at the end of philosophy where thinking might happen. But thinking can occur only where there is a place for the disclosure of truth. For Heidegger, truth can be disclosed only where difference is located. This difference is the ontico-ontological difference where (in his 1927 version) *Dasein* is interpretation and where (in the 1950s) language speaks.

Heidegger marks the shift from a theory of consciousness and self-consciousness to a theory of language. Sartre has no place for language until the late 1940s and 1950s. Merleau-Ponty had already spoken of the embodied and gestural expression of language in his *Phenomenology of Perception* (1945), but in the late 1940s, when he began to read (and lecture on) Saussure, he incorporated the idea of a "spoken speech" and a "speaking speech" as a sign. With Merleau-Ponty, the language of the speaking subject is the elaboration of an embodied sign system. But Merleau-Ponty's phenomenology of language is not yet a theory of textuality. When Roland Barthes (1953) provides a critique of Sartre's concept of literature (1947), he sets forth a theory of writing *at degree zero*, i.e., no longer wrapped up in a complex discourse of subjectivity and authorship. Barthes proposes a theory of writing as revolutionary and yet nonhistoricist, a theory of writing which is informed by style and period but not tied down or limited to them. When Barthes later moves to a theory of the text (in the 1970s with *The Pleasure of the Text*, for instance), he sets the stage for a postmodernist theory of textuality—differential, scriptive, and semiotic—which also marks in turn the writings of Derrida, Deleuze, and Kristeva. And these are just some of the names that will figure largely in this and other volumes in the *Continental Philosophy* series.

Furthermore the essays in this third volume of the series address the very question of the limitations and delimitations that postmodernism marks out. The volume itself is organized into two unequal sections. The first raises some general theoretical questions about postmodernism—"Problematics" as we call them here—while the second attends to particular "Sites," namely the various arts themselves (and the philosophical reading of them). In the first part, such themes as the "time of postmodernism" (Taylor), the "language of postmodernism" (Scott), the "contradictory character of postmodernism" (Kuspit), and the "politics of postmodernism" (O'Neill) are each taken up in turn and given special attention. The various inroads offered in the first part open up spaces of discourse rather than foreclosing further consideration.

In the second part, particular "sites," as Roland Barthes might have called them, are identified and elaborated in considerable detail. Here one finds specific readings of "architecture" (Watson), "painting" (Olkowski), "literature" (Bruns), "theatre" (Mc-Glynn), "photography" (Weiss), "film" (Wurzer and Silverman), "television" (Seitz), "dance" (Levin), and "fashion" (Faurschou). While each elaboration is different, some common themes recur. Matters of alterity, inscription, difference, discourse, and desire—to name a few—are repeated in each site.

The contributors to this volume are themselves incorporated into the whole enterprise. Some are well-known names from a variety of disciplines, including Donald Kuspit from the art criticism world, Mark Taylor from the domain of a/theology, Charles Scott, Wilhelm Wurzer, and David Michael Levin from among the postmodernist postphenomenologists, John O'Neill from radical theoretical sociology, and Gerald Bruns from the hermeneutical literary theorists. And while this list is not exhaustive of those who have contributed to the volume, the essays of the others will speak for themselves and for their relation to official philosophical practice. All of the contributors to this volume operate in relation to some important dimension of continental philosophy and its contemporary context.

While the postmodern debate operates in many corners of current intellectual spaces, the November 6th, 1988, front-page *New York Times Book Review* article by Todd Gitlin (entitled "Hip-Deep in Post-modernism") marks the significance that this set of concerns has achieved. And while Gitlin waxes eloquent when he claims that "post-modernism is more than a buzzword or even an esthetic," and when he goes on to affirm that it is "a way of seeing, a view of the human spirit and an attitude toward political as well as cultural possibilities," he is nevertheless opening up the frame for further consideration of its indifferences, discontinuities, splicings, surface-plays, self-decenterings, and dispersals. The essays in this volume of *CP* come at these multiplicities in order to articulate their diversity and to give a sense of the postmodernist frame.

As to the crafting of the volume itself, the work of the assistant editors is especially important. The series could not succeed without their devotion and commitment to seeing it through. The original trio of J Barry, James Hatley, and Brian Seitz have begun to establish their own names in concert with the growth of *CP*. James Clarke, who joined us in the fall of 1987, devoted endless hours helping to bring this volume to fruition—most notably while the editor was teaching at the University of Leeds (England) throughout the spring of 1988 and while he was conducting research in Vienna during the subsequent summer. And although their names do not appear yet on the editorial page, Nina Belmonte and Jeff Gaines have already put in their share of hours, thought, and energy to the *CP* project, including this very volume. The editor cannot overstate his appreciation for the extensive contribution of all the assistant editors. And of the associate editors, the contributions of Forrest Williams and Stephen Watson are also gratefully acknowledged. While Watson offers an essay for this volume, the work of Forrest Williams behind the scenes is equally valuable. The Philosophy Department at SUNY/Stony Brook continues to provide xerox facilities and we are glad to express our gratitude for this not insignificant contribution.

The encouragement of Stratford Caldecott of Routledge has been immeasurable. Now that he has left the company, he will be sorely missed by those of us who benefited from his wisdom and good judgment. If *CP-III* were to be dedicated to anyone, it should surely be Stratford—in profound appreciation. In the wake of his departure, we are fortunate to have the interest, support, and growing commitment of Maureen MacGrogan who has followed the series for the last couple of years from the New York office. We are delighted that she will be working with us in the future.

CP is also its readers as well as its contributors. We hope that they will increase in number and that this volume will entice others to join in. *CP* readers make the series come alive—indeed offer it the *site* that matters. To the company of those already incorporated, we are glad for their support. To those who are new to it we offer our warm welcome.

Hugh J. Silverman, *Editor*

PART I
PROBLEMATICS

Chapter 1

BACK TO THE FUTURE

Mark C. Taylor

I The return of time

He was locked in combat with something inaccessible,
foreign, something of which he could say: That does not
exist . . . and which nevertheless filled him with terror as
he sensed it wandering [*errer*] about in the region of his
solitude. Having stayed up all night and all day with this
being, as he tried to rest, he was suddenly made aware
that an other had replaced the first, just as inaccessible and
just as obscure, and yet different. It was a modulation of
that which did not exist, a different mode of being absent,
another void in which he was coming to life. Now it was
certain, something was approaching him, standing not
nowhere and everywhere, but a few feet away, invisible.
. . . He felt ever closer to an ever more monstrous absence
that took an infinite time to meet. He felt it closer to him
every instant and kept ahead of it by an infinitely small but
irreducible splinter of duration.[1]

Modernism . . . Postmodernism. What *is* the difference? The
difference might involve the question of difference itself. The
question of difference, however, is inseparable from the question
of presence or, more precisely, the question of the possibility or
impossibility of presence. To interrogate presence is to question
both space and time. To think difference—the difference that
marks the margin *between* modernism and postmodernism, it is
necessary to refigure space by imagining time without presence.
Time that lacks the present implies a space that is never present
(though it is not simply absent). The space of postmodernism is
"the becoming-time of space and the becoming-space of time."[2]

As Thomas the Obscure suggests, to approach this uncanny non-place, one must err back to the future.

How can the timely spacing of a present that is never present be thought? By following the trace of Maurice Blanchot's "*différence*," which is the little-known precursor of Jacques Derrida's "*différance*," the becoming-time of space and the becoming-space of time can be thought by rethinking Nietzsche's eternal return. If modern philosophy "ends" with the arrival of Hegel, postmodern non-philosophy "begins" with the return of Nietzsche. Nietzsche's return is, impossibly, always already before Hegel's arrival.

> Nietzsche (if his name serves to name the law of the Eternal Return) and Hegel (if his name invites thought concerning presence as all and the all as presence) permit us to sketch out a mythology: Nietzsche can only come near Hegel, but it is always before and always after Hegel that he comes and comes again. Before: because, while thought of as absolute, presence has never reassembled within the accomplished totality of knowledge; presence knows itself to be absolute, but its knowledge remains a relative knowledge since it is not carried out in practice, and thus it knows itself only as a present that is not practically satisfied, not reconciled with presence as all: thus Hegel is still only a pseudo-Hegel. And Nietzsche always comes after, because the law that he bears presumes the accomplishment of time as present and, in this accomplishment, presumes its absolute destruction, so that thus the Eternal Return, affirming the future and the past as sole temporal instances and as identical, unrelated instances, freeing the future of all present and the past of all presence, shatters thought until this infinite affirmation will return infinitely in the future to that which under no form and in no time would know how to be present, just as that which, past and never having belonged in any form to the present, reverts infinitely to the past.[3]

Coming *after* Hegel, Nietzsche exposes the immemorial *before* that the System is constructed to recollect. This unrepresentable *anarchie*, which is always (the) outside of thought, is nonetheless thought in what Blanchot labels the "non-conceptualizable concept" of the Eternal Return. "The 're' of the return inscribes as 'ex,' opening of all exteriority: as if the return, far from putting an end to it, marks exile, the commencement in its recommencement of exodus. To return, that would be to return again to ex-centering oneself, to erring. Only the *nomadic* affirmation *remains*" (*PA*, p. 49). When re-turn is eternal, the ex-teriority, ex-centricity, ex-ile, ex-odus, ex-cess, ex-position, and ex-pense of erring are unavoidable.

Considered in relation to other interpretations of Nietzsche, Blanchot's account of the Eternal Return is undeniably backwards. For most commentators, the horror of the Eternal Return grows out of the prospect of an endless recurrence of what is present here and now. Blanchot, by contrast, does not interpret the future as a re-presentation of the present but reads the future in the past and the past in the future in order to approach the present by way of the detour through past and future. If return is eternal, it will not only never end but it never began in the first place.[4] In the absence of any true origin, nothing is original, which is not to imply that the origin is merely nothing. When nothing is original, (*le*) *tout* is secondary. If, however, all is secondary, something is always missing and everything is always lacking. To think this "lack [*manque*]" is, for Blanchot, to think what Western philosophy has left unthought.

That which is always already missing is a past that is "infinitely past" because it was never present in the first place. What has not been present cannot be re-presented. In Blanchot's rereading of Nietzsche's Eternal Return, the irreducible anteriority of the past repeatedly recurs as "the terrifyingly ancient [*l'effroyablement ancien*]" that is not subject to *Er-inner-ung*. Since the absolutely ancient can be neither re-collect-ed nor re-member-ed, it is irrevocable.

> The irrevocable is thus not at all or not only the fact that what has taken place has taken place forever; that is perhaps the means—strange, I admit—for the past to warn us (while sparing us) that it is the void and that the falling due [*echéance*]—the infinite, fragile fall—that it designates, this pit [*puits*], is the depth of that which is without bottom. It is irrevocable, indelible, yes: ineffaceable, but because nothing is inscribed there (*PA*, p. 24).

"*Le vide du puits, la profondeur de ce qui est sans fond*": the void of the pit, the depth of that which is without bottom is *la tombe* marking *le non-lieu* where (the) all falls [*tombe*]. *L'espacement* of this *tombe* is a time without present. The Not [*Le Pas*] of this strange space-time is *le pas au-delà*.

> Time, time: the step/not beyond [*le pas au-delà*], which is not accomplished in time, would lead outside of time, without this outside being timeless, but there where time would fall, fragile fall, according to this "outside of time in time" toward which writing [*écrire*] would draw us, if it were permitted of us, vanished from us, from writing the secret of the ancient fear (*PA*, p. 8).

Since the "outside of time in time" is never made present, the *tombe* remains—remains empty. *Le reste* of the empty *tombe* is *le puits* surrounded but not contained by the pyramid.[5]

The writing *covering* the pyramid is hieroglyphic. The message re-turned from the desert of Egypt by the latter-day Moses is that hieroglyphs are images—the images of desire that are the non-stuff of which dreams are made. The terrifyingly ancient never actually appears; it only reappears as the dream of the "is" that is not, and the Not that "is." The presence of this dream is the dream of the present in which presence appears but a phantasm. Nietzsche's immemorial law "suspends or makes disappear every present and all presence"—especially the presence of Hegel (*PA*, p. 26).

> The time of time's absence is not dialectical. In this time what appears is the fact that nothing appears. . . . The reversal which, in the absence of time, constantly sends us back to the presence of absence, but to this presence as absence, to absence as affirmation of itself, an affirmation where nothing is affirmed, where nothing never ceases to affirm itself in the torment of the indefinite—this movement is not dialectical. Contradictions do not exclude each other in it, nor are they reconciled.[6]

In the irreconcilable contradiction of "an outside of time in time," the past for which we long "is" always future and the future we ardently desire "is" always past. In the absence of a past that was never present, the dream of presence returns eternally to create the nightmare of a future that never arrives. If the encounter with the past has never taken place, the past is, paradoxically, always still to come. "*L'avenir*," in other words, is "*à venir*."

> Under the law of the return, where, between past and future nothing joins [*se conjuge*]—how to jump from one to the other, while the rule [of law] does not permit the passage—how would this jump be possible? Past would be the same as future. Thus there would only be one sole modality, or a double modality functioning in such a way that identity, differed or deferred [*différée*], would regulate difference. But such would be the exigency of the return: it is *under a false appearance of the present* that the past-future ambiguity would invisibly separate the future from the past (*PA*, pp. 21–2).

Inasmuch as "the law of the Return" is eternal, it exhibits a ceaseless compulsion to repeat itself. As the play of Freud's Little Hans suggests, the repetition compulsion is tied to death. By repeating the impossibility of presence, the law of Eternal Return implies the inescapability of death. Absolute past and infinite future coincide in the "eternal beginning and eternal end," which is, in Mallarmé's terms, the "Act of Night." The time of this dark act is "Midnight."

> "Certainly a presence of Midnight subsists." But this subsisting presence is not a presence. The substantial present is the negation of the present. It is a vanished present. And Midnight, where first "the absolute present of things" (their unreal essence) gathered itself together, becomes "the dream of a Midnight vanished into itself": it is no longer a present, but the past, symbolized, as is the end of history in Hegel, by a book lying open upon the table. . . . Night is the book: the silence and inaction of a book when, after everything has been proffered, everything returns into the silence that alone speaks—that speaks from the depth of the past and is at the same time the whole future of the word. For the present Midnight, that hour at which the present lacks absolutely, is also the hour in which the past touches and, without the intermediary of any present time, immediately attains the extremity of the

future. And such, as we have seen, is the very instant of death, which is never present, which is the festival of the absolute future, the instant at which one might say that, in a time without present, what has been will be (*SL*, pp. 113–4).

Death is the absolute future in which the absolute past approaches, but only approaches, for death is never present. The time of death and dying "is the abyss of the present, the reign of a time without a present" (*SL*, p. 117). In early as well as late writings, Heidegger argues that to think after the end of philosophy, one must rethink being in terms of time. Time appears radical only in relation to death. *Da-sein*, Heidegger maintains, must be understood as "being-toward-death." To think time as death and death as time is to unthink being by uncovering *fort* in *da* and *Nein* in *Sein*.

Echoing Heidegger, Blanchot stresses the unsettling interplay of time and death. Being, which is never present as such, is a tendency toward *l'avenir*. From this point of view, being is being-toward "the nonarrival of that which comes toward [*advient*]" (*PA*, p. 132). By interpreting the absolute future, which approaches without arriving, in terms of "death and dying [*la mort et mourir*],"[7] Blanchot is led to an unexpected conclusion. If death only approaches, I (or the I) never dies. "One never dies now," Blanchot points out, "one always dies later, in the future [*l'avenir*]—in a future which is never actual, which cannot come except when everything will be over and done. And when everything is accomplished, there will be no more present: the future will again be past" (*SL*, pp. 164–5).[8] Since *la mort* is never present, it (i.e., *elle*) never actually occurs.[9] "Midnight is precisely the hour that does not toll until after the dice are thrown, the hour which has never come, which never comes, the pure, ungraspable future, the hour eternally past" (*SL*, p. 116). If Midnight never strikes, death is impossible. The impossibility of death does not mean that life is eternal. To the contrary, the silence of Midnight is the speechless tolling of *le glas* that echoes in and through all things and every one. The impossibility of death "is" the "non-event" in which the Impossible itself draws near.

The Impossible is a *"non-power* [non-pouvoir] *which is not simply the negation of power.*"[10] As a "non-power or non-ability," the

Impossible is inseparable from a certain impotence.[11] This impotence can never be mastered, accomplished, or achieved, but can only be suffered patiently. For Blanchot, as for Heidegger, that which is beyond being and nonbeing approaches when one "waits for something that will not have taken place" (*PA*, p. 88). What does not take place in this waiting is the *"es"* of *"es gibt"* or the *"il"* of *"il y a."* The gift of *es* or *il* is, in effect, *un coup de don* that faults the subject. Commenting on the radical passivity implied in Emmanuel Levinas's notion of *il-leity*, Blanchot writes:

> Passivity: we can only evoke it by a language that is reversed or overturned. In the past, I appealed to suffering: suffering such as I could not suffer, so that, in this non-power [*non-pouvoir*], the "me," excluded from mastery and from its status as subject in the first person, destitute, desituated, and even disobliged, could lose itself as a me capable of suffering: there is suffering [*il y a souffrance*], there would be suffering, there is no longer a suffering "I", and suffering is not present, is not born (even less lived) in the present, it is without present, as it is without either beginning or end, time has radically changed its meaning.[12]

This suffering is a "catastrophe" for the centered self. To undergo the impossible approach of death is to be ex-*il*-ed from oneself. The proximity of death is "the beyond [*l'au-delà*]" that "is in us in a manner that forever separates us from ourselves."[13] As the outside that is inside, *le pas au-delà* doubles every one/ One. The unmasterable double makes doubting Thomases of us all. The ghostly "twin"[14] is a repetition of the subject that interrupts self-identity.[15] To bear the unavoidable wound of *le coup de don* is to suffer the fate of dispossession. The one who is dispossessed is left to err in the non-place of a desert wilderness and the non-time of an interminable night. Blanchot describes this night as *"Nuit, nuit blanche."*[16] The white noise of this white night is the "murmur" echoing in all of Blanchot's writing. While the philosopher writes to silence this lacerating murmur, the writer writes to let it/*il* re-sound. The murmur of writing is the inhuman cry that eternally returns "in" *l'entretien infini*.

Thus we will choose our ideology. This choice will be the only one that can lead us to a non-ideological writing:

writing outside of language, outside of ideology. Let us call
this choice, without shame, humanist. . . . But what is
"humanism"?[17] In what terms can we define it without
engaging in the logos of a definition? In those terms that
will remove it furthest from a language: the cry (that is to
say the murmur), cry of need or protest, cry without word,
without silence, ignoble cry where, perhaps, the cry writes,
the graffiti of high walls. It is possible, as one likes to state,
that "man passes away." He fades. He even has always
already passed, faded, to the extent that he has always
been suited for [approprié à] his own disappearance. But, in
passing, he cries; he cries in the street, in the desert; he
cries while dying; he does not cry, he is the murmur of the
cry (*EI*, p. 392).

E-cri-ture: le cri écrit et l'écrivain crie.

II   The space of literature

Now, in this night, I come forward bearing everything [*le
tout*], toward that which infinitely exceeds the all. I
progress beyond the totality which I nevertheless tightly
embrace. I go on the margins [*marges*] of the universe,
boldly walking elsewhere than where I can be, and a little
outside my steps. This slight extravagance, this deviation
toward that which cannot be, is not only my own
movement leading me to a personal madness, but the
movement of the reason that I bear within me. With me the
laws gravitate outside the laws, the possible outside the
possible. O night, now nothing will make me be, nothing
will separate me from you. I adhere marvelously to the
simplicity to which you invite me. I lean over you, equal to
you, offering you a mirror for your perfect nothingness
[*néant*], for your shadows that are neither light nor absence
of light, for this void that contemplates. . . . I am the origin
of that which has no origin. I create that which cannot be
created (*TO*, pp. 107–8).

Bearing everything toward that which exceeds the all . . . beyond
the totality . . . on the margins of the universe . . . slight extravagance . . . this deviation toward that which cannot be . . . outside

the laws . . . outside the possible . . . mirror of perfect nothingness . . . the origin of that which has no origin. . . . The "I" of this text is not only the anonymous voice of Thomas the Obscure; it is also art. The origin of that which has no origin is the origin of the work of art. For Blanchot, as for Heidegger, the origin of the work of art is "the intimacy of [the] rent, tear, fissure, cleft [*déchirure*]" (*SL*, pp. 226, 236). To be open *to* this tear is to be opened *by* the work of the work of art. "This experience is," for Blanchot, "the experience of art. Art—as images, as words, and as rhythm—indicates the menacing proximity of a vague and empty outside, a neuter existence, null, without limit, sordid absence, a suffocating condensation where being ceaselessly perpetuates itself as nothingness" (*SL*, pp. 242–3). The excessive *dehors*, which the work of art neither reveals nor conceals, is the terrifyingly ancient. "But where has art led us? To a time before the world, before the beginning. It has cast us out of our power to begin and to end; it has turned us toward the outside without intimacy, without place, without rest. It has led us into the infinite migration of error [*erreur*] . . ." (*SL*, p. 244).

By "returning to a time before the world, before the beginning," art is, in a phrase of Hegel repeated by Blanchot, "a thing of the past." The interpretations of the past of art developed by Hegel and Blanchot differ significantly. According to Hegel, art is past because it has been surpassed in philosophy. What is imperfectly represented in the artistic image is perfectly presented in the philosophical concept. For Blanchot, by contrast, the work of art "is very ancient, terrifyingly ancient, lost in the night of time. It is the origin that always precedes us and is always given before us, for it is the approach of what allows us to depart—a thing of the past, in a different sense from what Hegel said" (*SL*, p. 229). The past of art is not a past present, which can be represented. Rather art is bound to and by the unrepresentable before that is always already past. From this point of view, all art can be interpreted as *"la recherche du temps perdu."* By persisting in quest-ioning, this "re-search" does not end in absolute knowledge but repeatedly "relates to the unknown as unknown" (*EI*, p. 442). Blanchot believes the privileged form of this endless quest is *literature*.

Literature is the work of art when art does not work. "The ideal of literature," Blanchot maintains, "is to say nothing, to speak in order to say nothing." Literature can approach this ideal only through "a strange slipping and sliding [*un glissement étrange*] between being and not being, presence and absence, reality and non-reality."[18] This *glissement* is the impossible pursuit of that which language always excludes.

> Literature, as we discern it, is held apart from every
> excessively strong determination, hence it is repugnant to
> masterpieces and even withdraws from the idea of a work
> [*oeuvre*] to the extent that it makes of it a form of non-work
> [*désoeuvrement*]. Creative, perhaps, but that which it creates
> is always hollow with respect to what is and this hollowing
> produces only what is more slippery, less sure of being,
> and because of that, as though attracted to an other
> measure, that of its unreality where, in the play of infinite
> difference, that which nonetheless affirms itself by
> withdrawing under the veil of the not (*EI*, p. 592).

Never simply work or a work, literature is (a) play—"*le jeu de la différence infini.*" The play of infinite difference, which affirms itself by withdrawing under the veil of the Not, is unspeakable. It/*il* must, therefore, be written.

Writing becomes possible only *after* the work of the author Derrida dubs "the last philosopher of the book."

> The cut [*coupure*] required by writing is a break [*coupure*]
> with thought when thought ascribes to itself immediate
> proximity, a break with all *empirical* experience of the
> world. In this sense, writing is also a rupture with all
> present consciousness, being always already involved in
> the experience of the non-manifest or the unknown
> (understood as the neuter). But let us thus understand why
> the advent of writing would only have been able to take
> place after the completion of discourse (for which Hegel at
> least has shown us a metaphor in absolute knowledge) . . .
> (*EI*, p. 391).

Always arriving late, the "after" of writing repeats the "before" that is forever outside the book. This *dehors* is an *Other* that can neither be sublated nor sublimated. "Writing," Blanchot argues, "is the relation to the *other* of every book, to that which would be de-scription or un-writing [*dé-scription*], a writerly [*scripturaire*] exigency outside discourse, outside language. To write [is to write] at the edge, margin, brink, border, rim, hem [au bord] of the book, outside the book" (*EI*, p. 626). That which is other than the book is not reciprocal or antithetical. Instead of a binary opposite, *l'autre* is "alterity itself [*l'altérité même*]" (*EI*, p. 634). This alterity, which cannot be "taken up into [*aufgehoben, relève*]" any book, is what Blanchot describes as "pure exteriority." "What summons us to write, when the time of the book determined by the beginning-end relation, and the space of the book determined by deployment from a center, cease to impose themselves? The lure of (pure) exteriority" (*EI*, p. 625).

To heed the summons of the outside, to yield to its lure is to approach the approach of the Impossible. In writing, the proximate draws near by forever withdrawing.

> Writing begins only when it is the approach of that point where nothing reveals itself, where, in the bosom [*le sein*] of dissimulation, speaking is still the shadow of speech, a language that is still only its image, an imaginary language' and a language of the imaginary, the one no one speaks, the murmur of the incessant and interminable that one has to *silence* if one wants, at last, to be heard or understood (*SL*, p. 48).

The word, which (impossibly) "reveals" nothing, exposes the "crisis of the word." "The current play of etymology," Blanchot points out, "makes of writing a cutting movement, a tearing or rending, a crisis [*un mouvement coupant, une déchirure, un crise*]" (*EI*, pp. 38–9). The lacerating movement of writing cannot be contained in fixed language or captured by proper words. Either recalling Levinas and anticipating Derrida or recalling Derrida and anticipating Levinas (genealogy, as always, is uncertain), Blanchot describes the improper, excessive, eccentric, extravagant, duplicitous word of the writer as "a trace." To write nothing or almost nothing, it is necessary to write and erase *at the same time*. This impossible double movement, which "is" the restless movement of the Impossible, is staged in the trace.

> . . . to write, that is to go, by the world of traces, toward the effacement of traces and of all traces, because signs clash with totality and always already disperse themselves.

. . . Traces do not return to the moment of the mark, they are without origin, but not without end in the permanence that seems to perpetuate them, traces which, even while becoming confounded and replacing themselves, are forever there and forever cut off from that whose trace they would be, having no other being than their plurality, as if there were not *a* trace but traces never the same and always repeated. The *mark* [*marque*] of writing (*PA*, p. 77).

As the endless repetition of traces, writing is incessant reinscription. Writing, in other words, is not original but always "secondary" or "supplemental" to an origin that is never present.

To write, in this sense, is always first to rewrite, and to rewrite does not refer to any preliminary writing, no more than to an anteriority of language or of presence or of signification. Rewriting—a doubling that always precedes or suspends unity while demarking it: to rewrite holds itself apart from all productive initiative and pretends to produce *nothing*, not even the past or the future or the present of writing. To rewrite by repeating that which has no place, will have no place, has had no place, inscribes itself in a non-unified system of relations that cross without any point of intersection affirming their coincidence, inscribing themselves under the exigency of the return by which we are torn away from the modes of temporality that are always measured by a unity of presence (*PA*, pp. 48–9).

By uprooting the unity of presence, writing interrupts the presence of unity. This displacement has both spatial and temporal dimensions. Writing "de-situates" presence by differentiating what is not here, and delays the present by "deferring" what is not now. According to Blanchot, the spacing and timing of "*différer*" coincide in the polyvalent term "*différence*." "*La différence*," he contends, "is the play of time and space" (*EI*, p. 243). The trope of this differential play in *writing*. Blanchot concludes: "writing is difference . . . and difference writes" (*EI*, p. 247).

As the knot in which space and time are interlaced, *différence*, which is neither present nor absent, is the condition of the possibility of presence and absence. Since it is never present, *différence* is always "*hors langage*." The one who tries to write "outside language," in order to evoke that which has no place and has not taken place, engages in "the practice of the impossible" (*EI*, p. 491). Blanchot freely admits that "writing is, perhaps, non-writing" (*PA*, p. 67). If writing is non-writing, then to write is, in effect, to write Not. Not, however, can be written, if at all, only in the absence of writing. To write (in) this absence, the writer must attempt to write the absence of (the) work. "To write [therefore] is to produce the absence of the work (the out-of-work [*le désoeuvrement*]). Or again, writing is the absence of the work as it *produces itself* through the work, throughout the work. Writing as unemployment (in the active sense of the word) is the chance [*l'aléa*] between reason and unreason" (*EI*,p. 623). The unemployment of the writer calls into question the economy of the book. Writing is not "productive," "effective," or "useful." To the contrary, it is "useless to the world where only effectiveness counts, and is useless to itself" (*SL*, p. 215). Paradoxically, precisely this uselessness makes writing so serious. *Le désoeuvrement* marks the trace of a remainder, "*un pur reste*" that is "*hors tout*" (*PA*, p. 62). This *reste* signals "the absence of the book"—the very absence that the book is intended to fill.

> Writing is absent from the Book, being the non-absent absence from which, having absented itself from this absence, the Book makes itself readable . . . and comments on itself by enclosing history: closing of the book, severity of the letter, authority of knowledge. One can say of this writing, absent from the book, yet in a relation to alterity with it, that it remains strange to readability, unreadable insofar as to read is necessarily to enter by the gaze into a relation of meaning or nonmeaning with a presence. Thus there would be a writing exterior to knowledge that is obtained by reading, and also exterior to the form or the demand of the Law. Writing, (pure) exteriority, strange to every relation of presence, as well as to all legality (*EI*, pp. 631–2).

The writing, which is exterior to reading, is irreducibly "fragmentary." "The attraction of (pure) exteriority or the vertigo of space as distance," is, for Blanchot, the "fragmentation that only sends us back to the fragmentary" (*EI*, p. 626). Like Kierkegaard's unphilosophical "*smuler*," Blanchot's "idle [*désoeuvré*] fragments" can be only written *after* the closure of the book. In contrast to the book, which "rolls and unrolls time" in the continuity of a present that unites beginning, middle, and end, the fragment is "insufficient, unfinished (because it is strange to the category of accomplishment)" (*EI*, p. 229). Always secondary, the fragment is an unphilosophical postscript calling for endless supplementary postscripts. Fragmentary writing resists both systems and structures. Its words cannot be unified, assembled, or reduced to "1"; they are irrepressibly equivocal because irreducibly plural.

> The plurality of the plural word [*la parole plurielle*]: intermittent, discontinuous word, which, without being insignificant, does not speak because of its power to represent and even to signify. That which speaks in it is not signification, the possibility of giving meaning or removing meaning, even a multiple meaning. From which we are led to assert, perhaps too hastily, that the word or speech designates itself beginning with the between—that it is, as it were, on guard around a place of divergence, a space of dis-location that it seeks to encircle . . . separating it from itself, identifying with this gap, an imperceptible interval where the word always returns to itself, identical and non-identical" (*EI*, pp. 234–5).

By opening "*l'espace littéraire*," the writer's fragments expose "*l'espace de la dis-location*" in which author, reader, and book withdraw. Writing spells "the death of the author." In a section of *The Space of Literature* entitled "The Work and the Errant Word," Blanchot argues that "the work demands of the writer that he lose everything he might construe as his own 'nature,' that he lose all character and that, ceasing to be related to others and to himself by the decision that makes him an 'I,' he becomes the empty place where the impersonal affirmation emerges" (*SL*, p. 55). Through such kenosis, the writer opens the space of an "anonymous third." Even when he apparently speaks for himself, the writer actually writes in the third genre. "I" do not write, the "I" does not write; it writes, *il écrit*. The writer's action is, therefore, a passion, his activity a passivity, his doing an undoing. The third "voice" of the writer does not reiterate the synthetic third of Hegel's *savoir absolu* but re-calls the insistent third of Lacan's discourse of the Other in which, as Blanchot emphasizes, "*ça parle; ça desire*" (*EI*, p. 449). Through the "ventriloquis-tic" ploys of the Other, the writer becomes the echo of a silence he cannot silence.

In the effort to make the Impossible readable, the writer makes reading impossible. The writer does not communicate a message that can be comprehended, penetrated, or deciphered by the insightful reader. The death of the author entails the disappear-ance of the reader. According to Blanchot, "writing gives nothing to read, nothing to understand" (*PA*, p. 89). This "*rien*" is "*le non-savoir*" that suspends all certainty "between parentheses." The only "thesis" of the writer is the non-thesis of a "parenthesis" whose *para* is an indigestible *hors d'oeuvre*. In writing, "ambiguity is delivered to its excess." This excess, infinitely exceeding every-thing . . . beyond the totality . . . on the margins of the universe . . . slight extravagance . . . is *le reste* that the book cannot assimi-late. Such a remainder makes the author of the book gag until he finally vomits.

For the writer, the book is not present but is always to come. "*Le livre est le livre à venir.*" In fragmentary writing, the end never arrives but is ever deferred. The infinite deferral of the difference inscribed in writing marks and remarks the delay of the *Par-ousia*. In the absence of the Word, exile is eternal, erring endless.

> Error signifies wandering, the inability to abide and stay
> because where the wanderer is, the conditions of a
> definitive here are lacking. In this absence of here and now
> what happens does not clearly come to pass as an event
> upon which something solid could be achieved.
> Consequently, what happens does not happen, but does
> not pass either, into the past; it is never passed. It happens
> and recurs without cease; it is the horror and confusion and
> uncertainty of eternal repetition. . . . The wanderer's
> country is not truth, but exile; he lives outside . . . (*SL*, p.
> 238).

If modernism has passed, postmodernism lies in ruins—ruins of cultural monuments that once seemed secure. If, as Blanchot insists, writing has become "*l'écriture du désastre*," the space in which we are destined to wander might be imaged as a *Paysage Foudroyé*. As if commenting on Blanchot's insight concerning the interplay of errancy and exile in the artistic imagination, the

27

controversial French artists Anne and Patrick Poirier preface the most extensive catalogue of their work by writing: "*From landscape to landscape, from ruins to gardens, our work is a series of errings: from lived landscapes to desired landscapes, from physical errings to mental errings, from exile to exile—real landscapes and oneiric landscapes mix and mingle.*"[19] The Poiriers insist that their "fascination with ruined towns and buildings is not a morbid nostalgia for the past but a fascination with the architectural place itself. . . . In a ruin ownership is abolished, rules disappear, all at once the eye can see through the succession of spaces" (*V*, p. 72). The "succession of spaces" exposed by the exploration of the arche-texture of ruins opens one to a past that is not only historical but is also psychological. As the architect of psychoanalysis so often stresses, the interpreter of dreams is always something of an archeologist. According to the Poiriers, "Archeology, architecture, and mythology are metaphors privileged in order to try to set in space or put on stage the phenomena of the unconscious." The unconscious *partially* disclosed itself in archetypes that haunt the human imagination and inform all its creations. "For our part," the Poiriers note, "this is what we seek in our errings across architectures, ruins, and gardens: to attempt to understand the relations of archeology and mythology with our mental universe. To try to penetrate, on the basis of physical and perceptible tridimensional images, 'poetic' spaces contained in a region of our being that is accessible only with great difficulty" (*V*, p. 118).

Paysage Foudroyé (1982–83), which measures $39 \times 19\frac{1}{2} \times 2$ feet, combines extraordinary expanse and minute detail to create an uncanny landscape that is profoundly unsettling. The Poiriers explain that the land "black, charred, in ruin—is the probable site of the battle of Jupiter and the Giants. A fictitious Mediterranean, an entirely mythical geography where different structures [are] assembled around a basin of black water. [These structures] do not refer to any locale in particular, but should evoke the viewer's memories of archeological landscapes."[20] *Thunderstruck Landscape* is bordered by works figuring the death of two of the rebellious Giants. On one side, the Poiriers place *Death of Mimas* and on the other, *Death of Enceladus*. The Giants were the sons of the goddess of the earth named Gaia. With the encouragement of their mother, who had long been at odds with the sky gods, the Giants attacked the Olympian deities. After a prolonged war, the gods defeated the monstrous maternal envoys. While Mimas was struck down by a thunderbolt released by Zeus (or his Roman counterpart, Jupiter), Enceladus was buried under Mount Aetna, whence he breathed flames through the volcano.

In the *Death of Enceladus* two huge eyes, which are fragments of a much larger statue, emerge from a pile of white marble. In the midst of the rubble there is a miniature replica of a temple, and at the top of the work there is a bronze arrow representing the deadly thunderbolt of Jupiter. The *Death of Mimas* is formed by an enormous bronze eye with water constantly trickling out of it and a large arrow on either side of it. Between the *Death of Enceladus* and the *Death of Mimas* lies the scorched earth of *Thunderstruck Landscape*. Representing no actual historical site, this deadly wasteland is the trace of a dark space opened by a dreadful event (or nonevent) that "occurred" "before the world, before the beginning." Describing their "*giantomachie,*" the Poiriers write:

> The myth that guided the conception of this space is that of the battle of the gods and the Giants, a myth of violence

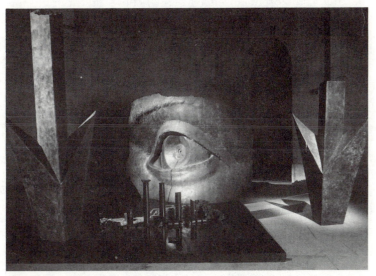

FIGURE 1. Anne and Patrick Poirier, *Mimas*. Courtesy of the artists and Galerie Daniel Templeton. Photographer, André Moraino.

and destruction. . . . It stages the combat between elemental and brutal forces attributed to the Giants, sons of Gaia, and the superior forces attributed to the gods of Olympus. In fact, perhaps [it stages] the incessant combat between the rational and the irrational, shadow and light, violent drives and sublimated drives (*V*, p. 118).

Even the struggle between such clearly defined opposites, however, is not absolutely primal. These ruins are a sign, no less and no more, of an absent origin that figures Blanchot's "origin that always precedes us and is always given before us." In their most revealing remark on *Paysage Foudroyé,* the Poiriers suggest the extraordinary complexity of their work:

On the earth, scattered in the disorder, a sort of pulverization of sculptural, architectural, and human elements (or fragments), as if [they had been] struck by an enormous shaking of an invisible origin. In fact, it is a question of traces [*traces*] of a combat on an inhuman scale of which there remain [*reste*] only some signs, which, in this chaos, are difficult to decipher (*V*, p. 118).

Like the "nonabsent absence" of Blanchot's "terrifyingly ancient," the Poiriers' "invisible origin" is the condition of the possibility of binary opposites like the rational and the irrational, light and shadow, presence and absence, etc. The "unrepresentable before" that is irretrievably past interrupts every present and disrupts all presence. Perhaps the recognition of the impossibility of presence/present "written" in *Paysage Foudroyé* helps to explain the tear trickling from the eye of Mimas. This tear might be the tear that issues from Bataille's thunderous "outburst of laughter,"[21] or the tear that is the tear [*Riss*] that Blanchot, following Heidegger, identifies as "the origin of the work of art."

The charred ruins of *Thunderstruck Landscape* trace the aftereffect of a *disaster* that is never present as such. "The disaster," Blanchot insists,

ruins everything, all the while leaving everything intact. It does not touch anyone in particular; "I" am not threatened by it, but spared, left aside. It is in this way that I am threatened; it is in this way that the disaster threatens in me that which is exterior to me—an other than I who passively become other. There is no reaching the disaster. Out of reach is he whom it threatens, whether from afar or close up, it is impossible to say: the infiniteness of the threat has in some way broken every limit. We are on the edge of the disaster [*au bord du désastre*] without being able to situate it in the future: it is rather always already past, and yet we are on the edge or under the threat, all formulations which would imply the future—which is yet to come—if the disaster were not that which does not come, that which has put a stop to every arrival.[22]

Suspended between *Death of Mimas* and *Death of Enceladus*, *Paysage Foudroyé* marks the "site" of a holocaust that is an absolute Disaster. In the postmodern world, the Disaster takes place (without taking place) *in* art *as* art. The time of the disaster is a time without present; its space, a space without presence. Forever exiled, the artist returns to a past more ancient than every past, where one encounters a future more distant than every future. To approach the *paysage foundroyé* that marks and remarks the space of postmodernism, one must follow Thomas the Obscure by going back to the future that always approaches but never arrives.

Thomas sat down and looked at the sea. He remained motionless for a time, as if he had come there to follow the movements of the other swimmers and, although the fog prevented him from seeing very far, he stayed there, obstinately, his eyes fixed on the bodies floating with difficulty. Then, when a more powerful wave reached him, he went down onto the sloping sand and slipped into the midst of the currents, which quickly submerged him. The sea was calm, and Thomas was in the habit of swimming for long periods without tiring. But today he had chosen a new route. The fog hid the shore. A cloud had come down upon the sea and the surface was lost in a glimmer that seemed the only truly real thing. Currents shook him, though without giving him the feeling of being in the midst of the waves and of rolling in familiar elements. The conviction that there was, in fact, no water at all made his effort to swim into a frivolous exercise from which he drew nothing but discouragement. Perhaps it would suffice for him to master himself to drive away such thoughts, but his eye found nothing to cling to, and it seemed to him that he was staring into the void with the intention of finding help there. It was then that the sea, driven by the wind, broke loose. The storm tossed it, scattered it into inaccessible regions; the squalls turned the sky upside down and, at the same time, there was a silence and a calm that gave the impression that everything was already destroyed. Thomas sought to free himself from the insipid flood that was invading him. A piercing cold paralyzed his arms. The water swirled in whirlpools. Was it actually water? (*TO*, p. 7).

Or something Other?

Chapter 2

POSTMODERN LANGUAGE

Charles E. Scott

The language of postmodern texts carries with it processes of self-overcoming by which, in the language, the reader undergoes movements that are different from those in metaphysical discourses. We will use the Nietzschean term *self-overcoming* and emphasize the Nietzschean inheritance in the postmodern suspicions of completeness, presence, unbroken continuity, identity, teleology. . . . Those suspicions are woven into patterns of words that bring the reader, who reads in the patterns, to the transforming horizon of the patterns, a horizon that verges on possibilities that carry the reader beyond the patterns. Postmodern words might leave one without the book that they seem to compose, or with a non-word (e.g., *différance*) to which the words seem to give place, or at a confluence of regularities that highlights the fragmentary and arbitrary histories of the regularities (e.g., Foucault's *The Order of Things*). The processes of self-overcoming are seldom noted in postmodern writing, partially because people in this strand of language have paid attention more to twentieth-century discourses and thoughts from which they continue to take their departures, and partially because self-overcoming has moved silently and unnoticed in much of postmodern language. Self-overcoming, however, governs the movements in postmodern language as authors make their various claims. These claims move within processes that simultaneously destructure, decenter, or deconstruct their own veridical presence. This is not a dialectical process. Reconciliation of conflict, self-positing, polarities, or subjectivity do not control the discourse. Postmodern discourses are processes that simultaneously form structures and lead to the alteration of the forming processes. In these processes metaphysical styles and thoughts may take place, not only as objects of discussion, but as aspects of the language that are also being overcome by movements that have been suppressed or overlooked by metaphysical discourses.

The horizon of finite time recurs repeatedly in postmodern language as the site of self-overcoming. Heidegger, not as a metaphysician of presence or a lyricist (as he is sometimes presented), but as the thinker of time, horizon, and ecstasis, constitutes one of the horizons of postmodern language. He repeatedly took phenemonology, dialectical thinking, and the metaphysics of time as they are developed in given texts through their most characteristic and disciplined language to the horizon of their own thought, where they and his own language not only encounter their own mortality, but where they also find themselves standing out into possibilities and questions that they could not previously have imagined or asked. These texts, in Heidegger's thought, are carried by their own momentum into issues and thoughts which site the texts beyond their limits. The horizonal transformations of language recur in his language not as a theme, but as the encounter of his thinking with given texts. The reader undergoes the transforming, destructuring processes, often without noticing them, and often repeats them unaware when treating of Heidegger. If this article had a sequel, it would be on Heidegger's language, and it would be an attempt to write about him by making place for the ecstasis that reverberates through his language. If it succeeded, one of his effects within postmodern language would become apparent, and the complex of failure, dying, speech, and emerging thought would take place. But Heidegger also is in the wake of self-overcoming as it takes place in Nietzsche's language.

Here we will take note of self-overcoming in Nietzsche's language. It is a process within figurations that puts in question not only the particular figurations but the significance of "figuration" for interpreting a discourse. It stresses formation by processes of deformation. It is a process that Heidegger as an interpreter of Nietzsche did not explicitly hear, i.e., it is a process by which metaphysics and nihilism are held in question even as they slip out of control in Nietzsche's discourse. But it is a process that, regardless of Heidegger's not thematizing it, appears to have given way to "de-struction" in *Being and Time* and indirectly to have given accent to Heidegger's account of temporal, horizonal ecstasis.

Further, the language of postmodernism has part of its parentage in processes of discourse that were at least partly independent of the author's motives and intentions. Self-overcoming takes place at times in spite of Nietzsche, and its work is not often dependent on the explicit awareness of post-Nietzschean writers. It has its continuing effect, at times in spite of the writers in whose language it occurs. It can put one's writing willy-nilly in question. It generates questions. Self-overcoming as it occurs in language is not a subject. It is not like a subject. It is not individual. It is not an identity. Is it a thought? It certainly is not an "it." But it takes place in Nietzsche's discourse, and we will have begun thinking of postmodern language, and only begun, if we highlight self-overcoming. By this emphasis we will have taken a step in postmodern language toward the emergence of postmodern language, an emergence which leads to a way of thinking in which dominance of accidental confluence, temporizing of time, and deferring in thought and speech make impossible a history structured by such metaphysical categories as Aristotle's five causes or a history written within either a "rational" scheme or a structure of "subjectivity." We will also have indicated that the temporizing effect of self-overcoming accentuates a strand of language within which schools and literal-minded followers seem unlikely. A postmodern author is usually overcome in the author's own discourse.

I Self-overcoming in Nietzsche's language

In the last paragraph of *Beyond Good and Evil*, Nietzsche pays homage to the life and death of his own thought. The previous paragraphs of the book mark processes of self-overcoming in which figurations of thought and speech come into their own effective power and, by their power, effect movement out of themselves into different figurations. Nietzsche had used the idea of self-overcoming to describe developments and transformations in Western thought, and we find that that process—self-overcoming—also characterizes the development of his own thinking. His concepts and images move with an energy that the formations themselves, no matter how self-conscious, cannot retain for long. The dominant ideas of these formations in Nietzsche's speech and thought, e.g., the dominance of the free spirit, the scientific importance of will to power, the death of God, can be repeated in post-Nietzschean litanies, in Nietzschean truths, in structures of action and feeling. They can maintain themselves in repeated judgments and habits of mind—Nietzsche could repeat himself and others can follow him and repeat him—but the repetitions and evaluations cannot hold and contain the energy that surged through them as they developed out of other formations and moved toward figurations that they could not imagine. These ideas and word formations could not make themselves sufficient, in their relevance, articulateness, and self-insistence, to their own power as they came to be. They could not persist through time with the power by which they came to expression. At best, if Nietzsche insisted on the truth of his thought, his words and ideas could repeat themselves in ways that deny their own passing and that produce by their power of denial a sickness of mind that Nietzsche, on his own terms, could hardly discern. If he made his thoughts into traditional, metaphysical truths, they would constitute a sickness that is housed within the truths and symbols, like those truths by which people lived together with certainty and traditional moral sensibility. His thoughts would be the "pale ghosts" that outlined residues of power that had largely withdrawn. The residue of the vitality of emerging thoughts is found in the formation of truths and virtues by which we give continual meaning to our lives, with little sense for the life and power with which the formations once moved. He says:

> Alas, what are you after all, my written and painted thoughts! It was not long ago that you were still so colorful, young, and malicious, full of thorns and secret spices—you made me sneeze and laugh—and now? You have already taken off your novelty, and some of you are ready, I fear, to become truths: they already look so immortal, so pathetically decent, so dull! And has it ever been different? What things do we copy, writing and painting, we mandarins with Chinese brushes, we immortalizers of things that *can* be written—what are the

only things we are able to paint? Also, always only what is on the verge of withering and losing its fragrance! Alas, always only storms that are passing, exhausted, and feelings that are autumnal and yellow! Alas, always only birds that grew weary of flying and flew astray and now can be caught by hand—by *our* hand! We immortalize what cannot live and fly much longer—only weary and mellow things! And it is only your *afternoon*, you, my written and painted thoughts, for which alone I have colors, many colors perhaps, many motley caresses and fifty yellows and browns and greens and reds: but nobody will guess from that how you looked in your morning, you sudden sparks and wonders of my solitude, you my old beloved—*wicked* thoughts! (*Beyond Good and Evil*, IX. 296).

These lines punctuate the self-overcoming of *Beyond Good and Evil*. As we reread and rethink the book—is it a book?—we might simultaneously undergo the book's nascence, its "morning," and its aging into more fixed formations. We also might simultaneously undergo its birth and its transformation on a horizon of change toward possibilities that are beyond its grasp. In that experience of self-overcoming we might live momentarily in the energy that Nietzsche called will to power. The words remain for return and rereading. They allow repetition, but *their* repetition and our undergoing again their self-overcoming resist their becoming definitive or even certain and sure of themselves in their formations. They do not constitute a monument to self-overcoming, although we can make them into an icon if we withdraw from their processes and invest them with ideological casting. Desires for longevity indwell the language of *Beyond Good and Evil*. Nietzsche too suffered nostalgia in his words, grammar, and thoughts for universalization. He too felt impulses for undying truth and for irreplaceable names and tropes. He too knew the remaining urge for indelible heroism in the fields of thought and science. "Perhaps," his words said to him, "we are true ideas, the true images of time and power." But *their* drive also left them to be traces of something they could not say. They are no less overcome in their own momentum, no less bereft of the joy of coming to be, than their own object of description—the structure of good and evil—which had itself been self-overcome and left as a trace of an energy that in its self-conscious-ness it did not want to know.

Thinking begins again in processes of self-overcoming. This last paragraph of *Beyond Good and Evil* marks a turn to genealogy, a more detailed and careful study of morality as such. Genealogy focuses our attention on the passing energy of our own funda-mental structures of evaluation and judgment. In *The Genealogy of Morals*, it repeats the thoughts of *Beyond Good and Evil* with philological and practical elaboration, and provides an even more compelling account of morality as a formation that has lost its creative power and is moved rather by self-insistent energy. *The Genealogy of Morals*, with its passion and preoccupation regarding morality, moves out of an identifiable Western moral posture to a nonmoral genealogical rehearsal of the generation and decay of morality. The emerging thoughts are that morality took its departure from active life-affirmation, that life-affirmation is lost to morality, and that in morality energy is spent in hostile reac-tion to life-affirmation. This reactive energy gives morality its self-conserving form and reverses its affirmative drive toward self-overcoming into life-denying hierarchies of self-preserva-tion. This account comes out of processes of self-overcoming in Western religion and morality in which the formulations of self-giving love, crucifixion, and obedience, for example, pervert the self-overcoming power of will to power.

The self-overcoming of *Beyond Good and Evil* also repeated, however, an interest in finding its own origination through a discourse that overcomes the truths out of which it emerges. Nietzsche's genealogical accounts are of practices and structures of thinking from which his own genealogies emerge. The "es-sence" of these practices and structures is an energetic process that produces them and goes on in them, but one that casts them toward their own overturning. As we reread and rethink the genealogies we also find ourselves moved beyond these ac-counts, due to the very effects of these accounts. Perhaps some-thing hardly thinkable gains relief, like a hyphen between "self" and "overcoming," something connecting and separating and not quite graspable in a given language. Perhaps a genealogy of genealogical thinking, instead of a genealogy of morality, suggests itself. The language of genealogical thinking forges ahead to another language and urges its thoughts to other figurations. It does not present itself primarily within the metaphysical formulations of truth or goodness. Its own founding ideas, like those of will to power and self-overcoming, forecast their own passage into other images, into beings outside of their present, comprehending power. If something eternal occurs, it occurs like a circle that means nothing in itself, like a mere "ever" without source or telos or intelligibility. Zarathustra's likeness to a monk, for example, his biblical cadences and the prophetic appearance which accompany his transformation of Judeo-Christian patterns of thought and life, are like the processes in *Beyond Good and Evil* and *Genealogy of Morals* in which the very thoughts of meaningful power and incarnation of the eternal in finite form undergo transformation within their own images and words. In Nietzsche's discourse, these and other traditional thoughts are driven away from themselves and urge other, contradictory thoughts.

Self-overcoming and the manner in which Nietzsche's discourse puts itself in question have exercised significant influence, both consciously and unconsciously, on twentieth-century style and thought. Self-overcoming is the most disturbing effect of his language. It prevents us from thinking with Nietzsche and through him, and at the same time from making his work either a model or a true and sufficient evaluation of Western culture. In spite of its accuracies and inaccuracies, his discourse makes its own formulations into remainders of a process it cannot contain. On its own terms the discourse is a complex organization of finite traces. Self-overcoming occurs through its analyses, descriptions, and arguments. It gives them moment and power and puts them into question, while possibilities for thought and speech emerge from the discourse and are welcomed in this discourse that anticipates its own overcoming. The simultaneity of assertion, power, mortality, and questionableness is the discourse's moment. When the questionableness of the discourse is not undergone, its moving power seems to have been removed and the pale reminder of this power, now merely staying power, has taken hold.

A discourse has within itself many elements that lead to the specific ways in which it overcomes itself. If, for example, a discourse is under the power of the good/evil formation, and if the discourse also posits power that is beyond good/evil, as in the case of Boehme's or Eckhart's mystical theology, the transcending power can put in question the good/evil structure and lead in spite of itself to a self-overcoming movement. The energy of the good/evil relation is beyond this relation and makes awkward the claim that power is good. In Nietzsche's discourse, a life-force beyond good and evil is accepted as dominant over the good/evil formation. That dominance defines a significant part of the self-overcoming of traditional theology and morality that takes place in Nietzsche's discourse. Its own value-judgments are also prevented from universalization by the freedom of their power from their structure, and its anti-metaphysical claims are as much in jeopardy as the metaphysical claims are by self-overcoming movements. If, however, the literal use of language in Nietzsche's discourse gains dominance over the language of irony, mockery, and parody, the literal claims will overcome the language of self-overcoming in the interpreting discourse. A Nietzschean metaphysics will emerge. When self-overcoming controls the discourse, there is no transcendence of the discourse to explain or justify its own processes. Will to power in its self-overcoming function has its origin and expected demise in its discursive course. In this sense, the thought of will to power traces its own energy within a pattern of historical formations. In the absence of any justification or being other than its own discursive process, will to power and self overcoming—two forces already active in Western language—combine in Nietzsche's discourse to produce one of its formative powers, a power by which it expects and affirms its own passage into other formations.

II   A language without truth

Nietzsche is deeply a part of the ideological history that he terms metaphysical. That word, *metaphysical*, functions for him by naming a broad confederation of thoughts and practices having in common the ascendant ideas of truth, reason, morality, and God. *Beyond Good and Evil* begins with the questions, who puts the question of truth? and, what wants truth? These questions in their context mean that we need to ask about the will that *seeks* and *wants* truth. In posing these two questions Nietzsche sets in motion a series of thoughts that are designed to work with and through metaphysical thinking, and in relation to truth. He is a part of the way of thinking that he is able to see as optional. He wants to pursue a different option, to be molded by a movement of forces that he sees coming together in a new organization of valences, knowledges, and insights. He intends to think his way through his own metaphysical "nature" to a way of thinking that he dimly foresees but that is still obscure in its details.

Truth is an issue of valences, of ordering forces, that give priority and status and thus also hierarchy and subordination to a group of thoughts, practices, and values. Ignorance and error, for example, are "lower" in this way of thinking and acting than truth: in the discourse of truth, the powers opposing truth are not conceived as differences on the same plane with truth, but as differences that are lower because they lack the value of truth. Nietzsche notes that *value* means the power, the valence, to evaluate, organize, and rank order.

How do "we" evaluate this will to truth? We meet this will—Nietzsche calls the encounter "a rendezvous . . . of questions" (I.1)[1]—in its power, and the issue is how we are to encounter it in a power of discourse other than that of the will to truth. To recognize that truth is a valence is a beginning. But that could lead quickly to our wanting to find the truth of truth, a desire that we will find Nietzsche undergoing frequently, and one that often holds him in the discourse ruled by the will to truth. The opening recognition can lead, however—it has the force to lead us—toward a way of thinking that is not governed by will to truth. *That* move, and not the one toward the truth of truth, is a "risk." If we are not asking about the truth of truth, what are we asking?

Nietzsche's exploratory move is designed to shift the discourse away from traditional, dominating interest in truth and honesty, pervaded as it is with the spirit of seriousness, and to alert us to self-deception in the name of self-honesty. We attempt to think of truth as originating out of its opposite. The traditional idea of an originary basis for truth functions predominantly in this effort. But if the originary basis is not being or a being, if it is nothing that can be thought literally or that has identity or order, then the idea of an originary basis is put into question by the way it is thought. Now it is in combination with absence of identity and order. Nietzsche is not creating an insoluble paradox on his terms. He is devaluing a valence by combining it with counter-forces. Thinking the value of the will to truth in this way results in a power situation different from that which accompanies thinking the value of truth within truth's rule. Both the ideas of truth and of originary basis are being thought through to a situation which denies them the power of being or of nondiscursive identity. In this reconstituted thinking, truth, being, and identity look like prejudgments in a history of evaluations or like strong assertions of belief founded in traceable interests and feelings.

Further, a different will is created in the new combination. As this organization operates, it wants to be. Its will to be, its immediate self-affirmation, drives in a direction quite different from the will to truth, which is the desire to *be* on the part of the truth-discourse. Different interests and possibilities emerge. In this changed discourse one begins to undergo a different thinking. Different attitudes and behaviors emerge as preferable in the changed hierarchy. This risk is underway as the long-lasting stabilities of the other discourses begin to melt away.[2]

The difference from truth that gives focus and estimate in Nietzsche's thinking is "instinct" (I.2–4). At times the concept of instinct proposes an identity for force that is different from the previously ascribed identity, i.e., instinct creates normative values different from those that the will to truth creates. Nietzsche then seems to be replacing one faith by another, i.e., he affirms the idea that life-force is not circumscribed by moral rules or laws. This force is not rational. It "guides" consciousness. It is not regulated by the principles by which we regulate ourselves. It spawns all manner of estimates. It is life and life-giving. It is "untruth." When he thinks this way, Nietzsche is a counter-metaphysics metaphysician. He develops a set of counterproposals that continue to make claims as to what the real and true state of affairs is.

The injection of instinct into the discourse of truth in Nietzsche's manner, however, moves toward an emerging discourse that is not counter-metaphysics, but a way of thinking that is nonmetaphysical. Falseness of judgment is becoming less of a problem: the issue is whether a group of evaluations are life-promoting and life-preserving (I.4). Often self-aware fictions that encourage play—fictions that love fictions—put people in touch with a liveliness that had been demoted below the self-unaware fictions of logic or reality-in-itself, a liveliness that now enjoys dominance over "true" judgments. The idea of instinct, which for Nietzsche means energy without truth or *a priori* law, leads to thinking that the idea of instinct needs to collapse on itself or lead away from itself in some way that prevents a literalization and a consequent metaphysics of instinct-energy. As the idea of instinct divests literal claims about being, universal laws, and self-identical reality of their power to convince, it can also function as a deliteralizing force regarding itself. It does not mean to be thought noncontingently. It too is replaceable. The idea of instinct is a force for transformation that gathers force as it drives one to think through it to a different idea in a different way of thinking: its power in a hierarchy of ideas transforms the will to truth into a new kind of desire and a different grouping of concepts that we will discuss.

Nietzsche was always under the sway of the ideas of noncontingency, ahistoricity, and timeless energy. Those ideas exercise a continuing power in his discussion of instinct and body, as well as of will to power and eternal recurrence. But those ideas are continually in question by virtue of the emerging organization of forces in which contingency (discussed as the function of will to power), historicity (discussed as the genealogical descent of all ideas, values, and practices), and field-dependent energy (discussed in terms of return and recurrence) have the privilege of challenging their previous masters. While Nietzsche is promising a higher honesty, he is also thinking that philosophy is "personal confession" (I.6) and that judgments are fictions (I.5). Even as one thinks that these two claims are themselves not fictions, Nietzsche turns to a descent of philosophical claims to show contingent plays of forces that generate and define the powers of thought, their efficacy, and that never show references beyond their efficacy and the organization within which they are effective.

Will and will to power are thought in two ways: as ahistorical energy and as drive that is found only in contingent organizations of forces. In the latter way of thinking "force" is nothing in itself, but is instead a relational occurrence. When we think in the first context, the instinctive basis of thought means that reasons and rules are founded in an indiscriminate energy that yields *all* differences and opposites. When we think in the second manner, the instinctive basis of thought means that instinct and its will are relational events in a hierarchical, changing order of forces. As the order changes, the instincts change. The life that instincts preserve on the first reading is something like a cosmic force. On the second reading "life" means *this* life at this time in this history. The second option makes "instinct" and "life" discourse-specific.

The difference in thinking that Nietzsche seeks, in contrast to the "self-development in a cold, pure, divinely unconcerned dialectic" (I.5), is a play of descriptions, evaluations, and senses for energy that experiments with combinations and hierarchies of claims. This different thinking does not have an overwhelming interest in certainty, literal truth, or speculative coherence. At least one side of his thinking is not looking for "truth," but for configurations that move through themselves with the energy they produce and promote. Not an energy that looks for its own *reflection* by reacting back on itself (not self-protective or dialectical), but a transvaluational one that instinctively moves beyond itself to other transforming configurations. In such thinking the idea of drive is like a battering ram that breaks apart the wall of certainty, an idea that need not revert back to itself by literalizing or by giving itself substantial endurance. Nietzsche often avoids the literalizing options by following out multiple drives, seeing their various and conflicting organizations, and interpreting them as a play for forces rather than as disclosing a reality outside of the given types of life.[3]

If we imagine nature to be deceptive, indifferent, wasteful, without mercy and justice, the effect of this idea may be to displace the inherited, broad notion of nature as an imagined regulative principle. It can incite one to replace that idea of nature with another idea that excites imaginative variations and the inclusion of references to nonregularities, to dislocations, violations of patterns, and processes of dismantling and reconstituting (I.9). Imagining nature in this way is not necessarily to propose a right teaching about nature. It provides, in Nietzsche's instance, a way of thinking that experiences the strength of the human desire to be in accord with "nature," and the strong but unconscious desire to violate "nature" and be different. The desire to violate "nature," i.e., to imagine things according to the interests of the human species, now becomes clearer. This thinking gives us occasion to think of our thinking as arbitrarily different from "nature," not as naturally like it. We may now think of "nature" as itself issuing from a species-desire to be measured, purposeful, certain, and just. The desire that generates "nature" is not founded in "nature." It is rather an insistent interest on the part of the human organization of forces in preserving its human difference in an otherwise unhuman setting. It is an interest in creating our own "nature." This self-creating and self-preserving creature creates a "nature" which lacks the distinctions of the human creature, i.e., a sense of justice, a knowledge of truth, the abilities to worship and to sin, etc. "Nature" functions in the service of the human will to distinction, privilege, and domination (I.9). "Nature" appears as a willful projection in the service of human willpower.

In the instance of those philosophers who think back to "the faith of former times," and who, in their desire for those happy certainties of immortality of soul and "the old God," feel mistrust, disbelief, disgust, and scorn for "modern ideas" and "modern reality," what is Nietzsche's suggestion? That one encourage the strength of their disgust, support their energy of refusal, because it is that energy, once increased, that can carry thinking and feeling forward and away, not back to the present holding point, but on and out to thinking with a power that does not yearn for the certainty of another era, for the past plays of energy and force (I.10).

Nietzsche takes a traditional idea, e.g., the idea of soul, and notes how it perverted a preceding idea of soul as breath of life, a perversion that develops in a combination of "metaphysical need" and an atomistic persuasion: the ideas of individuality and deathlessness merge with soul (I.12). He now retains the word, accepts the perversion in its history, and creates transvaluing hypotheses by using such ideas as "mortal soul," "soul as subjective multiplicity," and "soul as social structure of the drives and affects." He works with the submerged idea of a breathlike organization of affect and power, excising from it the later accretions of deathlessness, unity, identity, and ideological certainty. In a movement that conserves the idea of soul with its pervasive sense of life and breath, Nietzsche also transforms the "metaphysical need" for exactness of stance and the fearful need for individual reassurance into an idea that carries its tradition without control by fear of death, drive for certainty, or substantial identity. By this move he understands himself to have a situation, a collection of thought-forces, that encourages invention and discovery. Of what? Who knows? Certainly the metaphysical idea is both undercut and thought through to a group of directions and possibilities that, though dimly present, did not have priority in the metaphysical notion. A part of his inherited tradition is maintained while its hold is loosened, nuanced, let slip. In the play of ideas that accompanies this process, the idea's force wanes, is "forgotten." It no longer has the power to organize other ideas and feelings as it once did. This is not necessarily that kind of forgetfulness by which one does not know that the other idea existed. One can certainly know about it, but it will not have much power in the way it is known; it is similar, perhaps, to our knowledge of Victorian sexuality.

By pluralizing the idea of will into plays of forces, by showing, for example, that willing is physical sensing, thinking, and affect, that "it" appears always in a hierarchical stance with multiple dimensions and submissions—by thinking that will is no one thing, Nietzsche detaches will from identity and from an association of willing, subject, and essence (I.19). By this thinking Nietzsche makes optional the expectation that will is a state of being. The possibility emerges that willing is a "complex social structure of many souls" (I.19), not primarily the action of a commander or a state of being, but an optional, genealogically descended interplay of control and submission, fluid and without substance or projecting subject.

The order of thinking—Nietzsche compares it to the systematic relation of members of a continent's fauna (I.20)—occurs with the strongest powers arranging and organizing a group of other conceptual forces. Powers establish dominations. These power-dominations function through systematic structures characteristic of the particular organization. One is led to think some thoughts, but cannot think others that are natural in a different organization. Remembering unconsciously the originary powers in various settings is more likely than imagining something foreign to the established hierarchy of wills, ideas, possibilities, and pariahs. Into the thought of order, system, and necessity Nietzsche adds the image of contingent necessity—the fauna of a continent, an interruptable and thoroughly changeable "natural" order. In his discourse the emerging experiences of history, mutation, and relative necessities are added to the metaphysical discourses of order, eternity, and thought, thereby forming a new imbalance among the "animals," a different struggle for ordering-rights, a climactic change that weakens the strong and creates the conditions for different ordering powers and a changed species. Specifically, the verbs of temporal forces replace or bypass the nouns and adjectives of eternal verity. Origin and the images of mutation are joined. The chosen verbs suggest the dominance of impermanence. The ideas of orders now suggest insecurity, possibly fear, certainly a desire for expression that is localized in fluid relations and not in subjects. Instead of resemblance and intimacy with nonhistorical and noncontingent founding Orders, orders emerge through processes that resemble only other processes. In this changing mixture the expectation emerges that "owing to the unconscious domination and guidance by similar grammatical functions everything is prepared at the outset for a similar development and sequence of philosophical systems" (I.20). We are able to entertain seriously and with positive affect the likelihood that rules of speech and practices of expression mold all these "inevitabilities" that we find "metaphysically" convincing and obvious. Permanence, in contrast to change, may be rather more the function of grammar than of "reality." The ideas of transcendence, of essences outside of historical development, and of timeless necessities are caught in a transvaluational process.

Finally, by asking, From where do I get the concept of thinking?, Nietzsche raises in a preliminary way the issue of descent: What interests have helped to form this concept of thinking? What kinds of willing yielded the idea of an ego that thinks? What interests have made believable the claim that immediate certainty resides in thinking? From where does the associated insistence on truth come? In this way he displaces a felt certainty with felt uncertainty in the activity of thinking. We are thinking the questions and the issues of descent in a type of activity that one expected to be certain of itself. The dual thought that the state of immediate certainty is replaceable and that immediate certainty is a product of a traceable discourse, is itself a replacement that reorganizes a thinking-life and makes optional a felt and fundamental necessity in the previous thinking-arrange-ment (I.16). The arrangements themselves are interpretations. No "one" is doing the interpreting. And the interpretation alters when a displacement, a replacement, or another reorganizing event occurs.

But there is also an important aspect of Nietzsche's thinking that carries forward the metaphysical tradition. He states that the convictions of philosophers are based in personal or perhaps group interests—in specific dislikes, in privileges, distastes, or group leverage—and that we can understand those interests if we see that they are expressions of something much more fundamental, i.e., life or the will to power (I.9). If we understand the will to power as life's drive for itself, we look for a flowing, dynamic reality to replace personal and collective will. Our task then is to live according to the energy that is "wasteful beyond measure, indifferent beyond measure, without purposes and consideration, without mercy and justice, fertile and desolate and uncertain at the same time" (I.9). And that task pushes us to agree with Nietzsche's judgment that energy is just that way, as distinct from how it is construed in other teachings.

Or, when Nietzsche encourages the strength of disgust and disbelief regarding modern ideas and reality on the part of those who are "trying at bottom to win back something that was for-merly an even *securer* possession, . . . perhaps the 'immortal soul,' perhaps 'the old God' " (I.10), he appears to be saying that mistrust of those ideas is right and that by encouraging mistrust one will gain the strength to let go of the old certainties. That strength of conviction on Nietzsche's part, his own joyful cer-tainty that those old ideas are silly when they function as objects of faith—his own strength of belief—asks for agreement or dis-proof. It invites followers, as well as the enemies that Nietzsche said he wanted. It is not a doctrine, but it is clearly a position that can be assumed.

"A living thing seeks above all to *discharge* its strength—life itself is *will to power*; self-preservation is only one of the indirect and most frequent *results*" (I.13). *What* does Nietzsche mean? He appears to be talking here about some kind of *what*, and not addressing some power or other which happens to occasion the claim. He speaks of life itself, says that it *is* will to power, he claims that discharge and not self-preservation is its primary characteristic. The claim is opposed specifically to the scientific claim that self-preservation is the dominant instinct of an organic being, and by this opposition Nietzsche makes his claim a candidate for replacing the scientific one. He makes will to power a principle that one should maintain and defend, and the functions of fantasy, imagination, and pluralization fade in the background. The demands of method and systematic relations among principles with the power of explanation control the foreground. It is stated as a metaphysical interpretation.

Nietzsche further contrasts the idea that nature is a law-abiding organism—an idea that emphasizes sameness under law—with his own thought that the will to power exhibits not the *conformities* of "nature," but its tyrannies. Will to power, not law, is the continuing necessity of "nature." Will to power is not subject to law. This claim is a frequent one for Nietzsche and means that will to power exceeds all ordering principles; and to the extent that ordering principles are historical and genealogical, will to power appears to be non–historical. Nietzsche is willing to say, "Supposing that [this claim of mine] is only interpretation . . . well, so much the better" (I.22). On his terms, it must be an interpretation. But he appears not to have appropriated the possibility that will to power itself is to be interpreted as genealogical. Nietzsche's direction is clearly away from notions of substance and transcendental essences. Until, however, the will to power is thought as originative, optional, and only circumstantially necessary, it will tend to have the status of a transcendental energy that explains historical processes. Nietzsche's statement, "so much the better," indicates that he wants a process of disagreement in which ultimate laws and forms can be subjected to irony and made apparent as interpretations. His putting will to power in opposition to natural law, however, at best obscures its own dependence on contingent configurations and at worst suggests that it fills the space of "essential nature" previously filled by law.

He speaks also of the "doctrine of the development of the will to power" as the basis for understanding psychological states (I.23). On the one hand, Nietzsche has in mind that psychologists have feared and repressed anything that looks like will to power and have injected destructive "moral prejudices" into their research. He also means that will to power is the basis for all psychological development, that it is *the* fundamental drive, and that it is to replace the notion of human nature.

The "prejudices of philosophers" are thus borne forward in the first section of *Beyond Good and Evil* by different interpretations of ideas that are within the metaphysical tradition. The power of explanatory thought is retained; and so too are those thoughts that propose something that permeates all orders and hierarchies. But those "prejudices" are also thought in a process that develops a configuration of forces different from those that Nietzsche sees as definitive of metaphysical ways of thinking. Those forces begin to produce affections, concepts, and ways of thinking that function in a nonmetaphysical (as distinct from antimetaphysical) attunement. They begin to create a very different geography of valence and interest. We can follow in his work the tensions created by the presence of metaphysical ideas in a process designed to transvalue them, and we can see in detail how Nietzsche's discourse develops the transvaluational process in such a way that it undergoes transvaluation.[4] The self-overcoming that takes place in his discourse dominates other discursive functions and sets in motion ways of speaking and thinking that turn the momentum of modern discourses into formations that are alert to their own regional and mortal way of being. The foundational assumptions in modern thought that remain active in this discourse are temporized in the processes of self-overcoming.

III   *Jenseits* Nietzsche

Why have we discussed Nietzsche and self-overcoming when our topic is the *language* of postmodernism? In the processes of its formation the language of postmodernism has developed into a complex thought of finite temporality without the controlling force of the idea of subjectivity. The forces and mutations in the emergence of this language have eroded and replaced the control of subjectivity. Consequently, history is no longer a narrative of subjectivity in any sense of *subjectivity*. By virtue of the processes by which the orders of modern thought are broken apart, neither continuity nor meaning control the reading of past occurrences and their many connections and junctures. When the language of postmodernism confronts the language of postmodernism, as in the case of the present essay, the movement of discursive strands continuously offsets their fixation into authoritative patterns, logics, or teachings. In the movement of thought from Nietzsche to Husserl to Heidegger to Derrida, for example, the problem of transcendence is the focal point of rethinking and self-overcoming *when* read back from Derrida to Nietzsche. In Derrida's discourse processes of self-overcoming operate in his struggle to rethink presence and let metaphysical patterns of thought decompose in the discourse's composition. Something like self-overcoming rather than self-consciousness or reflection empowers this language. The time of Derrida's discourse is found through various processes of deferring and temporizing in which identity, meaning, and continuity arise only to be put off. Metaphysical thoughts occur within processes that are bound by these thoughts, but which are not controlled by their patterns. The passage of metaphysics, rather like a process of self-overcoming, gains control. This passage constitutes a temporality that lends a non-metaphysical horizon to metaphysics, a horizon that decomposes metaphysical orders by temporizing their orders of authority.

Postmodern thinking finds part of its own language by accounting for its developing processes in the specific texts of its discourses. Had we worked with Heideggerian texts, we would have found another aspect of postmodern language in a horizon of finite temporality where metaphysical language is overcome from within its own movement. That overcoming takes place in the momentum of originating questions and in the crises of metaphysical language itself. By following Nietzsche we have involved ourselves in a movement prior to Heidegger, and in whose wake Heidegger's thought developed. The "difference" of self-overcoming, rather than the "identity" of evolutionary and continuous development, has moved language. His is a discourse that offsets itself as it offsets the defining categories and thoughts that have cast the tropes and forms of its heritage. The power of Nietzsche's texts disempowers the structures and forces that generated the disempowering power.

What could have been accomplished in a summary essay showing, for example, the historical development of postmodern language in the works of Saussure, Lévi-Strauss, Jakobson, Husserl, Hegel, Marx, hermeneutical thought, Heidegger, and Nietzsche? Could we have thought in those terms without the suggestion of narrative continuity and the goal of full commentary? Perhaps we would have been driven to the Renaissance. We might have needed long footnotes to cite the important influences of Eckhart, Boehme, Fichte, Feuerbach, and Kant's *Third Critique*. Other thinkers would require mention, because a summary essay demands the effects of "wholeness" and "completion." This essay is hampered enough by its lack of irony, its serious avoidance of mockery, its directness, and its hope for descriptive accuracy concerning the movement of self-overcoming. It hangs by the thread of its partiality to the incoherence of events and the impacts of accidents in its own formation. It lacks theater and eliminates dialectical thinking. It does not even mention Foucault or Lacan. Derrida is noted in passing. Where are these heroes of postmodernism? Their texts are voided in a moment of obsession with Nietzsche's self-overcoming. Have these texts already been overcome in Nietzsche's self-overcoming? Do they repeat what cannot be said in Nietzsche? Do they happen in a space of Nietzsche minus Nietzsche, a crisis that marks a temporal stretch that is unspeakable in metaphysics? A time of Nietzsche minus Nietzsche?

Chapter 3

THE CONTRADICTORY CHARACTER OF POSTMODERNISM

Donald Kuspit

I The ailment called postmodernism

"The inflationary and often contradictory use of the term post-modernism does not have to concern us," writes Jochen Schulte-Sasse, "as long as it is understood that postmodernity and post-modernism refer to qualitative changes in society and their cultural manifestations."[1] Schulte-Sasse is wrong: the inflationary and often contradictory use of the term "postmodernism" does have to concern us. The term may be more significant for what it tells us about the theorists who use it than for what it tells us about society and culture. (The contradictory character of the term expands its meaning; its inflationary character follows from this contradictoriness. That is, the inflation signals that the contradictoriness is unresolvable—an idealistic over-expansion that empties the term of material meaning. The only historical reality "postmodernism" comes to signal is that of its exaggerated significance for theorists, which is one way of understanding how it is that a term can become a signifier without reference. A so-called free signifier is a term that has been so removed from circulation—practice—by its intellectual analysis that it can only signify that analysis. It has, one might say, been over-clarified, which reduces its usefulness. It achieves ideal, rather than realistic, status.)

Is there any way Schulte-Sasse can be sure that the social and cultural changes "postmodernism" theoretically designates have not been inflated—into qualitative ones—by the term itself? The

53

changes may not be what they seem to be in the light of the concept when the concept itself is obscure. The term "postmodernism" may pass its inflationary contradictoriness on to its object, making what may be social and cultural molehills into insurmountable mountains. It may be that our society and culture do indeed have an inflated, contradictory character[2]—and this is implicitly, if perversely, acknowledged through the inflated, contradictory use of the term "postmodernism." However, there is no way of establishing it except through an analysis of the contradictoriness of the term "postmodernism."

That Schulte-Sasse is compelled to suppress his own intellectually honest, unhappy admission of the problematic character of postmodernism should make us aware that it has ideological import and is protected by a mystique. Postmodernism is more of a program developed by theorists than the common reality of contemporary society and culture. Postmodernism is a rhapsodic, elusive, exhilarating concept, used with license, because the hopes and fears—anxious ambitions?—of theorists are riding on it. I suggest that the term "postmodernism" is deliberately kept flexible and enchanting—so rich with connotations that it dissolves on direct contact with reality—as a pretentious, pseudo-autonomous display of theory's critical power in its bourgeois situation of social impotence.[3] The creative use of the term "postmodernism" is the product of unconscious frustration rather than unfolding conscious insight. In order to deny this frustration, the meaning of the term "postmodernism" *must* be kept open—even if it becomes so porous that it can hold no meaning. The more outwardly complex the theory of postmodernism, the less the inner truth it signifies will have to be faced: it implies the collapse of a by now true and tried (even establishment) sense of criticality, namely, that of anti-establishment modernist (avant-garde) criticality. It suggests that there is no replacement concept of criticality in sight. We may be in a transition toward a new period, or deadended in the old one. The term "postmodernism" reflects the uncertain destiny of criticality in contemporary society and culture. This signals, I contend, a changed rationale for criticality, a change in its meaning and purpose. If criticality is to continue to be socially useful in a broad way—rather than simply serving the narcissistic needs of intellectuals—it must serve different human needs than it once did.

The *Sturm-und-Drang* debate surrounding postmodernism creates the impression that it represents some extraordinary understanding.[4] The theory of postmodernism is presented as a great critical innovation, fraught with consequences for society and culture. Its incestuous intellectual turmoil suggests that it is conceived in difficult labor: it weighs a great deal at birth. In fact, all the conflict about it, like its own contradictory character, indicates that social and cultural theorists are extremely unsure of themselves, and of the power of their theory. The theory of postmodernism represents a general crisis of theory's belief in its power and influence—theory's loss of narcissistic face, loss of elementary belief in itself, loss of self-idealizing self-esteem. The excessive conflict and contradictoriness—leading not to agreement, but to rancorous confusion—raises the suspicion that the conceptualization of postmodernism is more a matter of honor among theorists than of interpretation of phenomena. The theory of postmodernism is a kind of spectacle—another entertainment, as opaque as any in our society; it obscures more than it illuminates—and fails to provide a genuinely critical/activist understanding. The difficulties, both internal and external, of the theory of postmodernism, suggest that it reflects contemporary bourgeois society more by way of demonstrating problems involved in critical and activist engagement—activism through criticality—than by direct articulation and examination. In other words, the contradictoriness of the theory of postmodernism is not simply a matter of familiar epistemological uncertainty accompanying the attempt to fix a concept definitively. Nor does it indicate an intellectual incision along a dialectical fault. Rather, it suggests the problem that critical/activist theory has encountered in its attempt to maintain a critical cutting edge in society.

The inflationary, contradictory use of the term "postmodernism" also suggests its esthetic use; it is an artistic phenomenon of sorts. One might even be tempted to say, however tongue-in-cheek, that the theory of postmodernism is implicated "in the aesthetic of the sublime [through which] modern art . . . finds its impetus and the logic of avant-gardes finds its axioms,"[5] making it a species of avant-garde art. Even further, it seems to be more about the problems of presenting theory, even the unpresentable in theory, than about creating a theory, if these elements can be separated at all these days.[6] It is of course harder and harder to distinguish a theory's artistic character from its cognitive character: analysis is itself a mode of narrative. And there is apparently less and less need and desire to make the distinction—perhaps another sign of theory's impotence, self-defeat. But it is worth noting that blurring the difference between the artistic character and the cognitive character of theory can be understood as a manifestation of what Freud has called "omnipotence of thought."[7] If thinking about postmodernism has become a high art, then it must involve the omnipotence of thought, like all art.[8]

If this is the case, then the theory of postmodernism is an artistic illusion serving theory's most desperate infantile needs. I have already suggested that they are generally narcissistic; now, I want to propose that they are specifically a matter of secondary narcissism, a regressive response to various social dangers, from bourgeois indifference to outright appropriation of criticality.[9] The critical/activist theorist necessarily—tautologously—believes in his or her criticality, and in the power—necessity, validity, and efficacy—of criticality as such. That is, after all, what it is to be a critical/activist theorist, and to have self-respect. The theory of postmodernism is the latest attempt to reinforce the credibility of critical thinking as an activist mode of relating to the world as well as an inherently valuable activity. It argues for the socio-existential as well as high intellectual import of critical thinking. More precisely, the theorists of postmodernism argue that there is still a significant critical culture in bourgeois society, acknowledged and advocated by, and including, them.

However, the theory of postmodernism absolutizes a bankrupt vision of the critical as parodic irony. Culture is supposed to be a parody of society.[10] This is criticality in acceptable bourgeois form. Parodic irony is criticality without its poisonous sting, the empty shell of criticality, criticality that has been castrated. The postmodernist version of criticality as parody is an attenuated, compromised conception of criticality, designed to save critical theory's face in contemporary bourgeois society. Parodic irony is not only no longer effective against it, but is itself bourgeois, a tactic of bourgeois control, a sign of the cynicism of the bourgeois status quo. In contemporary bourgeois society, parodic irony means self-compromise; it is no longer subtly rebellious self-assertion, dialectical self-consciousness, ingenious self-transformation in the face of the status quo. Parody is thus an illusion of criticality. It is criticality without any teeth.

Postmodernist theorists hang on to the old idea of avant-garde criticality or resistance to bourgeois society. They assume that to rationalize and conventionalize modernist criticality into parody—to turn confrontational avant-garde anger into witty sniping—is to propose a whole new theory of criticality. They do not recognize the de facto bankruptcy of avant-garde criticality. As has been much noted, it has been institutionalized and co-opted by bourgeois society. Not only is the old criticality dead and the new criticality not yet born, but its birth is hindered by the postmodernist theorists, who refuse to recognize the obsoleteness of the old criticality. This puts the fate of criticality itself in jeopardy. As we will see, it is in architecture in particular—the most public of the arts—that parodic irony is supposed to be most alive and effective. Indeed, the term "postmodernism" has been applied most unequivocally to architecture. But even there, the avant-garde idea of criticality—even in its attenuated form of parodic irony—has become beside the point, a fact which architectural historians alone seem to recognize. As we will see, they argue that what is perceived as parodic irony is nothing of the sort.

In sum, I am arguing that the fundamental postmodernist issue is what the character and meaning of criticality are in the so-called postmodernist age. The truth behind the term "postmodernism" is that modernist criticality no longer works or makes sense in contemporary bourgeois society. The bourgeois have learned to resist it by assimilating and neutralizing—diluting—it. Their strategy of response is not unlike that of the Russians, who let invaders penetrate into their land as far as they can, until they flounder and die in the Russian winter. The bourgeois have made modernist criticality, with its confrontational melancholy and disruptive deconstruction of bourgeois modes of representation, their own.[11] They have introduced an almost overwhelmingly therapeutic—anesthetic?—response to melancholy, in effect surrounding it on all sides, creating the illusion that it is generally conquerable but in fact acknowledging its near universality.[12] And they have assimilated deconstructive modes of representation, which get their revolutionary power by playing upon the ambiguity of the difference between abstract presentation and concrete representation, as the spearhead signs of their own ideology of so-called "permanent revolution."[13] The theory of postmodernism reflects this—showing its own bourgeois character—by dogmatically advocating hypothetically deconstructive parody as therapeutic criticality, in effect combining the extremes in a single facile formulation. This innocent notion of therapeutic deconstruction plays into the hands of bourgeois society, for it amounts to criticality's self-limitation. Thus, the contradictoriness which theorists regard as a sign of the complexity of the phenomenon of postmodernism is actually the sign of the failure of critical theory to achieve a revolutionary criticality, such as avant-garde criticality claimed to be, whether in its melancholy or deconstructive modes. The real phenomenon of postmodernism is that neither theory in particular nor culture in general live up to their own great critical expectations of themselves. Theory imagines it has achieved authentic criticality—criticality serving the needs of contemporary society—by advocating a watered-down version of the old modernist idea of criticality, which today has become a quaint, historical aspect of what Harold Rosenberg called the tradition of the modern. And high culture seems to flounder in a melancholy deconstruction of all historical styles, a fact that seems especially evident in postmodernist architecture. Later, we will see that the decadence suggested by this fact means quite the opposite of what it seems to.

The inflated, contradictory use of the term "postmodernism" also marks the degeneration of activist criticality into futile, self-righteous rage signalling nothing but its own preaching thunder. It has been argued that this is the way it exists in the Marxist writings of Frederic Jameson and Terry Eagleton.[14] Activist criticality seems to be able to exist paranoically only as rage because it unconsciously experiences itself as peculiarly illegitimate or impossible—threatened in its very existence—in contemporary bourgeois society. It is lost in a kind of no-man's-land; more precisely, it has become irrelevant because class conflict has become peculiarly irrelevant in bourgeois society, so that activist criticality has no clear side or revolutionary cause to serve. Paradoxically, this is just because social differences have become perversely irreconcilable: class conflict has become hypostatized. Philosophically, this can be regarded as the collapse of dialectic, the much-acknowledged inability to achieve totality, or rather the recognition of a perverse totalization of society through the principle of permanent contradiction. Contradiction is institutionalized as irreducible, in effect an acknowledgement of the so-called instability of and discontinuity in all social relations, and the consequent diminishing of the sense of self.[15] This simply underlines the insurmountable differences that make for a lack of social and personal cohesion.

If criticality that is worth the name—criticality that is more than rabid and finally arbitrary and pseudo-apocalyptic negation, more than a displacement of one's death wish onto the other, a blind aggression against the other—implicitly aims at reconciliation with its target, then the hardening of differences into irreconcilability signals that activist criticality is no longer a "progressive," viable approach to social conflict. If contradiction has become a principle of social "conservation" and determination, criticality can no longer work through contradiction. This perverse social and cultural stabilization—"inflation"—of contradiction in postmodernism can be regarded as an ironical apotheosis of the unconscious bourgeois belief that the "difference" between itself and all other classes can and will be overcome, but on its own terms: everyone will eventually become bourgeois, creating a homogeneous society in which the lowest common denominator conception of life will be elevated as ideal. (Supplying this conception and performing this elevation is the task of popular culture.) This is certainly one ironical way of avoiding "catastrophic" revolution, maintaining the status quo, and trivializing activist criticality as beyond the pale—marginal in the extreme. It is a major way of de-legitimatizing critical difference in general and muting activist criticality in either its conservative or anarchistic forms.[16] The inflationary, contradictory use of the term "postmodernism" reflects this bourgeois hypostatization of irreconcilability and the simultaneous falsification of reconciliation. This theoretical as well as social and cultural triumph of the bourgeois is more than a class or ideological victory; it is a "metaphysical" triumph.

II The cure called postmodernism

The term "postmodern" implies contradiction of the modern without transcendence of it. This is, I take it, what Jean-François Lyotard means when he writes that "the postmodern . . . is undoubtedly a part of the modern."[17] Clearly, part of the identity problem of postmodernism is to identify the modern. Instead, postmodernism has reified the problem of identity, absolutizing identity crisis, as it were. Postmodernism implies not simply that it is difficult but impossible and *unnecessary* to achieve what Heinz Kohut calls a core self,[18] primitive "integrity," or what Schulte-Sasse calls "a homogeneous, fortified identity."[19] This is the import of the postmodernist argument about—one is tempted to say advocacy of—schizophrenia.[20] It is the one area of consensus in postmodernist theory. At the same time, postmodernism shows itself to be violently nostalgic for the various avant-garde strategies of achieving integrity. These range from the techniques of aggressive alienation as described by Renato Poggioli[21] and as summarized by Jürgen Habermas in his statement that "modernity lives on the experience of rebelling against all that is normative"[22] to Lyotard's view that the postmodern is the neo-sublime of unpresentability, namely, a neo-estheticism in the form of neo-experimentalism.[23] Habermas, in spite of himself, is a postmodernist, or at least he faces a postmodernist issue, in addressing the problem of legitimation—and its distorted mirror image, i.e. Peter Bürger's notion that the avant-garde is an attempt to re-integrate art and life by overcoming estheticism.[24] Postmodernism is in the contradictory position of yearning for the perhaps insane and ineffective rebellious integrity of the avant-garde—the tragic idealism of its activist criticality—and repudiating it. This is the essence of its, and unconsciously bourgeois society's, identity problem.

As I have emphasized, postmodernist theory is in a double bind: it acknowledges the social assimilation of the avant-garde as another cultural institution[25]—as noted, another bourgeois entertainment—and its dissemination in the schizophrenic field of society, yet it still clings to a belief in activist criticality that can only derive from the avant-garde. This condition of contradiction—which as I have suggested is as stable as contradiction in bourgeois society—signifies activist criticality's condition of social and cultural impasse, which is most succinctly articulated in the impasse of the self facing the problem of its own integrity. From a postmodernist perspective—which supposedly transcends pessimism and optimism—this problem is passé; yet on the individual level it is experienced as pressing, and the postmodernists indirectly acknowledge it in their theory of the individual as a schizophrenic "center" displaced by messages passing through it. The most significant aspect of postmodernist thinking—as exemplified by Habermas, who as I have suggested is more postmodernist than he realizes—is its insistence that the only way out of this impasse of activist criticality and self-criticality, the only way to establish a critical/activist relationship to society and to find a ground for personal integrity (reconciling these pressing needs or rather denying their inseparability), is through acceptance of intersubjectivity. That alone leads to critically significant individuality and social activism. The modernist rebel and experimenter refused the condition of intersubjectivity, which postmodernism embraces.

In summary, postmodernism has a double dimension: (1) desperate clinging to obsolete modes of hyper-individualistic yet conventionalized or institutionalized criticality (e.g., in the pseudo-rebel/hero of the rock world); and (2) recognition that the *locus vivendi* of activist criticality and sophisticated integrity is at once cognitive and empathic acceptance of intersubjectivity, with all its problems. In fact, the transition from the paradigm of modernist subjective consciousness to that of postmodernist intersubjectivity advocated by Habermas has been thoroughly worked out in psychoanalytic theory's transition from drive theory to interpersonalist and object-relations theory.[26] Above all, as I will maintain, with the empathic as the conduit for the cognitive—something that the historian of postmodern architecture, rather than its cultural interpreter, recognizes as a general truth of postmodernist intentionality. (Psychoanalysis has long since been postmodernist; whatever pockets of modernist thinking about the subject remain have been integrated into a postmodernist intersubjectivist perspective. I mention this because I will use postmodernist psychoanalytic concepts in order to understand what is basically at stake in postmodernist architecture.)

The difference between the two sides of postmodernism—and the correct (essentially psychosocial or intersubjectivist) inter-

61

pretation of its critical/activist dimension—can be made transparently clear by contrasting a cultural theorist's with an art historian's understanding of the critical/activist character of postmodernist architecture. As Linda Hutcheon, the theorist, remarks, architecture is "the one art form in which the label [postmodern] seems to refer, uncontested, to a generally agreed upon corpus of works."[27] For Hutcheon, postmodern architecture has an unequivocally "parodic relation to the art of the past."[28] This is a supposedly critical—rather then merely parasitic—relationship: "It contests uniformity by parodically asserting ironic difference instead of either homogeneous identity or alienated otherness."[29] (The former is the normative bourgeois conception of identity, the latter the avant-garde conception, both are supposedly quaintly modernist). The key word here is "contest," which echoes Lyotard's notion of "agonistics"[30]: without it, there is no criticality. As Hutcheon says, "contemporaneity need not signify wholesale implication without critical consciousness."[31] For her, there is a double aspect to postmodernist criticality in general: the return to the past (presumably the passive element in it), and the return to it in a parodic way (where the parodic is a way of avoiding sentimentality or directionless and speechless nostalgia, and is thus presumably the active element in it). The postmodernist return to the past is generally critical of modernism, with its presumed repudiation of the past. And the parodic relation to the past is particularly critical, for the return does not mean that one is taken in by the past, but rather that one maintains a "critical" distance from it. And to what point? Hutcheon has nothing to say about this. Parody shows that one is not taken in by the past, not really sympathetic to it, and recognizes that it is not really "appropriate" to the present. Then why bother with it? "Just as modernism (oedipally) had to reject historicism and to pretend to a parthenogenetic birth fit for the new machine age, so postmodernism, in reaction, returned to history, to what I want to call 'parody,' to give architecture back its traditional social and historical dimension, though with a new twist this time."[32] Is this just another swing of the pendulum, the inevitable return and recycling of the past that is repressed in collective modern memory?

What does this complex postmodernist criticality—the return

to the past, the parodic distance from it—really amount to? As Hutcheon presents them, both the return and its parody are superficial, gratuitous, seemingly self-reflexive acts of art. Where the medium of self-reflexivity was the material medium in modernist art, in postmodernist art it is presumably conceptual—the way of conceptualizing the past, more generally history, including the history of the present. But is the reconceptualization of the past—the establishing of a new critical/activist relation to it—accomplished by this kind of mechanical reversal of the modernist orientation and the emptily ironical, purely esthetic parodying of the past, as Hutcheon presents this re-orientation to the past? Both the "reaction" and the "twist" as she understands them seem to serve no other purpose than to afford the postmodernist architect the narcissistic self-satisfaction of cleverly asserting "critical difference" from the modernist architect. They are almost foreordained moves in the game of history, the first making them gain the prestige of knowing how to play the game—understanding the timing crucial to playing it. If there is anything truly revolutionary in the postmodernist giant step toward history and the small parodic step away from it, it has been lost in Hutcheon's treatment of the steps as esthetically experimental. For her, they are implicitly the latest way of generating artistic novelty in a critically credible way. For all her insistence on the criticality of the return to history and the use of parody, she shows this trivial criticality as having no other point than to celebrate itself. It may be "reductive" to think, as Hutcheon writes, "that any recall of the past must, by definition, be sentimental nostalgia," but it is also reductive of criticality to think that the parodic "ambiguity and irony" that result from "echoing history and its multivalent meanings" is its postmodernist essence.[33] On the contrary, the parodic is criticality deadended in itself, smugly lost in the labyrinth of its own knowing subtlety—criticality with no other purpose than to score points in a game of solitaire, to play that nostalgic game of Trivia called "ironic references."[34] The parodic is modernist ambiguity and irony reduced to the purposeless cunning of a generalized reason.

It never occurs to Hutcheon that there may be other reasons than esthetically ingratiating, cannibalistic, didactic ones for returning to the past and establishing what she mistakenly interprets as a parodic relationship to it. In fact, hidden behind the self-importance of the parodic return to the past, there is an attempt to achieve some kind of intimate relationship to it. Postmodernist architecture attempts to appropriate the past not as a dead, over-estheticized form but as a living, symbolic substance, charged with contemporary significance—which is the only way the past can remain viable. The return to the past is in effect a criticism of the present's lack of integrity, and is in purpose motivated by an effort to recover that integrity in symbolic form. For authentic postmodernism, the past represents lost integrity, the "home" the subject no longer inhabits but still yearns for, namely its own sanity and general good. The past is re-enacted less in the spirit of parody than of empathy, however incomplete. Pre-emptively to interpret the postmodernist appropriation of the past as parodic—a kind of witty "off" parroting of it—is to ignore the latent empathic reasons for seeking out a relationship to it, trying to establish a kind of introspective relationship with it. That empathy may miss the full reality of that past—and may be a form of knowing mystification to some—but this reality always exists archaeologically, through its reified information-signs and ideal constructs.

Is the inflationary, contradictory use of the term "postmodernism" a reverberation from this empathic use of the past for the purposes of achieving an elusive contemporary integrity? Does it perhaps signal the difficulties of using the past as a weapon against contemporary schizophrenia or lack of subjective cohesion? Does it register the difficulty of using the past intersubjectively? Is the reluctance of cultural theorists to accept this intersubjective, empathic use of the past as a symbol of integrity—the "true self" hidden under the contemporary "false self," in D. W. Winnicott's sense of these terms[35]—responsible for the inflationary, contradictory use of the term "postmodernism"? Will such empathic searching always seem inflationary and contradictory—overreaching and unstable—from the perspective of theoretical purity? This search constitutes the critical/activist content and intentionality of postmodernism at its best.

Pure theorists are ashamed of and refuse to admit the contemporary emotional needs that motivate the postmodernist return to the past. They have in effect estheticized and emotionally sanitized critical/activist theory—removed its psychological aspect. But some art historians are ready to admit it, if indirectly.

They implicitly acknowledge that postmodernism makes the past contemporary by using it to satisfy living needs symbolically. They realize the peculiar character of postmodernism's intimacy with the past—in effect a testing of its potential for symbolizing the integrity absent in the present, of making good the bad present environment[36]—and that its critical activism exists through this testing.

For them, genuinely "postmodernist" criticality is an effort to solve the problem of modernity, the problem that, it is now realized, the aggressive rebellion or anti-normativeness and alienation from intersubjectivity that avant-garde activist criticality signalled. It is the problem of the apparent impossibility of achieving integrity according to existing psychosocial norms, and yet it is a felt need *for* the integrity *without* the destruction of the intersubjective matrix of society. Under the auspices of this postmodernist articulation of the felt, pressing need for integrity—for cohesion in the face of a schizophrenic, idly pluralistic world—modernist rebellion can now be understood as an attack against the character-types that bourgeois society proposes as models to be followed. From the postmodernist art-historical perspective, the so-called nostalgia of postmodernism shows that an element of profound psychological pathos—misunderstood by the parodic interpretation of postmodernist criticality—is operational in the postmodernist manipulation of fragments of past styles. What appears to be parodic is in fact a loose and limited allegorical attempt to integrate sign-fragments of the past in a way that makes contemporary emotional sense. It is an effort to give a sense of dialectical inevitability to their relationship, as though their contemporary presence could only be explained by the fact that their reconciliation was imminent. There is no actual statement of reconciliation, only its proposal or rehearsal, as it were—no actual integrity, but its intimation. The amalgamation of historical styles is in part that of a constellation in the sky, in part that of a confederation of states.

Postmodernism thus represents an expanded sense of the possibilities of the past. Cognition of the art-historical past is worked through to an empathic relationship to it. There is the gold of integrity in the empathy itself. Integrity is, as it were, prosthetically achieved through this narcissistic appropriation of the past, in effect a combination of mirror and idealizing transferences to it.[38] The appropriation of classicism in Charles Moore's Piazza d'Italia in New Orleans (1976) does not parodically empty it, as Hutcheon thinks, but in fact establishes an empathic intimacy with it—no doubt ironic from the perspective of a professional classicist or fan of popular culture—and thereby gives it a special kind of fullness and accessibility, or usefulness.

The architectural historian Heinrich Klotz is closer to an understanding of the emotional gains of postmodernist appropriation of the architectural past than Linda Hutcheon. One can regard Klotz's approach as "conservative" rather than "radical" if one wishes, but that is to miss the critical import. Klotz calls attention to the "playful and humorous" character of Moore's postmodern architecture: "here the sonorous sound of the all-powerful no longer speaks, but the wit of the human-all-too-human." What was dismissed as unserious by modernism—"human license"— is once again allowed.[38] For Klotz, postmodernist architecture has something to say about the condition of being human— the creative play inherent in being human. Integrity is realized through this play.[39]

> Postmodernist architecture is not intent upon exclusivity and strict consequence, but is prepared for difficult compromises and proposes daring connections. It advocates . . . the fullness of life, not the orthodoxy of dogma. The "revolutionaries," who broke completely with history in the name of a new age, are today "revisionists" who have the dangerous purpose of reconciliation. They want to combine the memory of the long past with the pathos of innovation. . . . Revision is the third way between conservativism and revolution, which we would like to advertise as the term—already one of abuse—for "postmodern." We presuppose that an abundance of the achievements of the modern are still valid, and we presuppose that an abundance of the dogmatic, rigidified teachings of the modern are untenable. . . . Radically new, standing in sharp contrast to the program of the modern, is the demand for an architecture that no longer proclaims the abstraction of pure geometric form, but instead the diverse forms that are used to mediate contents and messages, that

is, an architecture that again permits the pictorial and the imagistic [*Bildhaften und Abbildhaften*], decoration and ornament, symbol and sign.[40]

It is appropriate that architecture, the most public of arts, once again openly serve human needs—the need of being human—and that it resist the tendencies of modernist architecture to annihilate all traces of humanness. Clearly, for Klotz, postmodernist architecture at its best is an attempt to counteract the annihilative anxiety that haunts contemporary bourgeois society.[41] Where the modernist building was the metaphor for the modern ideal of robotic man,[42] the postmodernist building is an attempt to make buildings once again like essentially organic human beings, however integrated with the machine. Freud has remarked on the uncanny effect of certain automata that seem human, suggesting that certain human beings operate automatically.[43] While not denying the machine presence in contemporary life, postmodernist architecture is an attempt to restore the human to predominance. The compromises and reconciliations it proposes, from the return to decoration (inseparable from the notion of improving decor or environment) and ornament (once thought of as a "necessary accident" of human existence[44]), to the symbolizing and signing of historical human presence, are all indications of the postmodernist path to integrity of self.

The fact that an irreversible intersubjectivity is suggested by the "theatrical" turn to history, in the form of remembered architectural styles, is perhaps the most dynamic part of postmodernism. Postmodernist architecture suggests that it is never possible to be an integral subject without remembering the intersubjectivity of the past. In this sense, it is a kind of healing of the wound modernist architecture gave to the human beings who inhabited it by asking them to forget everything but the present. Modernist architecture functioned like the commissar of a brave new world ruthlessly liquidating all traces of the old worlds that once existed. Now this mechanistic inhumanity is itself eliminated as criminal by postmodernist architecture. This is correlate with the assimilation of the technological revolution that inspired modernist architecture. In however strange a way—and that it is often an apparently comic way suggests that there was a tragic aspect to the old modernist architecture—postmodernist architecture struggles to articulate a sense of human self that, while appropriate to the present, takes its cues from older statements of humanness which it struggles to remember. These become its sources. In its encyclopaedic, quasi-museumlike character, postmodernist architecture shows a hunger for old ideas of authenticity. It is like Hamlet with Yorick's skull, in search of a half-familiar, half-forgotten truth about human existence. Until it finds that truth, it remains a demonstration that there is more in the heaven of art than modernism imagined in its philosophy.

Chapter 4

POSTMODERNISM AND
(POST)MARXISM

John O'Neill

It may well be that I will not honour my topic. This will depend upon your point of view. In earlier times, I might have presumed upon its direction. Today, however, Marxists are less sure of themselves and postmodernists would be offended by any other certainty than uncertainty. Here is a dilemma we have inherited from modernism, namely, that we cannot start from any certain sense of the public's authority nor of its morality. This is so because a modern audience cannot resist the seduction of its own decentering, of its irrelevance and its dispersion. So you would be no more satisfied if I were to presume upon your postmodernism as a perspective upon your Marxism than if I were to treat your Marxism as an antidote for your postmodernism. So I will not relate to you what you already know about these elements of our culture. Rather, I will try to keep the reflections that follow within and against the tradition of modernity, weighing its hopes while marking its melancholy. This, then, is an attempt to honor the question of their relationship by avoiding any dogmatic account of either postmodernism or of Marxism while nevertheless striving within the limits of each discipline to put oneself in question.

I will, however, set forth certain bold assertions at the outset so that they may serve either as a guide to or a summary review of the places (*topoi*) at which one must engage argument. At the same time, nothing requires that one's development of these issues should be concerned with them in any sequence or priority. They are, then, reminders or remainders of the postmodern condition.[1]

Theses on postmodernism

1 Novelty is the new conformity; yet
2 the return to history is rather an escape from history.
3 The open history of fashion and style is the end of all histories mirrored in our own; at the same time as
4 the norms of subjectivity and pleasure are conscriptions of repressive *jouissance*.
5 Fashion rewrites the body, assigns its moods, movements, and manageability in order to distract us from the corpse of politics.
6 Style rewrites the mind, appropriates authority and narrativity in order to subject writing to writing—grammatology without end.
7 Alienation and youth are no longer shocking in themselves or even together; this is because alienated youth is the norm—but without any sense of its alternatives.
8 No attempt to *épater la bourgeoisie* can satisfy the bourgeois capacity for shock, violence, and deception.
9 All such observations are met with indifference; this is because—
10 we no longer have the will to difference. Begin again at point one above . . . repeat until the cycle separates into stations of the Cross but with no Easter.

What is difficult in thinking about postmodernism is that it deprives us of the very resource of parody needed to situate it. This is because postmodernism celebrates the neutralization of all conviction from which even mimicry derives. Our predicament is that neither socialist realism nor bourgeois fictionalism will show our society to itself because its soup cans and its tractors are neither more dead than alive. Moreover, their reproduction actually confirms the production of the ideology of repetition and so convinces us of the foreclosure of history in the narrow future of the self's immediate future. Socialism appears no less to confirm our capacity for boredom than does capitalism. For whether alienation is banned or bastardized, it still eats away at our insides, voicelessly. Thus we are condemned to the present as our future, and no wind truly waves the bright flags of postmodernism or Marxism.

The fact is that our neo-liberalism will not allow institutional substructures to determine cultural superstructures any more than it will allow history to work behind our backs. And the same is true of our liberal politics. We will not prefer class to race or to gender, even if it means moving the political struggle indoors, floating it in the imaginary settings of commissions, television, and the university where insurrection is about as obscene as an erection. This is probably more true of North American practice than of European politics, even though such practice nicely fits with the linguistic excesses and the withering of truth and history celebrated in post-structuralist theory. The awful thing is that our political space has been foreclosed in the name of both theory and practice. Under these circumstances the common sense of British Marxists is little better than the hedonism of their French counterparts or the postmodern puritanism of their American commentators. In Canada, meantime, we seem curiously bent on moving from postmodernism to premodernism, while living off the remains of a colonized modernity with its comfortable disdain for its surroundings at home and abroad.

However we refer to it, there can be little doubt that we now experiment with postmodernism. Indeed, this may so far be the case that no one can recall—let alone be recalled to—modernism. Yet we know enough to know that despite its mock seriousness, postmodernism could hardly be responsible for itself. Postmodernism displays energy that is frivolous and wasteful. We know that it has solved no historical problem, that it has not come into any utopian end of history and that, above all, it is prematurely aged with its own pretence that youth has neither a past nor a future. Yet there is a complaint, however thin its voice, that postmodernism cannot fail to bring against its parent. It is the charge that it is, after all, nothing but the child of modernism. It therefore cannot be understood unless the compulsion that drove modernism to yield to its own after effect can be understood. Why do parents weaken themselves with the hope of their offspring who are in turn burdened with a future for which they lack strength and against which they must rage? Viewed in this way, postmodernism wastes itself with the reproduction of the past in an infantile hope of monumentalizing a moment outside of its own memory that might somehow trigger its identity, its past and future now. Postmodernism is therefore extremely verbal, despite its weak capacity for language; it is a master of gesticulation but otherwise inarticulate. Architecture is its empty soul; and film and literature its wandering ghosts.

Yet it appears that modernity (or pre-postmodernism, if you will) has been sick all along with its own dead end. Now it is mocked by its own children for not having delivered their development, their endless progress, their reasonableness, their polymorphous bodies of desire, their love and peace, their seals and whales. The children divide their complaint into consumerism on the right and anti-communism on the left and in between the older children rejuvenate themselves momentarily in Live Aid concerts. Everything testifies to the insanity of postmodernism. Politics, art, and the economy turn into fragments of light spinning off a glass globe at the center of a dark world where the children dance to their own deafness. Everything glitters in a world without vision. Language fractures in the same way. Our stories do not hold but instead they proliferate without priority. Unable even to order their own elements, our narrative arts begin nowhere, end nowhere, and are a puzzle to their own fictional inhabitants. The farm, the factory, and the family are wastelands of character, order, and progress and no longer serve the engine of postmodernity any better than a disco. Terrorism, racism, and the unofficial wars in Afghanistan, Nicaragua, Lebanon, and Ireland divide the political realm, scatter its sites and scramble the language of revolution in the disorders of the disfigured but twin enterprises of capitalism and communism. In such observations we, of course, overwhelm ourselves, entangling ourselves in the ceaseless flux of events without a history or a space—or rather of events that have been deterritorialized and dehistoricized by the failure of modernity to include them in its geopolitical order. The war in Afghanistan no more captured our attention in Canada than a sale on Bloor Street and for the same reason our own past is as remote from its present as are the Maritime provinces from Toronto's Yorkville.

The question that postmodernism turns upon is, how do we justify the repudiation of the past that gives modernism its sense and yet not accept everything around us in the present—including modernism and its generation of antimodernism, if not postmodernism? Can we really set aside our Cartesianism and Kantianism, or our positivism, as though they haven't withstood our

Hegelianism, our structuralism, our mediations and totalities, and although these, too, are worn around the edges, ought we to discard them into the bargain? If the bourgeois humanist tradition is bankrupt, shouldn't we also call in our loans to socialist humanism? Of course, the Left continues to be braver in its philosophy than in its politics. What I mean is that anti-humanism may look well on one's office door while the university enjoys civil liberties and good salaries in exchange for its responsible academic irresponsibility. But where the political consequences of anti-humanism are practiced by soulless bureaucracies and state machineries of confinement, censorship, and torture—such a notice would merely mark one's own disappearance. Between the alternatives of philosophical bravado and political impotence, there lies the intermediate realm of the economy, class, race, and illness, as well as the outer horizons of colonialism and nuclearism, where it is harder to pronounce the death of humanism and yet difficult to hold on to the birth of socialism. In a sense, we exclude ourselves through the very practice of such panoramic surveys which are to the intellectual what the supermarket is to the consumer—our ersatz freedom of choice exchanged for abandoning productive choices in the economy and the polity. Of course, the university and the rest of our mass-media culture supplement the shopping center in the maintenance of a society without history, where everything jostles everything else in an unseasonable present. We suffer our moral poverty as that *embarras de richesse* we call pluralism and perspectivism because we no longer assign to the self and its situations any authority beyond its own renunciation, and then we fall into style.

There is in postmodernism a certain will to willessness—a failure of nerve that gives it its nerve. How is that? It reveals itself in the *primacy of language,* in the objectivity of institutions resistant to intention, affect, and hope. Such institutions turn language against itself, making it an autonomous discourse resistant to context and common sense. The dead-end of history, the foreclosure of community, and the trivialization of the self and family are the rubble upon which we construct our glass corporations. Here speculation is doubly spectacular. We have gambled against ourselves while constructing glass towers to reflect everything we have lost—a corporate Babel where language holds to

73

no center. Reflecting our reduced polytheism, the glass corporation miniaturizes us with its welcome, its disposability, its accommodation of our wants generated on its behalf. Such events, so far from being extralinguistic, are inconceivable without a similar incorporation of language in a self-sufficient structure. Paradoxically, it is then the language paradigm to which appeal is made in order to comprehend the objectivity of our corporate institutions, whose self-contained discourse is productive of our deepest alienation from meaning, context, and purpose. The naturalization of the language paradigm is the ideological counterpart to the dehistoricization and the depoliticization of the capitalist process. Thus meaning-and-value-production exceed us as much as the ordinary labor of work; and in each case we are dispossessed by what we need. The implicit complaint in this observation, however, cannot be articulated once our language has gone on a post-structuralist holiday, abandoning its own history to the rituals of meaning without values.

The cry that there is nothing outside of language or that there is not extratextuality (*hors texte*) is insufferable because it is we who are outside of language once the flow of its signifiers exceeds our attempts to identify their referents. It is our history, our community, our hope that is abandoned with the embrace of the quasi-natural language reproduced in the discursive machines of our corporate and governmental institutions. Our commercialism, like our intellectualism, mesmerizes us and, precisely because we make ourselves central to its spectacles, we thereby lose our historical and social bearings. Thus the power of the media over us is the power we have in the media, providing we surrender to its desires as our wants. What else we might truly need will also be supplied by the media in morality plays and subsidized corporate high culture.[2] In the latter, the struggles of the family and the individual with some authority are specularized in compensation for their abandonment in the commercialized and politicized ethics that rule the day. Thus the culture industry produces an ethics of nostalgia which spiritualizes us as passive spectators of the world we have lost, while simultaneously foreclosing any insight into how our past morality might be rendered continuous without future moral needs. The result is that fundamentalism prevails over utopianism. Or else we have to refurbish our religions, and in this regard, Marxism and

Christianity are on the same footing in needing to reconnect the events of human suffering with institutional mediations that translate work, reason, and love into meaningful lives for persons, families, and communities fulfilling the present with the continuity of past and future hopes.

The postmodernist rejection of mediations, the search for immediate presence, is haunted by the unfulfillment of this desire. The rejection of Christ's mediation of human history left not only the Jewish people waiting and thirsting in the desert—it has scattered all interpretation. However discreetly we make our assumptions, the dance of polytheism surrounds them and the outer edges of knowledge and value darken. Neither nature nor mind nor the body has replaced the theological text with self-certain readings because in them we have only rediscovered the blind spot in ourselves. For such insight we pay to ourselves a price that disclaims any redemptive value. Having reduced language and history to our own uses, we are as unsure of our place among their shifting signifiers as we are of any other thing no longer signified except as it clings to exchange value. Here nothing stands unless it be style, and then even style must hope it will be recycled, affirming the second time around its celebration of absolute irrelevance. In such contexts, the self loses its depth; everything becomes a surface—our mirrors reflect nothing but a glassy superficiality of looks, arrangement, decor, montage. Between the spaces lie the dead gods of divinity, authoriality and paternity without which grammar itself falls apart. Thus we no longer observe any canon and our master narratives fragment into hysterical case histories whose incompleteness marks our impotent and uncertain point of view. Lacking a storyable literature, we also lack a politics and thereby any sense of history, place, and family except as we append these to madness and exploitation. Or else we retreat to our libraries and blindly explore their labyrinths, entombing desire in dead languages that will never again gather any community beyond the bone heaps of literary criticism.

Postmodern artists reject the aestheticist autonomy of modern art. However, while problematizing both the subjective and objective referents of art, it cannot be said that postmodernism has reduced the elitism of art, escaped from its commercialism, or abandoned itself to the interpretative will of a new political public.[3] Moreover, the gesture of killing off God and ourselves as fellow artists surely no longer astonishes a bourgeoisie that long ago emigrated into the labyrinths of bureaucracy, into the irre-sponsibility of the market, realpolitik, and fashionable histories in which everything is degradable. In short, it is difficult to hang on to postmodernism's claim to be transgressive given the capacity of late capitalism to absorb and to neutralize every shock it imposes upon human truth, justice, equality, and beauty, and even to replay these outrages in anything from a rock video to a commercial or new release. The faster the culture industry runs to outrage its bourgeoisie, the surer it can be of its own embourgeoisement. After all, vulgarity in the appropriation of wealth by those who are successful in the culture industry cannot be considered to have revolutionized our society or its values. When the children of rock video sing out to the starving children of the world, charity itself has been reduced to a postmodern gesture of having fun on behalf of the world's immiseration. We have to ask whether Jesus would have done better as a Palestin-ian disc jockey. The idiocy of such questions reflects the uncer-tainty we experience in wanting to believe that any of our institu-tions work towards our humanity. It may well be that "we"—intellectuals and artists—are paid to suffer this question without politicizing it in order to square it with our ordinary moral convic-tion that the world's humanity is still worth working for and that it cannot be trashed by the present disvalues of any major society. Postmodernism is perhaps the penance we pay for abandoning politics. But such a *mea culpa* reverses the order of things. For we have no politics that has not already abandoned us in its pursuit of greed, triviality, and borderline insanity. It isn't just that the king has no clothes—he is naked because he is a corpse, mindless and speechless.

Hal Foster has suggested that we can distinguish two lineages in postmodernism, somewhat as follows:

1) *Neoconservative* postmodernism;
2) *Post-structuralist* postmodernism.[4]

The nomenclature is, however, a little clumsy. On the one hand, neoconservatives would probably consider post-structuralism part of the culture of antimodernism which they deplore. They would also be surprised at being considered postmodernists rather than, say, neomodernists. This is because they remain enamored of the modernist will to subjectivity, action, and history. Post-structuralists, on the other hand, appear to be beating the dead horse of modernism whose corpse is perhaps more rotten, even if more recent, when found in the streets of socialism. Post-structuralists seem to believe that the cart of history and politics can lurch along without any horse in front of it— they do not notice the masses pushing from behind. The same is true of the more flamboyant cultural antics of postmodernists. Their pretence to *épater la bourgeoisie* merely starves out the ignorant masses while scarcely feeding the voracious appetite of the bourgeoisie for shock, outrage, and violence. By the same token, the bourgeois consumption of violent culture protects it from its own productions of historyless violence, which have colonized the domestic imagination as well as our extraterrestrial dreams. Thus the Super-Id of late capitalism expands in the wasteland created through the collapse of the modernist Super-Ego, giving rise to a neoconservative lament for lost spiritual authority. Late-capitalist technologies no longer manufacture history and selfhood, any more than the professions and bureaucracy can reproduce society and the family.[5]

Late capitalism unleashes an unbounded narcissism for which it is simultaneously produces the liquefactions of an ahistorical, asocial mass culture, economy, and politics. Such a culture is marked by its identification of opposites, its ability to collapse contraries, to combine sentimentalism and indifference, exploitation and emancipation, to psychologize the political process while deepening its disciplinary politicizations of the psyche and its therapeutic culture.[6] Thus the psycho-text and the skin surfaces are inscribed within circuits of symbolic exchange whose own cyclicity of highs and lows provided all there is of orientation, history, and value. Experience surrenders to the autonomy of the instant which in turn cracks all memory. Suffering cannot be recalled except through the rosy glasses of nostalgia. Denunciation sounds manic and, like the bitter critic, excludes itself with an apology. Capital is, after all, self-critical, bitter and self-mocking, cruel and kind, intelligent and zany. How should we exceed this god-term? How are we to refuse it its proper idols?

As Weber saw, our reason has divided once and for all into the subrationalities of science, art, and ethics. But we have not experienced any detotalizing settlement in this process. On the contrary, our science tries to rule our politics and economy, while our economy largely dominates our art and morality, if not our science. At the extreme edge, our art and morality try to impose their rule upon our science and political economy—but they generally lack the stamina, as in the university; or else they scandalize us, as in the case of liberation theology. Surely, we can hardly hope for postmodern literary criticism to rise above these contradictions—to unmask social difference (class, gender, race) and to regenerate "our" humanism. The more literary criticism achieves social consciousness, the more it dissipates—like everything else in the postmodern experience. To return to Weber, we might say that the crisis of modernity consists in the empty voice of its double vocation for science and politics—men are no longer sure of their ruling knowledge and are unable to mobilize sufficient legitimation for the master-narratives of truth and justice. The fact is that philosophy, history, religion, and art have lost their authority.[7] This has been known for some time. Yet we seem to need Lyotard and Rorty to tell us this—despite their own bad faith. Lyotard tells us the news, having learned that the physical and biological services are tactical, prize-seeking enterprises in which truth is entirely strategic. Rorty chats away in a post-Wittgensteinian room whose mirrors reflect nothing but the lost contexts of his own good sense. The lesson is that we never would have been surrounded by so many corpses— Reason, Desire, Woman, God, Society—had we asked less of the seminar and the bedroom.

Such is the news from Paris and Princeton. We must recognize that words and things have come unstuck. Thus we are all schizophrenics without logos: the flesh writhes, shouts, screams, or sinks into speechlessness. Or perhaps women, hitherto excluded from language, will resuture words and things for us, if there is still time left for such gynesis.[8] For it now looks as though European men have declared themselves as much out of style as Hollywood men. Stallone and Clint Eastwood notwithstanding, the men are no longer as sure as a gun. Rather, the gun itself assures their death—over and over—and the death of the Western (revived, of course, in the new genre of films on pre-post-Vietnam) is on a par with the death of the Western metaphysics that once underwrote it. Whether feminized women can turn themselves into a final metafiction, or at least a fiction that will buy us more time, remains to be seen. In the short run, of course, they are in vogue, talking, writing, and voting themselves into the vacancies advertised for women. Whether these former troglodytes can make the workplace, the university, parliament, and the TV any more true or just remains to be seen. What is currently undecidable about women might then be what is currently undecidable about the exhaustion of modernity and the birth of postmodernism.

Yet, who can say? And when the story begins to take shape, will it be a good one or will we have to put out our eyes for nothing?

PART II
SITES

Chapter 5

IN SITU: BEYOND THE ARCHITECTONICS OF THE MODERN

Stephen H. Watson

Poetic forms in architecture are sensitive to the figurative, associative, and anthropomorphic attitudes of a culture. If one's goal is to build with only utility in mind then it is enough to be conscious of technical criteria alone. . . . Could these two attitudes, one technical and utilitarian, and the other cultural and symbolic be thought of as architecture's standard and poetic languages?

In its rejection of the human or anthropomorphic representation of previous architecture, the Modern Movement undermined the poetic form in favor of nonfigural geometries.
—Michael Graves, "A Case for Figurative Architecture"[1]

18. Our language can be seen as an ancient city; a maze of little streets and squares, of old and new houses, and of houses with additions from various periods; and this surrounded by a multitude of new boroughs with straight regular streets and uniform houses.

203. Language is a labyrinth of paths. You approach from one side and know your way about; you approach the same place from another side and no longer know your way about.
—Ludwig Wittgenstein, *Philosophical Investigations*[2]

I

I begin by citing two texts, one by Ludwig Wittgenstein, a famous philosopher (and sometime architect) of the twentieth century, and another by Michael Graves, a famous architect (and sometime philosopher). And I will be concerned with what hinges these two texts and what they say about 'habitable space,' and hence about 'habitability' and 'spatiality.'

Still, one should proceed cautiously in standing between here, that is, in taking up a position between these authors, and perhaps even their disciplines. And more to the point, one should perhaps always be leery when "philosophers" and even "architect-philosophers" look at the "arts." It concerns the problem of the relation between theory and practice. And perhaps, more specifically, it concerns the status of 'criticism' in general and the relation between the language of the critic and the language of art. One should, that is, be leery of the space which intervenes, the space which divides, the space which distances texts from things—even other texts, if we follow Graves. And, consequently, one should be leery of texts which claim to be 'about,' to be textual 're-presentatives'—'meta-texts,' the philosopher might call them—*claiming* in fact to bridge the distance involved, the space which, after all, the text articulated here, therefore, *figures* too. And it should be attended to just because, perhaps always, and certainly in the confrontation which Graves attributes to modernism, this distance was covered over—not just by those 'outside' philosophy, but also, most pertinently, and most ironically, by those occupying the position of philosophy itself. And yet, it rested perhaps upon a covering-over which is itself by no means modern.

Plato, the philosopher's philosopher in this regard, the *eidos* or archetype of this 'covering over,' in fact recognized this distance without perhaps taking seriously what is at stake. The distance, he acknowledges, involves a quarrel (*agon*) that is ancient,[3] that between the philosopher and the poet, or, in any case, between himself and the legacy of Homer, who too had already felt it in defending the figural against the onslaught of the canons of reason in pleading, "Why grudge this faithful bard the right to please us by any path his fancy takes?"[4] The quarrel nonetheless is not simply ancient, it is *archaic*, one which concerns the *arche*, the principles, the origin, and certainly the space we inhabit, the space the poet 'figures,' as Graves puts it, and the space which both the philosopher and the architect, by 'architectonics,' 'construct.' Accordingly, as will become evident, if this *agon* affects the ancient texts of philosophy, it is not without its effect in the domain of the architectural as well. Still, what is it that the space of the figural and the space of construction have in common? And is there, to speak Miesian, a 'universal' space which might homogeneously combine both, the space of the figural and the space of reason (already canonized by Plato by means of the paradigm of geometry)? Is there then a solution to the conflict which concerns this difference, a double encoding which might bring this *agon* to rest?

II

The problem of construction should be considered first. For reasons which are not simply accidental this notion plays an overdetermined role—perhaps even 'overdetermined' in the Freudian sense, such that more than one cause or origin stands behind this term, invested within and figuring it, as can be exhibited simply by looking at its history. If, as is normally or canonically the case, we distinguish architecture and building, declaring with the *Oxford English Dictionary* the former to be "the art or science of building or constructing edifices of any kind for human use," and the latter, the practice of "constructing a building," we ought to look more closely at this "construction," which seems to provide "the common root" intervening between the two domains, providing what is common to both stems. A more common lexicon yields its effect in defining "construction" as "the action or business of building," but precisely in a way which covers over the overdetermination in its past. The *OED* marks a simple 'architectural' usage for "construction" in English dating from as early as the fifteenth century, in referring to "the construction of the city of Rome" under the general rubric of "putting together of parts," this perhaps entirely in accord with its Latin etymological past as *construere*—literally, a "heaping-together."

Nonetheless, too much intervenes before the 'science of architecture' could accept this definition. First a definition dating from the sixteenth century should be mentioned, one which Webster's lists as primary, but obsolete (*pace* Graves and Wittgenstein): "the act of construing (as in translating)," a matter which would make construction (already) a wholly linguistic matter. Secondly, in a definition dating from the eighteenth century, the *OED* links "construction" with science, or at least the science of figure, i.e. geometry: "to draw, delineate, or form geometrically." Finally, an entry from the nineteenth century promotes the practice signified by the term to a full-fledged science: "the art of distributing the different forces and strains of the parts and materials of a building in so scientific a manner as to avoid failure and insure durability."[5]

III

While it would be easy to argue that these transformations are by no means innocent (in fact progressively promoting an increasingly formalized and decreasingly figuralized practice), such tracings are at best ambiguous. If they can open up a certain (necessary) polysemia concerning the practice of "construction" and the theoretical *topos* to which it adheres, it does not tell us much about what is at stake, nor why problems affecting architecture and building might be mediated in terms of it. More to the point, it is not at all clear how the science of forces, i.e. mechanics, impacts upon what the *OED*'s final definition quite innocently calls "the art of distributing the different forces and strains of the parts and materials of a building." Moreover, it does not tell us whether that *art* might itself take place in "a scientific manner," how the 'science' of figural construction impacts upon the art of construction, nor *how*, finally—since art has to do with the latter—we are to inhabit the space that results. . . .

Further, and not insignificantly, it would be mistaken to claim that this diachronics, this historical tracing of the additions and transformations affecting such an apparently innocent notion as "construction," had to do simply with the 'architectonics' of architecture, and not those concerning "construction" more broadly—even those concerning the construction, the construals, of language and the art of theory. That such is the case, and that it impacts upon both sides of this hinge, the hinge between theory and practice—but also between the art of theory and the theory of art—can be witnessed in reading the works of Immanuel Kant, the most important aesthetician of the eighteenth century (the century of "construction"'s elevation to a science). Kant's work can quite properly be claimed to open up the overdetermined space of aesthetic modernism.

Writing precisely in the wake of the elevation of this 'geometrical constructivism,' Kant claimed that mathematics presented "the most splendid example of the successful extension of pure reason" (A712/B740). This method proceeds by the "construction of concepts" (*Konstruktion der Begriffe*) and hence is free from our reliance upon the fallibility of our senses and the limitations of the faculties of apprehension (*apprehensio*) with which we are endowed (preventing us consequently from knowing what things might be like apart from those conditions—as things in themselves).[6] "I construct a triangle by representing the object which corresponds to this concept either by pure imagination alone, in pure intuition, or in accordance therewith also on paper, in empirical intuition—in both cases completely *a priori* without impairing its universality" (A713/B741). The results are consequently universally and infallibly sound. Hence it was not at all coincidental, all things considered, that Kant chose the figure—and what seemed to him to be almost a demonstrable schema—of architecture and architectonics as paradigms for rationality, now sure of their apparent connection with the *more geometrico*:

> By an architectonic I understand the art of constructing systems. As systematic unity is what first raises ordinary knowledge to the rank of science, that is, makes a system out of a mere aggregate (*Aggregat*), architectonics is the doctrine of the scientific in our knowledge, and therefore, necessarily forms part of the doctrine of method (A832/B860).

Architectonics, then, provides the condition for the possibility of the emergence of absolutely necessary, apodictic knowledge—'science.' It does so precisely by moving from the mere aggregate—the "heap" of our rational practices—to the etymological past of "construction," to its new, demonstrative counterpart, or by moving from mere narrative or historical knowledge to what Kant calls "knowledge by principles" (A836/B864).

Still, if Kant was not among the first to import the trope of architectonics (literally, 'pertaining to architecture') into the realm of the rational through his concern with problems involving the systematization of knowledge in general, he was, perhaps, the first to see the failure of this attempt. The languages or narratives of human reason would not manifest the homogeneity that could provide a true reflection for the archetype of this architectonics. They could not synthesize the aggregate of our rational practices in such a way that its parts could be brought to unity, fully grounded, demonstrated, systematized, and hence, made fully scientific. If it is true, as Kant claimed, that "human reason is by nature architectonic" (A477/B508), this did not mean that the narratives of human reason would become demonstrably rational (*cognitio ex principiis*). Moreover, the way in which Kant perceived this failure of architectonics in the realm of the scientific was not without implications for the realm of the artistic, since the conflict was not irrelevant to it and to the nature of its 'hinge' with the scientific.

The conflict in question essentially concerning the attempt to universalize the principles of mechanics—which were deterministic—irrevocably conflicted with the spontaneity and freedom which characterized both the basis of human responsibility in the moral sphere (freedom of the will) and human creativity (the free play of imagination) in the aesthetic. Hence, there must be a real question as to whether the architectonic modelled after the paradigm of mechanics could provide a science of aesthetics, and consequently, an art of architecture. It concerned whether, in short, this architectonic based upon "the most splendid extension of pure reason" could produce a building of value in the realm of the rational, since the scientific thesis only seems to arise in conflict with the sphere from which it borrowed its paradigm and which gave rise to an insurmountable antithesis concerning its principles. "Since, therefore, the antithesis thus refuses to admit as first or as a beginning anything that could serve as foundation for building (*Grunde des Baues*), a complete edifice (*Gebaude*) of knowledge is, on such assumptions, altogether impossible" (A474/B502–3).

IV

While this failure concerning rational architectonics seems to be confined to the realm of pure theory in the Kantian text, a close reading exhibits its effect in the realm of the aesthetic as well. It should first be acknowledged that, notwithstanding its exemplary function in the realm of pure reason, Kant has little to say about architecture itself. And yet, the first example of the *Critique of Judgement*, which is to delineate the sphere of the aesthetic, is precisely "a regular, purposive building."[7] Further, all of his criteria concerning the adjudication of the beautiful will remain in accord with this 'purposive regularity'—pure 'form' as he calls it. Architecture, nonetheless, remains an example of merely adherent beauty, since it remains bound by use, a specific purpose, and not by considerations which are purely aesthetic. Consequently, Kant claims, when speaking of the beauty of a *place*, we must abstract any *use* it might have. Moreover, we must abstract any moral interest we might have regarding it, say, *à la* Rousseau in "rebuking the vanity of the great who waste the sweat of the people on such superfluous things" as the palaces of Paris (39). All that is left then, Kant claims, is the pure satisfaction which arises in the harmony instilled in the perception of their mere form, the beauty of what is "universally communicable" (60), and thus, what is in some respect, he thought, objective.

It is often pointed out by Kant's commentators that his commitment to pure form by no means follows from his commitment to the harmony and the 'disinterested' satisfaction which the experience of the aesthetic instills; that, in "no case do Kant's substantive formalistic opinions express views which we must accept simply on the basis of his explanation of aesthetic response alone."[8] Pure sensation ought to do the same thing, as painters such as Rothko and musicians such as Schönberg have shown. They attest to a simple harmony between perceiver and perceived, an 'equality' of "one to one," as Augustine argued in *De Musica*.[9] For Kant, on the contrary, "the purity of colors and tones or their variety and contrast" add to an object, making it "worthy of contemplation and beautiful" simply "because they make the form more exactly, definitely, and completely intuitable" (61).

Still, pure form is by no means innocent in all this, nor are the predicates of clarity and distinctness which are invoked to describe it as well as architectonics in the rational. The purity of line, the mathematical line, *mathesis* is in question here: "delineation (*Zeichung*) is the essential thing" (61)—even when it is "free delineation," such as in the outlines of flowers.[10] Nor is the connection of form with Kant's claims concerning 'objectivity' innocent in satisfying the requirement that beauty be a matter of what "admits with certainty of universal communicability; for we cannot assume that the quality of sensation is the same in all subjects" (60). Precisely because of these commitments, Kant was forced to *subsume* sensation, the imaginary, and the imaginatively figural—one might say the specifically human—beneath form, and deny it all but accidental access to the realm of the aesthetic.

V

Still, before condemning all this as an overly restrictive account of rationality, an impoverished account of sensation, a philosopher's account of the aesthetic, and, from the perspective of a number of artistic practices, just a bad description of art, we should follow Kant's Pythagoreanism all the way through—if for no other reason than to avoid continuing the Freudian economics—the disguised symptoms that arise from elsewhere. We need then to follow the irony which awaits the mathematical in the realm of the aesthetic, for its elevation was not Kant's last word. Even his examples become overdetermined here. If, as has been seen, the construction of the figure of the triangle was paradigmatic of the most splendid extension of pure reason, its appearance in the realm of the aesthetic did not occur easily under the auspices of pure form. The pyramid, that construction delineated by four isosceles triangles rising from a square base, became equally the paradigm for the failure of aesthetic Pythagoreanism. For the Pythagoreans, the pyramid was the object of their greatest success, while the problem of the surds, the irrationals, their greatest misery. The sheer satisfaction attaching to the contemplation of pure form failed, when confronted with an event whose comprehension (*comprehesio aesthetico*) was in the strict sense impossible.

Kant's explanation of this event seems more than trite, dependent still upon a certain understanding of the visual, and a certain mathematical perspectivism to which we will return. Still, the failure that emerges in this experience is significant:

> We must keep from going very near the Pyramids just as
> we must keep from going too far from them, in order to get

the full emotional effect from their size. For if we are too far away, the parts to be apprehended . . . are only obscurely represented, and the representation of them produces no effect. But if we are very near, the eye requires some time to complete the apprehension of the tiers from the bottom up to the apex, and then the first tiers are always partly forgotten before the imagination has taken in the last, and so the comprehension of them is never complete (90).[11]

Kant again put the full 'value' of the aesthetic event upon a contemplation and its "completion" and "comprehension," an event which once again would make the beautiful depend upon our ability to *enframe* and ground it comprehensively. But the failure which is involved here, our failure to comprehend and measure the event at hand strictly, brings about a rupture and a "bewilderment" (91), one which instead of attaching simply to the inharmonious and that which, as opposed to pure form, could be subsumed beneath the 'ugly,' attaches instead to a different realm, the sublime. Rather it was for Kant precisely an indication of the human—or at least all that remains transcendent within the human—the encounter with our "moral destiny," as Kant put it, and thus the need to envision imaginatively what transcends these fragmented conditions. Moreover, in this regard, the 'de-lineation' of the involvement—or more precisely, the withdrawal—of the human in the event itself indicated in the aesthetic realm that "imagination is a necessary ingredient of perception itself" (A120n), and that the "figurative synthesis" (B151) which intervenes between sensibility and understanding was itself a revelation of human possibility. As such, the failure of the experience of pure form and the failure of its architectonic pretension to completeness, to science, unleashes all that "astonishes" here. This accounts for Kant's "attraction and repulsion," as he describes it (97), before an event which cannot be brought to unity, cannot be completed, an event for which a direct *mensuratio intellectus ad rem* cannot take place. In this regard, the event released the work of art's 'power' as 'symbol,' as figurative potential to reveal what escaped the scientific construct.[12] And thus, if the pyramid seemed a symbol of mathematical perfection and stability, it was equally a feeling of 'otherness,' as attested throughout its history, beginning with the Greeks and their sun cult at Heliopolis (marked by a stairway to the heavens), or with the Enlightenment, as Kant attests—and still today, if one takes Charles Jencks seriously, with what he calls "symbolic architecture."[13]

VI

This fracture that arises in the space which differentiates form and figure is 'systemic.' What the division in Kant's text foretells is precisely the failure of modernism: the failure of the attempt to *deduce* and perhaps even to regulate the art of architecture by the science of forces, the failure to evacuate the human from the domain of the architectural, to create a space which might in the end be non-figural, and consequently, to turn 'place,' and all that figures in its 'habitation,' into simple *position*.[14] In the realm of theoretical architectonics it was the recognition of the failure of the model of the mind as an immutable *tabula rasa*, a blank slate—or again, fully in line with geometrical perspectivism, a "plane of representation" (A658/B686), as Kant calls it—which might fully recuperate an outside image, without figuring or distorting it. In all this, as Kenneth Frampton has put it—following Giulio Argan's analyses of Brunelleschi, the split between form and figure, seeing and doing, theory and practice was of a piece.

> This willful creation of distance between conceiving and building pervades the entire Renaissance. It was as much present in Brunelleschi's invention of perspective or in his machines for the building of the copula over Santa Maria dei Fiori in Florence in 1420 as it was in Galileo's invention of the telescope in 1610, with which men first established the proof of the Copernican universe. The effective split of appearance and being that was the consequence of this proof, served to institute Cartesian doubt as the fundamental basis of the new scientific perspective.[15]

Despite all that had been facilitated in the sphere of conceptualization, the recognition of this 'split' could not licence either the subsumption or the dissolution of the human within the algorithms of scientific regularity. As Kant realized, we could not simply choose either one or the other in order to overcome the conflicts in the foundations of our narratives concerning science and the human. Whereas an art which purely compartmentalizes and privileges the formal becomes simply boring, as has been subsequently learned time and again, Kant himself did not allow it until the last pages of his analytic concerning the aesthetic:

> If the beautiful arts are not brought into more or less close combination with moral ideas, which alone bring with them a self-sufficing satisfaction, this latter fate must ultimately be theirs. They then serve only as a distraction (*Zerstreuung*), of which we are the more in need the more we avail ourselves of them to disperse the discontent of the mind with itself. . . (170).

The elevation of the formal over the medium, of the conceptual over its content, of syntax over semantics, led to the delusion that the latter could be identified on its basis, and this could be deduced, inferred, and regulated on its basis. As Portughesi quite rightly reminds us in this regard, Walter Gropius thought the new architecture was "not a new style, but a victory over every possible style," a matter of "absolute rationality."[16] Hence, the failure of modernism, it could be said, along with Graves, was a matter of not seeing the difference which intervenes between them, a failure to keep the formal—Graves's "internal requirement"—separate from the "figural" or "anthropomorphic," a conflation, or "subreption," to speak Kantian, by which things intellectual are confused with things 'sensible,' imaginary, and artistic. It led to the delusion that the formal might itself dictate a *style*, that stylistics could be turned into a schematics, could become objective, instead of being a matter of the 'symbolic,' the "indirect presentation" or figurative expression of the conceptual (197), when what was at least as important was the difference which intervened between them, and, perhaps allowed the formal and the figural to be meted out. What had been forgotten in all this was perhaps just this difference.

What the 'modern' lacked was the recognition of the problem of *interpretation*, the figuring which haunts all engagement with the formal—the recognition that there is a kind of abyss between the formal and the figurative which calls upon the freedom of the interpreter and demands a certain 'translation.' Interpretation in this sense is not simply an in-forming of a particular 'semantic' medium, but (to cite Louis Kahn in relation to the architectural and writers such as André Malraux and Maurice Merleau-Ponty in the realm of the aesthetic) a kind of "de-formation" of the formal requirement, particularly in its *'application.'* The resulting "constructions" become a matter of 'construal'—precisely that rendering of "construction" which the *O.E.D.* had marked as obsolete, an obsolescence, which may not have been accidental within the history of the modern and its elevations of the mathematical. The application of the sciences which inform the architectural does not proceed, to invoke Kant's characterization of the rationality of the aesthetic, "just mechanically, like a tool controlled by the understanding and the senses, but *artistically.*"[17] While the separation of conceiving and doing (science and its application) made possible the informing of art by science, it could not be reduced to the latter. And if in this regard the metaphorics of the mechanical, of mechanism, instrumentality, and the machine which afflicted both architectural and scientific cosmologies was or at least seemed apt, it was, as we now know, illusory in both domains—that is, precisely a trope, a figure, and not a schematism for the objective application of mechanics itself.[18] The tendency to see this metaphorics as itself 'scientific' was thus unable to grasp the figurative synthesis at work in the production which resulted and all that intervened by means of it, all that was specifically human, the moral and artistic at work (and at risk) within it, instead dissolving the *topos* of the human within the *u-topia* of the model.

What ensued when the project became writ large has perhaps now become clear. With the transformation between conceiving and doing, being and appearance, Argan claimed, "[i]t became possible in the Renaissance to think of the city as a unified form (in a utopian but not absurd manner), willed into being by a prince and created by his architect . . . which made it possible theoretically to construct a city within a man's lifetime."[19] The purity of the modernist aesthetic created in its city a macro-space which as much as possible avoided all reference to the figural for the sake of its canons, thus in a sense denying the specificity of the city as anthropomorphic, as 'habitable.' The *eidos* of the city became precisely the u-topian construction of mathematical space, merely a "filling in" of its mathematical grids which would provide precisely and ideally "a continuous and uniform production of reality" (A143/B183), rather than the heterogeneous and dynamic spatiality of the figural for which one would need an energetics and a certain "vibration," to use a word Kant invokes in his attraction and repulsion before the pyramids (97). The space of this de-formation thus was, to return to Merleau-Ponty, the experience of "another space and time" than that of the mathematical and the merely conceptual.[20] More perhaps, if one follows Christian Norberg-Schulz, the space of Prague, Khartoum, Rome, and Chicago, than say the majestic steamliners which were to set sail down the sea of Le Corbusier's grids.[21] The point is that the turn to the *genuis loci*, instead, allows space to be figured and depends upon the articulation of natural place as something other than the space of construction. It is a space which allows the Wittgensteinian labyrinth of architectural and linguistic difference to be articulated, and even welcomed. As Wittgenstein put it at the end of a similar battle with the architectonics of formal logic, "ordinary language is all right."[22] A recognition here which refuses the concepts of the city, habitability, or construction to be "circumscribed,"[23] to be simply grounded by a function, a model, or a metaphorics which might be eternalized, and hence precisely recognizes the labyrinth as necessary and not without its virtues, and certainly not without its own characteristics. . . .

VII

Still, if the modern was, again to speak with Wittgenstein, "captivated by a picture"[24] (literally, an *ab-bildung*),[24] there remains the problem of the rigor that it upheld, its commitment to purity, as critics always claimed. And, consequently, there is—perhaps as a result—the question of what guides artistic production beyond those codes. It is all very well, it might be replied, to talk about questions concerning "double encoding," the modern and its "other," as Jencks puts it, the formal *and* the poetic, but if one dissolves the possibility of their simple identification, or denies that any simple synthesis can be found to unite them—if, that is, there is a certain "heterology" which is intrinsic to what arises in its failure—what forbids the possibility of 'anything goes' here, what ensures that eclecticism and the tolerance of difference is not merely the ideological front for mediocrity? If, to take an uneasy example, Norberg-Schulz can find a *genius loci* at work within such diversity, why isn't it the case that he can find it anywhere? If he can claim for instance that Mies van der Rohe's "personal idiom fitted Chicago perfectly,"[25] does he see no connection with the disastrous *lack* of place which afflicts the slum housing of the South side? Moreover, recent writers (not without a certain irony) have even called for a re-reading of the Miesean project to be undertaken precisely along the protocols of Kant's notion of the sublime, one which thereby would justify its 'purism,' since Kant claimed that "there is a certain spirit of minutae (*esprit de bagatelles*) which exhibits a kind of fine feeling but aims at quite the opposite of the sublime." Hence the argument: "The factor of sublimity that makes Mies's 'splendor' possible rules out the 'spirit of minutiae' and affirms simplicity as a function of care in respect to elements of larger wholes. (What could be less 'reductive'?)"[26] Further, we recall that this "splendor" is precisely the term by which Kant originally characterized the most successful extension of pure reason, mathematics.[27] Still, without strict criteria here, without either ideology or algorithm for critical evaluation, how are we to decide such issues?

The difficulty must be affirmed. Criticism after all is figural, too, and equally interpretative. The search for a simple algorithm for decision will have to be foregone. We will need, that is, to step beyond modernism in our critical expectations as well— which does not at all necessitate that we give up the past here, even if we will need to be limited by what we can expect from it. In 1930 Wittgenstein claimed that "Today the difference between a good and a poor architect is that the poor architect succumbs to every temptation and the good one resists it."[28] The point is perhaps a trivial one. Nonetheless, *that* Wittgenstein too put the question of architecture in moral terms may not be insignificant. If it is true that the failure of the modern involved a certain failure of the *science* of architecture, a certain failure concerning the rationality of artistic canons (*nomoi*), it was also the failure of forgetting what Graves calls the anthropomorphic dimension of architectonics. And precisely in this regard, it was a certain failure regarding 'architecture' itself, or in any case an overly simplified betrayal of its past.

If it were the case (and perhaps this is what made its forgetfulness so easy) that the canons of Greek architecture were based upon *mathesis*, this by no means meant that they were *scientific*. Quite to the contrary, for the Greeks, as the name *architektonike* attests, it was from the beginning a matter of human affairs and not scientific ones, a matter that is of *techne*, skill, not of what is universal and demonstrably true, but of skill in dealing with the particular. But it was too perhaps a question of *prohairesis*, of rational deliberation in a realm which was always already context-specific. Thus, it was a question concerning the right thing to do at the right time in the right way, a question of the potential of the human and of human excellence (*arete*), that is, a question of human virtue. It was then, as Kant put it in reflecting on this same past, a matter of our "moral destiny," a question of "production through freedom based upon rational deliberation" (146).[29]

The ancient *architekton* was precisely a "chief constructor," and *architektonike*, a major art, not yet confined to the *techne* of building. Moreover, the 'art' of production itself was not simply construction, but a bringing into being, a *poiesis*, poetry in its most original form. Given this latter point, it is not surprising that even the mathematization of the canons did not prohibit their functioning at a symbolic level, that is, that the figural and the formal did not conflict—and would not be seen to conflict until after the scientific revolution.[30] In this regard, as Erwin Panofsky (among others) has recognized, the ancient canons were in fact "anthropometric."[31] Mies's Seagram Building, by contrast, does not alter the mathematical line, and it does not do so because it *constructs* its object, or to be more precise, because it *figures* its object precisely *as* a construction.

None of this should be taken as an attempt to exchange the modern for its predecessor, that is, as a romantic retrieval of the classical past. The conflict of our rational narratives, *inter alia*, the conflict still unresolved regarding the value of the modern, bars that *de facto*. If we have a particular narrative about who and what we are, what separates us from the Greeks is precisely its status as one narrative among many, and thus as belonging to a domain which is, again to use Wittgenstein's term, "uncircumscribed." What is in question now is a problem which concerns, as Kant's account ultimately recognized, the "pluralistic" (*plural-isticsh* [xx119]) and a situation in which in the strict sense "nothing can be decided by proofs" (183). Nonetheless the question of "proper rational deliberation" and the question of "production through freedom"—in short, the problem of "art," as Kant defines it—remains (145). And, in this respect at least, it is true that since its Greek inception architecture has involved the venture of the human precisely in the same moment in which it became a figuration. A human construction was at stake.[32] Likewise, if it is the case that surpassing the rationalism of the modern again forces that figural moment to prominence, it must be equally said that in broaching once more the question of the human it broached again the potential of discourses regarding the ethical and the sacred. Moreover, it was one of Wittgenstein's own virtues to have seen that this question of the ethical, the *ars vitae*, belongs essentially both to the architectonics of philosophy and the architectonics of architecture itself: "Working in philosophy—like work in architecture in many respects—is really more a working on oneself. On one's own interpretation (*Auffassung*). On one's way of seeing things. (And what one expects of them)."[33]

VIII

It is just this interpretation (and perhaps the question of self-interpretation) which has always seemingly remained absent in this domain. And the absence in question is perhaps as ancient as the *agon* between the rational and the figural traced earlier through Plato. If one looks, for example, to the *locus classicus* of architectural theory, the ten books of Vitruvius's *De architectura*, its overdetermined effect can already be seen, a conflict between the demand of scientific demonstrability and the play demanded by the practice of building—one in which, moreover, the Greek past had not yet been fully subsumed. In Book I, for example, architecture is referred to scientific principles in a way which would categorically deny the need or the possibility of interpretation. Science provides the significance and the intelligibility of architectural practice. "In all matters, but particularly in architecture, there are these two points—the thing signified, and that which gives it significance. That which is signified is the subject of which we may be speaking, and that which gives significance is a demonstration on scientific principles."[34] For Vitruvius the scientific principles, the canons or laws, were already classical, Pythagorean and—as they would be for Kant—formal: proportion and symmetry must guide throughout. Still, these laws submit in the *De architectura* to a strange alteration. On the other hand, in Book III Vitruvius is categorical about these canons: "Design . . . depends on symmetry, the principles of which must be most strictly observed by the architect."[35] But the question of symmetry arises quite differently in Book VI, and the difference—the figural difference, if you will—between the two treatments is startling. If in Books I and III the significance of the architectural in exhausted in the demonstrable and the canonical, Book VI seems to deviate. Initially, it agrees: the first thing to settle, Vitruvius claims, concerns the standard of symmetry. But this standard neither exhausts, nor in the end determines architectural practice. We should look at the sentence in which this deviation arises: "The first thing to settle is the standard of symmetry, from which we need not hesitate to vary (*sine dubitatione commutatio*)."[36] Not hesitate to vary—to alter, stray, or deny? What could license such a departure from the *nomos*, from the *kanon*? How could architecture proceed if variance from the *kanon*, from the demonstrable, from the scientific is justifiable? And how could Vitruvius—whose "teaching on proportion was treated throughout the Middle ages and the Renaissance, as having the force of a revelation"[37]—seem in this regard so little concerned with his modernist counterparts and their claims regarding the formal and the language of formality?

What intervenes between the two books is precisely the problem of the human, the problem of use and context: "After the standard of symmetry has been determined . . . it is next the part of wisdom to consider the nature of the site, or questions of use or beauty, and modify the plan by diminutions or additions. . . ."[38] Moreover, the problem of this 'modification,' the problem, again, of "de-formation" in Vitruvius is in a sense entirely reminiscent of the failure Kant encountered concerning *mathesis* in his experience of the pyramid: "The look of a building when seen close at hand is one thing, on a height it is another, not the same in an enclosed place, still different in the open, and in all these cases it takes much judgment to decide what is to be done."[39] Beyond the canons of "mere science," the problem of the human, the problem of interpretation, remains and summons the figural as a solution to the extension of the rational. Before this requirement, in fact, Vitruvius did not hesitate, indeed demanded that the canon be altered, knowing perhaps what was at stake—namely the question of stylistics, of the human, and of the habitable. And what is perhaps most disturbing here is that we moderns still see that variance and its 'flashes of genius,' the difference and the space which results, as somehow irrational, while Vitruvius, precisely to the contrary, declares that it requires *more*—not less—judgment. But geometry and building are perhaps themselves quite different in Vitruvius, notwithstanding, as has been seen, the ambiguity which divides his text and which will ultimately have portentous consequences for his modern counterparts. Geometry is of use to the architect, not as "the most successful extension of pure reason," nor even in the end the strict criteria in accordance with which all human matters can become rationally intelligible, but rather, as Vitruvius flatly states, because "it teaches us the *use* of the rule and the compass."[40]

Still, to allow architectonics to undergo such deformation, to admit that neither the art of theory nor the practice of art may be made determinate—to allow, that is, that in neither domain could there be a *Konstruktion* which might ultimately ground the task at hand—is not without consequence. If the recognition of this 'de-construction' does not in fact render all art (or all truth) derisory, if, that is, returning the task at hand to the appearances reopens the possibility of their legitimation, it does so only to the extent that it forces thought beyond the topos of the universal precisely in order to confront within its failure and dispersion both the heterogeneity *and* the potential of its remainder.

> The bold undertaking that we have designated is thus bound to fail through lack of material, not to mention the babble of tongues, which inevitably gives rise to disputes among workers in regard to the plan to be followed, and which must end by dispersing them all over the world (*in alle Welt zerstreuen musste*, leaving each to erect a separate building for himself according to his own design. (A707/B736).

100

Chapter 6

A POSTMODERN LANGUAGE
IN ART

Dorothea Olkowski-Laetz

In the essay "Origin of the Work of Art," Heidegger traces the subject-predicate structure of language and the substance-accident structure of things to show how both are derived from the analysis of the "mere thing" into some matter that stands together with some form: a form always determined by the use to which the thing will be put. This allows both the appearance of the thing and that of language to remain constant. Regardless of what *we* try to say, discourse concerns itself with some subject related to some predicate in a manner indicating either that it is useful or that it is stripped bare of usefulness.

Therefore, within the law of contradiction, that is, insofar as "S *is* P," our thought is always already structured by this obscure origin. The system (of discourse) always signifies and represents; the appearance of the thing becomes constant, language becomes constant: form and matter, subject and predicate.

So, for example, the painted image of shoes (in a work by Vincent Van Gogh), detached from any owner-user, leaves us speechless. Both the work of art and the shoes it "depicts" require reattachment to an owner or, at least, to an origin in order for discourse to be able to articulate them.[1]

The Derridean reading of Heidegger indicates that this is due to the pre-comprehension of time in discourse (located first in the texts of Aristotle) in which a being can be grasped only in its being as presence, and meaning is understood only in reference to the present as the determinate mode of time. Time represented *in act* is spatial; it is the circle which encompasses its origins and end and whose borders have come to delineate the logic and grammar of Western discourse.

The circle, as actualization of the "now," is the discursive nothing of time, the repetition of each "now" in another. It is thus the creation of time through the mechanism of representing each present moment in another: a loss of origins, and the inevitable domination of beings by spatio-temporal discourse. What is not given to thought as a representation has no hope of being recognized, while all attempts to oppose the discursive system directly result in co-option.

Yet Kant and Hegel already make way for the spatial and temporal (and thus discursive) counter to the significational system. They do this not by directly confronting it in order to produce yet another level of signification, but by opening up a space for thought, opening up the possibility of other logics and other grammars. They do this by dissolving and completing space and time, the very categories they are thought to have raised to the highest levels of reality.

Hegel dissolves the substantiality of the object, its spatial determinations, with the notion of the interrelation of forces. The movement of the relation between the one and the many of the thing is force. Yet, force is *nothing* apart from its relation to another force, a perpetual exchange of determinations precluding substance. Kant anticipates this with the discovery of the acategorical sublime. The "sublime" is a stranger to the categories of consciousness: *no sensible form* is sublime, no object of nature as mechanism in accordance with laws is sublime. Rather, the sublime emerges as a surplus never completely enframed by the categories of discourse, never subject to determination by time or space.

There is no doubt that the dissolution of spatial and temporal categories poses an important question, that is: Is this possible? Can we think "otherwise," or does the detachment of the work of art continually compel us to think within the circle of representation? Is there any other way for thought to get its orientation when the work of art is detached from any owner-user or origin? Is there any point of departure that allows the work of art to be its own orientation and to provide an orientation for thought not bound to presence or absence, to substance and its accidents?

Marcel Duchamp offers us the art work stripped bare of the

character of usefulness and of the structure of presence. Duchamp's paintings, readymades, gestures, and silences (after 1923 he primarily played chess), are stripped bare of any vestiges of humanity, the illusion of either time or of eternity, the personal presence of the artist, the possibility of identity. Octavio Paz remarks that Duchamp's paintings, such as *Nude Descending a Staircase* or *Tu m'* are the decomposition of movement and time. They are thus the image of delay, dispersion, static representations of changing objects.[2]

The *Large Glass*, also known as *The Bride Stripped Bare by Her Bachelors, Even* functions in a similar manner. Drawn with a compass and ruler instead of with a brush and paint—in order to eliminate the hand of the artist, the subconscious, the accidental[3]—the *Large Glass* engenders a plurality of readings in terms of its own forms. It is no object, but a relation, a series of relations, or physical, sexual, and linguistic dimensions. As such, it maintains itself in its incompleteness, the void upon which the work depends. This void is not simply a negation of the representation that brings to presence, rather it is that of a work of art detached from the representational network, stripped bare of any use, unavailable for identification or restitition to an owner-user. This non-mechanistic machine functions in an unpredictable way, according to laws of exception, but it is not chaotic insofar as "each one of its moments is definitive in relation to those that precede it and relative to those that come after" (*MD*, p. 80).

Insofar as the *Large Glass* is a picture of the mechanical Bride undressing, forever separated from the masked and uniform(ed) Bachelors, it is an image of eternal delay, spectacle and ceremony, a physiological and psychological event, a mechanical operation and physicochemical process, an erotic and perhaps spiritual process (*MD*, pp. 7, 16, 80).

But what is important here for thought is that all these elements are totally detached from the desire of the spectator who cannot bring this work of art to presence and who cannot make it speak the language of his or her ownership (see below, on Van Gogh).

The "Readymades" are ordinary objects: a pitch fork, a ball of twine, a corkscrew, detached from their original contexts, freed of use but not yet submerged in new interpretations, new ideologies. The "practice" of Readymades demands absolute disinterest, not merely a useless or out-of-work disinterest. They must be articles without visual interest, without meaning, articles without desire of any nature. Thus the choice of a Readymade amounts to a "rendezvous": an encounter in a time that is arid with indifference (*MD*, p. 28). This is the death of desire. This is why Duchamp introduced very few of them, and this is why the best way for him to maintain their integrity would have been to destroy them before the viewing public grew used to their forms and began to interpret them within the significational system.

Can we, however, orient our thought according to the demands of this extreme body of work? Is the *Large Glass* absurd because no engineer can construct it, because it is a glimpse into meaningless repetition, a testament of indifference? And is it, as Paz claims, a critique, a form fated to lead us toward the abyss? Working out these questions demands the laying out of a number of issues. The issue of detachment and alienation, the separation from representation, and representation itself. This demands moving through several layers at once, through the linguistic and archaeological dust to examine other sites, other works of art, in order to place ourselves in front of them, to read their writing, to hear them speak, to see them move or, by refusing to move, refuse space and time.

Characteristically, it is Heidegger who offers us an instance in which the work of art is not thought within the circle of reattachment imposed by the painting's representative function. He states that the more cleanly ties to the human are cut, the more detached the work is from origins, the more dehumanized the work, the more it leads us into the "open," where a totally unique being can be brought forth. In this sense, truth arises out of a nothing that is not time, but detachment,[4] and detachment brings to light the characteristics of an alienation that is not oriented by presence.

Ortega Y Gasset had already noted how such art is not only unpopular, it is necessarily anti-popular, since for most people the pleasures of art are not distinguishable from ordinary pleasure. The object of their attention is always people and their passions, thus an art without such sentimental attachments leaves them without a clue as to what it is about. But a work of art that is dehumanized, or antihumanistic, forces a maximum of distance and a minimum of feeling of personal intervention in the work of art, a freedom from real events.[5] The work of art is no longer a sign, a means to think about some other reality and to make it present; rather, it is itself made the object and aim of thought (*DHA*, pp. 18-9).

The painted representation of shoes (in Heidegger's essay) can only illustrate the reliability of equipment, but the dehumanized, detached work of art acts to transport us out of the ordinary, out of the representative, and out of space and time. It is a displacement that disrupts our ordinary ties to world and earth, a deformation of reality that shatters the human-lived aspect, so that knowing is transformed into a "standing in the openness" that happens in the work, and a "knowing what one is willing to do" in the midst of it (*OWA*, p. 67).

If we take detachment seriously, without trying to reattach via some projective understanding, then things are never present and ordinary. Heidegger, however, retreats into the "open" of language. Language, by naming, projects a clearing for the openness of what is. But the noun is given on the basis of the verb, and so to name is to name present beings, to reattach the shoes, and to forget the work of art as a work of art. Heidegger is compelled to claim that whenever art happens there is a beginning, and a thrust enters history, so that history either begins or starts over (*OWA*, p. 81). Art, not surprisingly, is then historical: otherwise we must remain speechless in front of it.

But what about the work of art itself? Is there a work of art that speaks for itself without the necessity of interpretive projection? Jacques Derrida would insist that the painting by Van Gogh (of shoes) is fluent in the language of difference, detachment, and reattachment. Derrida concurs that detachment, or the process of fetishism as he prefers to call it, is described by Heidegger as *aletheia*, letting the thing show itself, the uselessness of the work and product. The painting as fetish is useless to the apprehension of utility (*VP*, p. 358). The painting serves only as a reference. Because of the detachment, the fetishization of the painting, nothing authorizes this, but *nothing forbids it either*.

Julia Kristeva writes of another detached, fetishized painting, or rather, of a series of paintings showing the same figures again and again. This is Bellini's series of the *Madonna and Child*. In Bellini's paintings, as in Van Gogh's series of shoes, we have no direct access to the space of the figure. In Bellini's case, it is the space of the Madonna that is beyond narrative, psychology, lived experience, beyond the signifying economy of figuration.[6] The gaze of the Madonna is never centered on the child. Thus, the spectator suffers a loss of identity, a shattering of the image, while color, constructed volume, and light break from the thematic representation to insist that they are the real and objectless goal in the painting (*DIL*, p. 248).

The result is a "fetishized" image, floating over a luminous ground, evoking inner experience rather than referential objects. Identification with the fetishized image must be abandoned in order to experience what Kristeva calls *jouissance*, that is, pleasure, in the sense both of mastery over technique or a body of knowledge, and passage through the work, play, finding the right of way through materials (colors, sounds, phonemes, words) where meaning has not yet appeared, no longer is, or functions to restructure thought (as it does in art) (*DIL*, p. x). Reattachment of the fetishized maternal image in the form of desire for the body results in a figuration that reduces color and volume to a technical device in service to the representable, desirable, fetishistic form. This is fundamental to humanist realism and to the founding of signs and sign systems (*DIL*, p. 243).

Like Heidegger, Kristeva attributes each different sense of fetishization (detached and reattached) to a different orientation of thought. There is a split subject, a split between conscious and unconscious motivations: physiological processes opposed to social constraints, the phenotext of traditional narrative and science opposed to the genotext, which effects semantic displacements in the given fabric of language. (*DIL*, p. 7).

But Kristeva, again like Heidegger, parcels out these two realms in an irreconcilable and unrelatable manner. Drawing, the conscious process of mastery, produces the representational fetish. Color transforms the narrative representation from material for identification into the search for surface and light, the juxtaposition of colored masses, producing a minimal signifying structure (*DIL*, pp. 263, 25). Color is identified with poetic language, a rhythm which, as a *presence*, necessarily precedes the repetition that produces signification.

> The word is experienced as work and not as a simple substance for a named object nor as an explosion of emotion. . . (*DIL*, p. 31).

It is a presence which acts as an upheaval of present place and meaning, a present dependent on the future. It is, however, an impossible future, because it is measured against the present language-structure which it always eludes. It is the promise of meaning, utopic, contesting the violence of the present sign system, the current social contract.

For Derrida, it is necessary to underline this conflict (in Van Gogh's painting of shoes) between the indetermination of painting and the attribution of an owner-user (*VP*, p. 368). The system of the indeterminate painting is such that the work of art is detached, yet it initiates reattachment. The logic of detachment is a logic and dialectic of opposition whose effect is to restore difference. The painting and what it "depicts" are both attached and detached.

Heidegger and Kristeva maintain the detached work of art in a significational silence, punctuated only by the rhythm of the material word. Derrida, however, makes the claim that art both can and cannot speak for itself. This operates in two ways. One projection operates in the choice of the model in a *parergonal* fashion. The part (what is depicted) overflows the whole (the painting). But, simultaneously, the work of art, as work as art, does not reveal the truth of what is depicted; its discourse is about the picture, about the *parergonal* structure of the picture. Second, the detachment of what is depicted opens it up to the unconscious of the other (*VP*, p. 435). As such, the work of art is open to anyone's interpretive understanding and to Derrida's difference.

However, openness to the unconscious of the other can never be resolved in possession or preservation. The depicted must always be returned to the painting; no one understanding can ever claim it (*VP*, p. 435). But what if the goal is not to "understand" what is depicted at all, nor to return it to a purely utopic space? Derrida quotes Artaud: "Listen to the painting. It delouses us of the obsession to make 'others' out of the objects, and to dare to risk the loss of the other" (*VP*, p. 435). What if there is no noble demand to "understand," to "admit," the passions of others? What if,

> The goal is neither to further the conflict (by associating through similitude), nor to reduce it (by sublimating, sweetening or normalizing the passions), nor yet to

transcend it (by "understanding" the other person), but to exploit it for the greatest pleasure of all and without hinderance to anyone. How? By playing at it; by making a text out of the conflictual.[7]

This is not Kristeva's *jouissance,* because it does not demand a psychoanalytical reading of the motives of the artist, an under-standing of the conflict that results in the abandonment or deni-gration of one mode of language in a turn to utopia. Nor is it Heidegger's *alethia,* letting the thing show itself as useless, out of work, work and product; a projection of understanding, a reduction accomplished on the basis of rejection of the norm.

Nor is this the *Derridean* sense of the play of difference. If a cri-tique of any of the concepts involved in laying out the circle of understanding always leads us to the point of reconstituting the same system in another configuration, to the "false sortie," then perhaps a "critique" will not give thought its orientation with re-gard to things, with regard to beings. The Heideggerian critique brings thought into the circle, compelling us to orient our thought according to metaphysical notions of being as presence and repre-sentation. The Derridean reading leaps over this reconstitution by pointing it out and simultaneously affirming and denying it, confirming the impossibility of thinking otherwise.

Does the conflict, the hinge between the differential concepts become the text? There is no idiomatic reading of a painting, Derrida tells us; detachment always leaves the work open to the unconscious of the other. Yet is it not the case that the Derridean reading *does not* refrain from hindering no one—that, rather, it demands its *own* idiomatic reading?

In *The Colors of Rhetoric,* Wendy Steiner illuminates this conflict between the differential elements of the *parergon* in works of art.[8] Like Kristeva, she notes that prose stresses the already established signifying system, while painting stresses the work of art as a thing. The more it is a thing, the more trouble it has being meaningful within the system of the signifying norm. This is because structuralism has made language the model for understanding all cultural phenomena, even though the struc-ture of painting is not dependent upon the phonemic-morphemic relation, nor upon the rules of syntax. Units in painting are combined according to laws which may or may not be invoked.

No painting is geometrically ill-formed insofar as the forms evidenced in painting are a question of style, a semantic convention, and not a signifying system (*TCR*, p. 123).

Steiner points to the odd paintings of René Magritte to make this clear. The *Key to Dreams* presents mislabelled images that are also misillustrated nouns. The words and the pictures remain independent of one another so that even a correctly matched pair seem as arbitrary as any other (*TCR*, p. 145). Magritte "names" his paintings in a manner that brings into question the act of naming, undermining the obvious relation between the title and the work, the name and the thing. This upsets the subject-predicate relation projected by language onto things, and leads us to question substance, presence, and time, as they have imposed themselves upon the work of art. Graphic and plastic elements are superimposed within the paintings in order to contest the obvious identity of the figure and the name we give it, while dissolving both.[9]

Magritte's painting plays on resemblance and representation to the point where the leaf of a tree assumes the shape of a tree (*L'incendi*), where the hull and sails of a ship are also composed of waves (*Le seducteur*), and where the representation of a pair of shoes or a dress begins to resemble the anatomical features they cover (*La philosophie dans le boudoir*) (*TNP*, pp. 38-9).

The point, for Magritte, is that between words and things, new relations can indeed be formed. Michel Foucault writes that, in a painting, "words are of the same cloth as images" (*TNP*, p. 39). This means that they are *not parergonal* (implying a logic of contradiction affirmed) as Derrida would like to maintain; they are "similar." One can no longer affirm that "this" painting, word, or image is or is not a pipe, because similitude (insofar as it is *neither* subject-predicate logic *nor* ontological) renders identity and its difference meaningless.

Resemblance (and so the *parergon*), Foucault points out in *This Is Not a Pipe*, his study of the paintings of Magritte, presupposes a model, an original substance, a first cause that orders and hierarchizes the increasingly less faithful copies, whereas the similar simply exists in a series without indication or necessity of a beginning or an end. It is not a circle, but a certain kind of event, singular insofar as it is not framed by past or future, and thus not subject to the determinations of presence and absence, substance, matter, form, or usefulness. Words and things (and by extension words and words, and things and things) stand together in indefinite relations of similar to similar. The *simulacrum*, always reversible, ranges across the surface, eliminating the original, and forcing a reorientation of thought (*TNP*, p. 35).

Such thought requires neither knowledge (based on concepts) nor judgments (based on the original); it is, rather, the repetition of an event without origins, the production of the *simulacrum*, the exhibition of what Gilles Deleuze calls the ghost, the phantom, that is, the linguistic surface of metaphysical bodies that is not able to be characterized by the metaphysics of presence, nor compelled to follow the circle.

For Foucault, Magritte's painting *Decalcomanie* offers a transfer of images in which similitude reveals what recognizable objects and familiar silhouettes hide, prevent from being seen, or render invisible. The body is the curtain, the right is the left and the left is the right. The resemblance between the (original) figure of a man in a bowler hat and his (derived) silhouette cut out of the fabric of the curtain to reveal the waves on the beach, and the clouds that the original faces, vanishes in the open network of similitudes, open not onto the "real" man who serves as a model for the painting and exists independently as the "true" original, but rather, open out onto all other similitudes, including that real man (*TNP*, p. 47).

But to characterize these relations in terms of similitude understood as *resemblance* is to place these works upon the projected surface of representation, to embalm them within the signifying system. To think Magritte's images in terms of similitude, says Foucault, is an act, "thinking" the double.

> For though this double may be close, it is alien, and the role, the true undertaking of thought will be to bring it as close to itself as possible; the whole of modern thought is imbued with the necessity of thinking the unthought. . . .[10]

If "knowledge" is partial because it is surrounded by an immense region of shadow that demands elucidation and illumination in an *act* of thinking, then it is irrelevant whether this representation is conscious or unconscious. If a new discursive unity must be thought, then it makes no sense to say that between a painting and what it represents there is no distance, that the model invades the canvas and the reference point is lost.

What must be made clear is the hold that language has over what it describes in the pictorial image, over the vast realm of the unthought. The "unity of discourse" reasserts itself (along with logic and ontology) the moment thinking takes place *in act*, that is, in the now present moment of the circle of representation. It is only when there is nothing left to know, nothing to affirm and nothing to deny, that all images and words, all beings, can remain within the realm of probability as events lacking necessity, yet subject to constant and predictable repetition.

Only the dispersion of representation (and with it, the *parergon*), can bring us to a confrontation with "stupidity," where there is nothing to know (for the categories of knowledge have been fragmented), and there is no history (for time and space have dissolved).

Yet this stupidity is precisely a place for thought. It is thought facing its own dogmatism, recognizing that there is "something happening" rather than nothing, and seeking its orientation from this "it is happening," rather than from discourse dominated by a single logic, a single grammar, a single truth. But for language in art, what can this mean?

In the postmodern world, it seems that history no longer provides identity or autonomy but is another commodity served up in television reruns, nostalgia, and endless repetition, so that instead of improving upon the work of the previous generation, each new generation merely repeats it with only a slight variation.[11] By repressing "material," history is reduced to a wardrobe, out of which we select each season's costume. Just as art historians reject Duchamp's anti-art stance by appropriating his objects into the realm of aesthetic forms, so philosophy, under such elegant appellations as the "sublime," has "colonized" art, translating it into popular generalities, repeated and recognizable forms.[12]

Like Foucault, Jean Baudrillard observes the reduction of this repetition in the form of the *simulacrum*, but he does not reduce it to representation. Instead, he points out that the *simulacrum* was valued in the Renaissance precisely because it was able to imitate Nature.[13] This is a repetition based on likeness, the likeness of the image to the real, and the determination of the real by the representation. This is followed by the rise of the industrial simulacrum, a fabricated image, opening up the possibility of an infinite number of identical objects, equivalent and interchangeable, and doing away with the need for the original, doing away with the value of the original (*JB*, p. 45). The photograph appears to be the paradigm industrial *simulacrum*, for an unlimited number of copies of any image may be produced without concern for the original of these images (*JB*, p. 45). The original print is always the same as the most recently made copy, so "original" is rendered meaningless.

In its current incarnation, says Baudrillard, the *simulacrum* precedes reality. The signifier has completely detached itself from the signified, from the "natural," from the representational structure, breaking apart both subject and object. Signs no longer refer to either a subjective or an objective reality, but to themselves, because there is no reality left to represent, and because what we accept as reality is already a massive simulation, "a fabrication of effects," "an artificial world without meaning."

> 'Reality' is constructed by the codes of society, by the already written, by the received languages and conventions that assume the subject's place (*JB*, p. 46).

Insofar as our experience, our knowledge, is constituted and limited by these codes, by the "solid anteriority" of language and things (*OT*, p. 334), it is wholly finite and positive. The abyss opened by the simulacrum is that in which "man" appears as a finite, determined being, trapped by what he cannot think, by what refuses to submit itself to discourse, and subject to the dispersion of time, that is, the linear flow of representations that are no longer gathered into the organizing unity of the system of language, but are dispersed.

With the dispersion and fragmentation of representations, there is nothing to know; there is only the distribution of information. There is no longer any history, only the parodying repetition of the past: a repetition visible in art, culture, styles, political posturing. The model dominates, but the return is governed by no historical necessity. Italian art critic Mario Perniola reminds us that today, "If I tape something live to see it two minutes later, the situation completely loses the impact of actuality. And conversely . . . if everything can be delayed, nothing is actual, and if everything can become instantly present, then everything is available as repetory."[14] On videotape and television everything is infinitely repeatable.

The confusion between past and present makes the attainment of an original impossible, but equally, it does away with the unquestioned and unquestionable validity of a system of language predicated upon the supremacy and stability of the "present." This confusion operates in the art world as a time containing all art, and an art that contracts all times into one single time containing all forms mixed together, with no one form predominating (*TTA*, p. 54).

This situation is what André Malraux refers to as the "museum without walls," the place where, by means of the photograph, a miniature takes up the same amount of space as a mural painting, where tapestry is admired for its lack of illusionist realism, stained glass for its color, and Islamic art for its lack of concern with history, hierarchy, or meaning.[15] The photograph, the book, and the museum have isolated works of art from their context; they have suppressed any sense of a model, and they have gathered as rivals works from diverse locations and time periods, inviting critique and comparison among them (*TVS*, p. 25).

The extreme confusion of forms and styles in contemporary art is directly related to the dissolution of any bond between artistic form and the social-historical time in which it exists (*TTA*, p. 54). Thought has been set adrift and wanders aimlessly among the multiplicity of forms, unable to distinguish past, present, or future. The "out-of-control parodying" of aesthetic and cultural forms belonging to other places, other times, may not be, however, simply a celebration of power or technology, but may also reflect despair.

Embedded in the postmodern sensibility, enfeebled by the multiplicity of formless forms and objects available for nameless utilizations, hidden in the current cynicism toward innovation, left behind in the rapid movement of social and technological advancement, is surely the great despair. History advances; it acts as though things can happen, and it takes action to make them happen.[16] Despair, however, arrests. It is the despair that nothing will happen in the dismantling of time which Jean-François Lyotard suggests characterizes the postmodern (*SAG*, p. 43).

Despair: repetition rather than nothing, a melancholy that obscures what is, perhaps, a barely recognizable virtue requiring the colonization of the troubling aspects of our *own* being, the rebellious regions of the self. "Responsibility is claimed for oneself, absolutely. It is not passed on."[17] But what poet and critic Carter Ratcliff calls the "modern will" is not the communication, expression, or conveyance of "meanings" from one psyche to another (*SF*, p. 52). It is not the temporal and spatial reunification of the fragmented, dehumanized, detached image. This will is, instead, a brutal recognition that "Pictorial space is in unceasing competition with the space we occupy, the 'space' of political and military power, space in all its configurations" (*SF*, p. 57).

It is in space in all its configurations that the struggle for power takes place, that the artist, philosopher, lawyer, businessman and -woman compete to define the arenas we inhabit, think, observe, manipulate. But today, space, like time, is completed, and to attempt to restore it is to restore the dismay, depression, and disorientation felt by artists and thinkers in the face of the totalization of thought, discursive systemization, and the rationalization of being. We begin in a condition of deep alienation, "fomented by military, ecological and media violence."[18] Is it the task of contemporary thought further to shock the public?

The work of art has been temporal, as the site of a speechless and shocking encounter between artist and audience; it has been spatial, a thing independent of human circumstances, an object always there to refer to, to be subverted to some use, even if only as aesthetic form. But with the dissolution of spatiality and temporality, the detachment of the work of art from fixed social, aesthetic, or metaphysical objectives, its resolution into a position where it is "not salvation, not philosophy," but "just art,"[19] an object brought into being by the thought and effort of an artist, we abandon the spatiotemporal discourse in favor of another.

Carrying out this project requires that clear distinctions are made between the logic and grammar of codified knowledge and those of exploration, discovery, creation. Deleuze insists that, in this regard, philosophy errs grammatically (and so logically too). As noted above, to speak in the form of "S is P" is to enclose events in the cyclical pattern of time, treating the present as if it were framed by a past and future in order to preserve the identity of content via the representation of that content.

Within this framework, the confusion of past and present, the forgetting of history, the parodying of old styles, are inevitably a part of the subversion of the system of discourse ruled by space and time. If we are to be able to speak without repeating the rationalized formula that forces us to say that "some subject is related to some predicate in a manner indicating usefulness or uselessness," we must search out a more complex logic than that of substantiality, and a grammar with a different type of organization.

Deleuze suggests we consider a metaphysics that is not a metaphysics of substance, but a metaphysics of the event. Discourse dealing with the substantial aspect of bodies, a substance that supports accidents, is not metaphysics, according to Deleuze; it is physics. Physics concerns itself with causes, situating accidents within a network of cause and effect.

Transposed into discourse, physics produces a logic and grammar centered on the referent, *designating* a state of affairs by associating words with images that must *represent* states of things as founded upon a judgment of the "I"; manifesting or *expressing* a state of affairs by means of causal inferences that commence with the "I" and aim to prove the existence of that state of affairs; *signifying* or demonstrating a state of affairs for an "I" by invoking a proposition whose signification is found in relation to other propositions which it either concludes or provides premises for.[20] In each case, we are in the order of *la parole,* the spoken word, and the "I" presents itself as first in relation to concepts, to the world, or to God (*LS,* p. 26).

But the "I" is first and sufficient in the order of *la parole* only insofar as it participates in significations that must be developed for themselves in the order of *la langue.* If these significations are not established in themselves, personal identity (the "I"), God, and the world founder (*LS,* p. 29). This also means that signification alone (the form of a proposition), is not sufficient to provide a foundation of truth for designation and expression. Neither the objective nor the subjective representation guarantees the referent. What may be necessary is a metaphysics of the "event" insofar as it does not exist *outside* of the proposition that expresses it.

It is for this reason that Deleuze introduces a "logic of meaning," a fourth dimension of the proposition, the pure "meaning-event" that insists or subsists in the proposition and is that incorporeal something (meaning) at the surface of things. The attribute of a proposition is a qualitative predicate, dependent on Being in relation to the verb "to be" (for example, "it *is* returned"), but meaning-events are not attributes of propositions. Rather, they are attributes of a thing or of a state of affairs *designated* by a proposition. As such they exist only *within* the proposition that expresses them, and take the form of a verb. This verb, this logical attribute, is not a physical state of affairs, nor a quality or relation; it is *not a being* at all (*LS*, p. 33), such that Being is not understood with regard to the verb "to be."

The meaning-event, in the infinitive form of the verb, (for example, "to lead," "to return") is directed toward the proposition as what is said about it, as its *meaning*, and it is turned toward things as an event, as what *happens* to them ("they lead," "they return"). What is important is that because it is always singular, the meaning-event given by the proposition cannot be categorized in terms of individual states of affairs, particular images, personal belief, universal or general concepts. It is neutral, neither mental nor physical (*LS*, p. 31), but always singular, because it is the verb's capacity to be infinitely repeated.

Deleuze suggests, then, that the event need no longer play the role of Being's attribute, but must be articulated in terms of the infinitive form of the verb. This allows meaning to circulate in discourse as a neutral, that is, *non-appropriating* element of the present tense, which alone posits an event without "to be," as in this fragment from William Carlos Williams's "The Hunters in the Snow" (which serves as a map for Breughel's work of the same name).

> The over-all picture is winter
> icy mountains
> in the background the return
>
> from the hunt, it is toward evening
> from the left
> sturdy hunters lead in (*TCR*, p. 81)

Here, the present tense ("the return"; "hunters lead in") indicates an event, something that happens, without referring to the verb "to be" as an attribute, that is, without designating some substantial being. Instead, the present tense serves as a displacement of the "now," of being in act; it is the eternal repetition of the infinitive. While the verb form "they are returning" designates a quality of "things" (in space and time: substances), the infinitive form of the verb "to return" is not a quality; it does not exist outside of the proposition that expresses the thing (*LS*, p. 34). The event serves to displace what can be said about the hunt and the hunters by what is indefinitely repeated, by what is said in the proposition.

This means that in the thought of the pure event, the *parergon* disappears with the identity of the subject and object (S is P). There is no *parergonal* structure in the poem or the painting. Rather, there is the event repeating itself as a singular universal, as an indefinite and "phantasmic repetition of the event,"[21] the individual encounter with repetition, thought as mime; repetition without a model (*TPH*, p. 179).

Temporality accounts for the "coherence" of the substantiality we attribute to substances. But the event is without substance, without this thickness. This is why we must be alert to the "surface," the domain of intangible (nonspatial and nontemporal) objects, the "phantasm" of which Foucault remarks that it cannot be reduced to a primordial fact but arises in the reversal that causes every interior to pass to the outside and every exterior to the inside. It begins in the oscillation that makes it precede, follow, and accompany itself, finally depriving outside, inside, before and after of significance.

The questions posed here are not about the reality of art, but about the reality of philosophy, the language in art. Is philosophy only effective at the borders, the margins of reality (as Derrida must claim), because it must think in terms of the logic of noncontradiction, the either/or, both/and of concepts and generalities tied to the significational system and determined by an absent-presence, the impossibility of thinking otherwise? Or, may it not take its orientation from the dissolution of the spatial and temporal discourse of substances that dominated the canvas and still rules thought?

Perniola clearly indicates that the dissolution of "space" and the completion of "time" fostered by modern art and presupposed by the metaphysics of the meaning-event has profound implications for all thought.

The completion of time implies the passage from a
European, or European-derived aesthetic to a planetary
aesthetic. This, in turn, implies the dissolution of many
oppositions, such as those between origin and copy,
genuine and spurious, function and ornament—points of
reference of the European aesthetic that are falling apart,
increasing the sense of disorientation and confusion (*TTA*,
p. 55).

Even the *parergon* dissolves in the dissolution of the oppositions that once constituted its borders. The European-derived
aesthetic can allow confusion and spectacle (for example, in the
collusion between capitalism and the sublime suggested by Baudrillard) but not a mingling of cultures, a thought that considers
the intersections among the diverse formal traditions, without,
however, accepting everything and without claiming "meta-his-
torical values" (*TTA*, p. 55).

Instead of despairing over this state of affairs, Roland Barthes
asks us to risk even more. "Imagine someone who abolishes
within himself all barriers, all classes, all exclusions, not by
syncretism but by simple *discard of that old spectre: logical contradiction;* who mixes every language, even those said to be
incompatible. . . ."[22]

What remains, says Barthes, is what comes "to me" out of the
disfiguration of language. And what comes, what stings, cuts,
wounds, bruises; what I see, hence notice, think (the "punctum")
is what Barthes paradoxically discovers in the photograph, that
paradigm of the industrial *simulacrum,* which, insofar as it is
without origins, is *also* the *absolute particular,* the singular universal.

What the Photograph reproduces to infinity has occurred
only once: the Photograph mechanically repeats what could
never be repeated existentially. In the Photograph, the
event is never transcended for the sake of something else:
the Photograph always leads the corpus I need back to the
body I see; it is the absolute Particular, the sovereign
Contingency, matte and somehow stupid.[23]

The photograph as meaning-event is the referent, one which
is "not the same as the referent of other systems of representa-

tion" (*CL*, p. 76). In the photograph (as in the meaning-event) something has *posed* and remains there forever; nothing has passed (been present) (*CL*, p. 78). The photograph, "as punctum," authenticates (that this has been only once) and never represents (*CL*, p. 89).

The photograph, heretofore the most public visual medium (the "studium"; the photograph insofar as it informs, represents, surprises, causes, signifies, provokes desires, affirms cultural norms: *CL*, pp. 26-8), becomes the most private, but only insofar as it wounds me, that is, only if it retains the slightest of ideologies that come to me. This is precisely what constitutes the "punctum"; and that is why it constitutes a science of the singular. It is, perhaps, only this bit of "ideology" that keeps the possibly infinite repetition of the event from becoming impossibly stupid and driving us back upon the firm ground of representation.

Recourse to the event and the surface may have induced a one-dimensional, reductionist reading of history, culture, artworks, but only when read on the borders of the significational system determined by space and time, substance, the present. This allows critics and philosophers to attempt to attach works of art to an owner-user or to an origin and to insist upon the language of subject-predicate grammar. Yet from the sublime to the "stupid," from Bellini to Duchamp and Magritte, philosophers have found the dispersal of significational systems and the simultaneous eruption of repetition. Together they operate to fragment unified language predicated on Being, and to reveal, on the surface of beings, a postmodern theory of language; one that has come to be formulated as a language in art.

Chapter 7

THE OTHERNESS OF WORDS: JOYCE, BAKHTIN, HEIDEGGER

Gerald L. Bruns

The movement toward the negation of meaning was exactly what meaning deserved.
—Adorno, *Aesthetic Theory*

Discourse is thus the experience of something absolutely foreign . . . a traumatism of astonishment.
—Levinas, *Totality and Infinity*

I

Let me begin by returning to *Finnegans Wake,* or rather to where I left off in *Modern Poetry and the Idea of Language* (1974), where I took the *Wake* to be the fulfillment of Flaubert's modernist dream of writing "a book about nothing, a book dependent on nothing external, which would be held together by the strength of its style, just as the earth, suspended in the void, depends on nothing for its support; a book which would have almost no subject, or at least in which the subject would be almost invisible."[1] Modernist writing means letting go of the foundations of discourse; it means letting discourse run its course independently of the laws of signification. Modernist writing is a species of "negative discourse" that tries to prolong "the moment before speech" (pp. 192–5). Blanchot has put it as bluntly as anyone can:

Language can only begin with the void; no fullness, no certainty, can ever speak; something essential is lacking in anyone who expresses himself. Negation is tied to language. When I first begin, I do not speak in order to say something, rather a nothing demands to speak, nothing speaks, nothing finds its being in speech and the being of speech is nothing. This formulation explains why literature's ideal has been the following: to say nothing, to speak in order to say nothing.[2]

In the light (or shadow) of this ideal, *Finnegans Wake* becomes perfectly intelligible for the sense it does not make. If, for example, we think of meaning on the structuralist's model as the product of a system of differences, the *Wake* will begin to make sense for the way it escapes the system, that is, for its effacement of difference, including the difference between sense and non-sense, as when every word is an echo of every other. Who can anyone be when everybody is somebody else? Of course, there is never a sense that cannot be made of any portion of the text—it is not that exegesis cannot occur—but what absorbs us, what matters, is the sheer materiality of the *Wake*'s language, which requires the word "reading" to be put in quotation marks as something that takes place only in a certain manner of speaking, under conditions of considerable resistance.[3] Years ago I quoted Clive Hart's line: "There is never any question of reading through the prose."[4] That is, one no longer reads consecutively because everything is happening simultaneously. Metaphor drives out metonymy. As in a fantasia of formalism, "all discourse is aligned along the several staves of a score."[5] The words of the *Wake*, says Hart, inscribe purely formal motifs, and the task of reading is to trace the itineraries of these motifs as they circle and twine through or upon the text. There are no such things as hidden meanings in *Finnegans Wake*, no concealed narratives, nothing behind or beneath the handiwork; everything is out in the open, riding the surface of expressive expressionless forms.

II

So one could say that the history of reading came to an end with *Finnegans Wake*, and that since 1939 readers of the world have been congregating in front of the text as before a Chinese Wall that blocks every access to the future. Since we cannot break through to the other side, there is nothing for it but to study how the thing is made. Some people call this going "beyond hermeneutics." *Finnegans Wake* turns us against interpretation and onto the path of structuralist analysis, where the end of reading is no longer to determine the meaning of anything but rather to lay open to view the deep structure or mode of production that makes meaning, or whatever, possible. So hidden meanings are replaced by tacit rules. Accordingly, mainline semioticians like Umberto Eco figure *Finnegans Wake* as "a model of the global semantic system" or as "a metaphor for the process of unlimited semiosis."[6] Which simply means that the *Wake* is structured as a language. Its surface formations are self-interfering and opaque like the surfaces of everything else—the body, natural language, history—but logical analysis can penetrate these formations to grasp an underlying rationality. The spirit of such analysis is captured by Althusser's idea that "the religious myth of reading" begins to dissipate with Marx's discovery that "the truth of history cannot be read in its manifest discourse, because the text of history is not a text in which a voice (the Logos) speaks, but the inaudible and illegible notation of the effects of a structure of structures."[7] Something other, deeper than the expression of meaning is at work. Call it, after Nietzsche, power; or, after Freud, desire. Questions of power and desire are technological rather than hermeneutical. "The question posed by desire," say Deleuze and Guattari, "is not 'What does it mean?' but *'How does it work?'*" "Desire," they say, "makes its entry with the general collapse of the question 'What does it mean?' No one has been able to pose the problem of language except to the extent that linguists and logicians have first eliminated meaning; and the greatest force of language was only discovered once a *work* was viewed as a machine, producing certain effects, amenable to a certain use."[8] Thus Jean-Michel Rabaté: "The metaphor of the machine describes not only the [*Wake*'s] theoretical functioning, but also the labour which constructed it. . . . Joyce means to capture in his machine all the fluxes he diverts, the flux of language and the flux of history."[9] So from the standpoint of technology one may put it that *Finnegans Wake* works like a text whose "inaudible and illegible" manifest discourse displaces the question of reading form the signified to the signifier, from meaning to desire, from consciousness to the unconscious, from faith to suspicion, from "What Does It Mean?" to "How Does It Work?"—in short, from surface to deep structure.

The unkillable idea, of course, is that *Finnegans Wake* works like a dream, and that what the reading of it requires is something like a Freudian model of analysis in which a latent content is constructed by recombining (as by free association) the surface debris of the manifest discourse. The text is not something one "reads through" but, like the dream, something to be reconstituted on another level. A recent example of this sort of thing would be John Bishop's *Joyce's Book of the Night*, which is uncontroversial and even routine in its critical observations and results but worth a second look for the way it incorporates the *Wake*'s own language into its discursive procedures:

> "How many of its readers realize" (112.1–2 [*really* realize]) "that [it] is not out to dizzledazzle with a graith uncouthrement of . . . the lapins and the grigs"? (112.36– 133.3). The referentially secure languages of "Latin" and "Greek," of course, are helpful to the reading of the *Wake*, but less so than a knowledge of "*lapins*" (Fr. "rabbits") and "grigs" (Eng. "crickets"), which leap all over the place, "runnind hare and dart" (285.4), rather like the nocturnal thought of the "quhare soort of mahan" who sleeps at the *Wake* (16.1). Because it is an "imitation of a dream-state" and not rationally discursive thought, *Finnegans Wake* is written in "coneyfarm leppers" (257.5–6 ["coneys"="rabbits"]), and not "cuneiform letters," or, again, in "some little laughings and some less of cheeks" (125.15 [and even less "Latin" and "Greek"]) What it really requires of its reader is the ability to pursue "distant connections" (169.4–5) and, in doing so, to leap all over the place. *"Read your Pantojoke"* (71.17–18 [and not the "Pentateuch"]).[10]

Bishop likes to say things like "all the printed letters and words in *Finnegans Wake* are mere 'vehicles' leading to hidden meanings and letters that are nowhere explicitly evident to a reader's literate consciousness" (p. 310), but all he means by this is that we should not try to read the thing the way we would a proposition or a narrative. The method of reading that Bishop counsels is not formally different from the sort proposed by Hart—what Hart

calls "motifs" are "long chains of association" for Bishop (p. 40)—
and the idea is simply to trace these chains (or rather construct
them) by piecemeal attention to the combinatory power of the
text's elementary particles. Since this power is considerably in
excess of what normally fits under the category of linguistic
competence, reading has a lot to do. The question is: What
motivates such reading? Bishop says:

> Any reader wishing to "read the Evening World," as
> opposed to "the dully expressed" [the Daily Express], must
> therefore learn to "stotter from the latter" with the hero of
> the *Wake*, by slipping from the literal surface of the text and
> becoming a freethinker of sorts. Making "infrarational" and
> "freely masoned" connections is ultimately more important
> to an understanding of the *Wake*'s "slipping beauty" (477.23
> ["sleeping beauty"]) than making literate distinctions,
> which is the business of the "day's reason" (p. 307).

One has, so to speak, to let go of the desire, or foundation, of
explanation.

In an essay called "Within the Microcosm of 'The Talking
Cure,'" Julia Kristeva talks about the way an analyst tries to come
to terms with her patient's "borderline discourse".[11] This is a
discourse that exhibits "the maniacal eroticization of speech, as
if the patient were clinging to [language], gulping it down, suck-
ing on it, delighting in all the aspects of an oral eroticization and
a narcissistic safety belt which this kind of non-communicative,
exhibitionistic, and fortifying use of speech entails. The analyst
notices a tendency to play with signifiers: puns, portmanteau
words, the condensation of signifiers, which are not always, not
only, or sometimes not at all cultural acquisitions" (p. 42). How
to read such a discourse?

> The analyst often feels called upon, especially in the
> beginning of the cure, to *"construct relations,"* to take up bits
> of discursive chaos in order to indicate their relations
> (temporal, causal, etc.), or even simply to repeat these bits
> of discourse, thereby already ordering these chaotic
> themes. This kind of logical, even associative, task could
> give the impression that we work at constructing
> repression. More precisely, and in light of the "sign"

function and its perturbations, these constructions serve to give the speech act a *signification* (for a subject—the analyst, the patient). This repetition or reordering by means of an interpretation that builds connections does not serve to reconstruct either a real or an imaginary biography. Instead, it reestablishes plus and minus signs and, subsequently, logical sequences and thus the very capacities of speech to enunciate exterior referential realities (pp. 45–46).

So, on this model, one might imagine a reader of the *Wake* trying to repair Joyce's text, making it readable by rewriting it according to the model of the proposition, the narrative, or the signifying system (the interplay, for example, of metaphor and metonymy).[12] In fact it is this sort of repair work that makes up the bulk of literary criticism, not just of Joyce's difficult texts but perhaps of all that is written, as if all texts were "borderline discourses."

But Kristeva goes on to speak of "condensed interpretations" that bear a more "erotic" relationship to the borderline text; instead of trying to repair the text, condensed interpretation embraces it in all of its materiality: "It separates non-sense from the restrictions of meaning and colludes with the manic or narcissistic manipulation of the signifier in the borderline patient" (p. 46). Thus, for example, as a work of "constructive interpretation," *Joyce's Book of the Night* simply re-invents the wheel; as a species of "condensed interpretation," however, it is a tour de force. For it is not so much that Bishop tries to penetrate the materiality of Joyce's language as the other way around: the language of the *Wake* is internalized—it would not be too much to say "cannibalized"—in Bishop's "reading" of it:

"It is a mere mienerism of this vague of visibilities," "for inkstands" (608.1 [Fr.. *vague*, "empty"], 173.34), that terms like "shade," "tar," "coal," "pitch," "soot," and "ink" should everywhere occlude words that are otherwise "basically English" (116.26). With intricate particularity, these "blackartful" terms (121.27) enable the *Wake* to adopt its own peculiar "dressy black modern style" (55.14–15), a "blackhand" "sootable" to the portraiture of *"a blackseer"* who is given to envisioning only vast "blackshape[s]" and lots of "pitchers" (495.2; *L*,III,147; 340.13; 608.29; 233.1, 438.13, 438.13, 531.15, 587.14, 598.21) (p. 219).

To be sure, this sentence is explanatory after a fashion, but taken just as explanation it would be pretty trivial, a piece of seminar-room philology. But Bishop's obsessive quotation from Joyce's text is more erotic than analytic; it does not try to rebuild the text within a framework of signification but "colludes" with its "manic or narcissistic manipulation of the signifier."

Naturally we want to know the point of such reading, what justifies it, what its cash-value is: but the point of such reading is just to free itself from the "restrictions of meaning" and the justifications of reason and explanation.[13] This means entering into the region of *délire*, which is Jean-Jacques Lecercle's word for "a form of discourse which questions our most common conceptions of *language* (whether expressed by linguists or by philosophers), where the old philosophical question of the emergence of sense out of *nonsense* receives a new formulation, where the material side of language, its origin in the human body and *desire*, are no longer eclipsed by its abstract aspect (as an instrument of communication or expression). Language, nonsense, desire: *délire* accounts for the relations between these three terms."[14] *Délire* describes the opposition between the dictionary and the scream. It occurs "at the frontier between two languages [as] the embodiment of the contradiction between them." On the one hand, there is the language of signification, that is, language as the functioning of *langue*, language as system and rule, as "an instrument of control, mastered by a regulating subject," language as the mechanism of repression that makes consciousness possible; on the other hand, there is language in its materiality—"unsystematic, a series of noises, private to individual speakers, not meant to promote communication, and therefore self-contradictory, 'impossible' like all 'private languages.' It is an integral part of the speaker's body, an outward expression of its drives. It imposes itself on the individual, controlling the 'subject': it is not the transparent medium which the instrumentalist describes, nor the means of consensus which the conventionalist conceives, it is, to misquote a philosophical phrase, a (material) process without a subject" (pp. 44–5).

If we think of the *Wake* as belonging to the region of délire, it

becomes evident that the reading of the *Wake* can no longer be
conceived as an analytical process, that is, as a process of getting
down to what is essential (say its "deep structure"). In *Finnegans
Wake*, as a work of *délire*, the essential has been displaced by the
excessive. The *Wake* is a product, not of *langue*, but of *lalangue*,
which is Jacques Lacan's word for that which *langue* excludes.[15]
Lalangue is language in its otherness, its heterogeneity, its irreducibility to consciousness and use, its uncontainability within
any system or framework of signification, its resistance to analysis or grammatical description, its materiality, its collusion with
the unsignifiable, its freedom. It is that which must be repressed
if consciousness is to form. In Lacan's lingo, it is that which
blasphemes the Name of the Father and plays havoc with the
Symbolic Order. Not surprisingly, *lalangue* is Joycean: it is not a
concept but an "infelicity" of speech, a *Wakean* stutter (cf. *Wake*,
36.20–34). In his Preface to *The Four Fundamental Concepts of Psycho-analysis* (1973), Lacan writes: "I shall speak of Joyce, who has
preoccupied me much this year, only to say that he is the simplest
consequence of a refusal—such a mental refusal!—of a psychoanalysis, which, as a result, his work illustrates."[16] Say that psychoanalysis—that is, normal, "constructive interpretation" of
borderline discourse—aims at the reinsertion of a text into the
order of signification. *Finnegans Wake* (here a synecdoche for the
history of poetry) refuses such analysis, invites erotic transgression into "condensed interpretation" where the reader lets go
into the "madness of words."[17] A current name for such letting-
go is "deconstruction," which, however, sets up its erotic relationships not with borderline discourses like *Finnegans Wake* but
with mainline texts out of the histories of philosophy and criticism. We may think of Jacques Derrida's *Glas* (1974) as "condensed interpretation" that brings the *Wake* out of the Hegel by
working out and joining in an erotic relationship between texts
by Hegel and Genet; anyhow this is the way Derrida thinks of it
("a sort of Wake").[18]

III

Lecerle aligns *délire* with the private languages of psychosis. And
indeed what is borderline about borderline discourse is just its

sociality, its communicative aspect, its integration into the order of signification. However, one might want to supplement or open up this way of thinking by replacing *délire* with Bakhtin's notion of the *carnivalesque*, which is a historicized rather than strictly psychic category of discourse.[19] That is, the carnivalesque brings *délire* into the open; the carnivalesque is the *délire* of the public realm. Whereas, following Hannah Arendt, we normally imagine the public realm philosophically as a space opened up and sustained by argument, the carnivalesque describes a public realm shaped by the sort of "maniacal eroticization of speech" that produced *Finnegans Wake*. In fact we may think of the *Wake* as opening just such a public space (into which, for example, all critical commentary on the *Wake* must enter, even if at its peril as serious or legitimate discourse). Bakhtin redistributes the distinction between surface and deep structure horizontally along a social axis instead of vertically according to descending planes of consciousness. In this respect he may be said to have freed language from the residual mentalism, or anyhow Kantianism, of the various semiotic, psychoanalytic, and deconstructive structuralisms. Thus unitary language and heteroglossia are social rather than logical categories of speech; they compete with one another along the same plane for control of the public realm.[20] They are like the distinction that Derrida draws between Husserlian and Joycean language.

> Both try to grasp a pure historicity. To do this, Husserl proposes to render language as transparent as possible, univocal, limited to that which, by being transmittable or able to be placed in tradition, thereby constitutes the only condition of a possible historicity. . . . The other great paradigm would be the Joyce of *Finnegans Wake*. He repeats and mobilizes and babelizes the (asymptotic) totality of the equivocal, he makes this his theme and his operation, he tries to make outcrop, with the greatest possible synchrony, at great speed, the greatest power of meanings buried in each syllabic fragment, subjecting each atom of writing to fission in order to overload the unconscious with the whole memory of man: mythologies, religion, philosophies, sciences, psychoanalyses, literatures. This generalized equivocality of writing does not translate one language into

another on the basis of common nuclei of meaning
(*Introduction to "The Origin of Geometry,"* pp. 103ff.); it talks
several languages at once, parasiting them as in the
example of *He war* [258.12] to which I shall return in a
moment. For there will remain the question of knowing
what one should think of the possibility of writing several
languages at once (*Post-structuralist Joyce,* p. 149).

A "pure historicality" would be one which is completely outside
the ideality of meaning, an open, unstructured, unstable space
of colliding or intersecting surfaces that cannot be mapped by
any external geometer (cannot be thought). Only by entering
into this historicity, however, can the ideality of meaning be
actualized as objective (that is, as actually saying something);
only when this happens does historicity become intelligible, if at
all. Husserlian language enters this space seeking total intelligibility; it tries to bring historicity under control, shaping it in its
own image according to a geometry of pure relations or the pure
forms of meaning; Joycean language lets itself go, turns itself
loose in this space and pervades it in all of its heterogeneity and
irreducibility to sense. Thus on the one hand we may imagine a
social order superintended by a universal grammar into whose
forms everything can be translated and understood by everyone
no matter what the time and place; and on the other hand we
have a world in which *all* words are alien, where no one is saying
anything except in "several languages [all languages?] all at
once." Here the kingdom of Babel is at hand.

Bakhtin's linguistics (or anti-linguistics), sets these two languages into ideological combat. He describes an "elastic environment of other, alien words" that must be brought to order—
dominated, if only momentarily, at some point or intersection—
if anyone is to make sense to anyone else.[21] There is, at all events,
no making sense anywhere except within this environment, that
is, there is no setting up an alternative semantic space where
sentences cohere transparently around a logical form. Husserl-
like, Bakhtin imagines a word trying to connect up with its object,
but, Joyce-like, he imagines this taking place in a sort of radio-
culture of intersecting societies:

Indeed, any concrete discourse (utterance) finds the object
at which it was directed already as it were overlain with

qualifications, open to dispute, charged with value, already enveloped in an obscuring mist—or, on the contrary, by the "light" of alien words that have already been spoken about it. It is entangled, shot through with shared thoughts, points of view, alien value judgments and accents. The word, directed toward its object, enters a dialogically-agitated and tension-filled environment of alien words, value judgments and accents, weaves in and out of complex interrelationships, merges with some, recoils from others, intersects with yet a third group: and all this may crucially shape discourse, may leave a trace in all its semantic layers. . . (Bakhtin, *Dialogic Imagination*, p. 276).

The idea is that intentions are never alone with their objects in the purely logical (or monological) space of the proposition; they belong to the "dialogized heteroglossia" where they always proliferate from the outside in. Imagine the proposition, not as a sealed-off logical form, but as porous and exposed not only inwardly toward psychic otherness and figural difference but externally toward an alien sociality, a "Tower-of-Babel mixing of languages" (*Dialogic Imagination*, p. 278). Husserl-like, Bakhtin picks out the relation of word and thing; Joyce-like, he situates this relation within the otherness of "alien words":

On all its various routes toward the object, in all its directions, the word encounters an alien word and cannot help encountering it in a living, tension-filled interaction. Only the mythical Adam, who approached a virginal and as yet verbally unqualified world with the first word, could really have escaped from start to finish this dialogic interorientation with the alien word that occurs in the object. Concrete historical human discourse does not have this privilege: it can deviate from such inter-orientation only on a conditional basis and only to a certain degree (*Dialogic Imagination*, p. 279).

So there is no pure, pre-Babel relation of word and thing: "The word is born in a dialogue as a living rejoinder within it; the word is shaped in dialogic interaction with an alien word that is already in the object. A word forms a concept of its own object in a dialogic way" (*Dialogic Imagination*, p. 279).

As if the word were more like a voice than a logical term, that is, more like a Joycean word made of other words than a semiotic unit of phonemic differences. On paper words are just terms; as soon as one speaks, however, words break their logical boundaries and begin speaking in tongues. We always think of what we say as if it were on paper, that is, simply and silently in terms of what we mean; but we are never ourselves alone, never *in propria persona*. In part this is the hermeneutical idea that we build our sentences out of words with a history, several histories, words that come down to us in a tradition of "multifarious voices," filled with the echoes of conflicting and crumbling contexts.[22] One's discourse floats in a Sargasso sea of usage. But Bakhtin's idea is that one's voice is always intersected by other voices, laced with other intentions, other worlds, as if one were always caught up in an urban noise of marketplace and fishmarket, street corner and train station, pub and union hall where everyone is talking at once and nobody is anyone who does not sound like someone else ("wi'that bizar tongue in yur tolkshap" (499.20–21).

Julia Kristeva says: "Dialogism is coextensive with the deep structures of discourse."[23] It is hard to see how this could be so, unless it were in a crazy linguistics (or anti-linguistics) where deep structures turned out to be only so many intersections of heterogeneous surfaces. Actually, this is not far from what Kristeva has in mind. Deep structure is not, as in Husserl or the analytic tradition, logical form; it is a textual mosaic of "once current puns, quashed quotatoes, messes of mottage, unquestionable issue papers, seedy ejaculations, limerick damns, crocodile tears, spilt ink, blasphematory spits, stale sheshnuts" (183.22–24); or words to that effect. Every sentence transforms the lacings of a text whose center is everywhere and whose circumference is expanding infinitely hourly in every direction. This is your basic theory of intertextuality.[24] Or think of Borges's great "Library of Babel." But Bakhtin likes to think of texts as stratified. On the surface they exhibit the logical form or poetic decorum of unitary language, but as you descend you will uncover layers of heterogeneous vocabularies. The point to remember is that your descent is not taking you deeper into the inner world of preconscious grammars or, below these, into the body where one hears the warm, undifferentiated murmur of the mother tongue. On the contrary, you are heading into the outer world of the "social heteroglossia" (p. 292). The deeper you go, the more open things get. Only now it becomes difficult or pointless to retain the concept of deep structure. As if one needed to be told.

IV

In *What is Called Thinking?*, Heidegger distinguishes between common speech (*gewöhnliche Sprechen*) and the speech of poetry and thinking (*Dichten* [not *Dichtung*] and *Denken*).[25] At first this sounds like the usual formalist's distinction between everyday and literary language, or between philosophical discourse and the way you and I talk to ourselves and others; or, in other words, "the language of the tribe" and its various possible poetic or logical purifications, its various efforts at "authenticity." As if poetry and thinking were expressions (as Bakhtin would say) of "unitary language." But for Heidegger poetry and thinking are not containable within unitary language. What Heidegger wants to distinguish are words (*Worte*) and terms (*Wörter*), and it is not easy to say what this distinction comes to. Terms are what we use in order to speak about this or that. We can fix the usage of such words, that is, determine the sense in which they are to be taken in this or that context. Terms are what dictionaries are made of; they are got together out of signifiers; they enable us to get into our mode of nomination with respect to whatever is at hand, gathering things into statements, bringing them under conceptual control. Terms are the building-blocks of propositions. They are the ingredients of every lexicon ("terms of art"). So one might say that they are foundational for unitary language. Heidegger calls them "buckets or kegs out of which we can scoop sense" (WD88/129). But we need not think of them only as logical entities or products of rigorous conceptual definition. Heidegger speaks of them as if they were simply the familiar words (*gewöhnlichen Wörter*) around which we feel comfortable, that is, words that never catch us by surprise or get away from us, words that will do us no harm, that we can rely on, that answer to our intentions not so much in the logician's strict sense as in the sense of what we just mean to say (*vouloir-dire*): in short words to communicate with because what they say seems self-evident or closed to interrogation and dispute. Terms are words that give us, in the words of Beckett's *Watt*, "semantic succor."[26]

Not so with words in the sense of *Worte:* "Words are not terms [*Die Worte sind keine Wörter*], and thus are not like buckets and kegs from which we scoop a content [*Inhalt*]. Words are wellsprings that are found and dug up in the telling [*Sagen*], wellsprings that must be found and dug up again and again, that easily cave in, but that at times also well up when least expected" (WD89/130). This figure makes words sound originary and primordial, as doubtless they are, but mainly in the characteristically Heideggerian sense of "not of our own making." The point of the figure is that words are not something under our control; we do not connect up with them by way of linguistic competence. Rather we should think of the word as that which struggles to withdraw from usual and customary usage, as if it belonged elsewhere. Not that words are always or ever materially distinguishable from terms. There are words in every term, and if you listen you can hear them, as if words were puns that we had to wrestle with in order to turn them into terms, that is, in order to insert them into the order of signification where they can be of some use to us. But words are not intrinsically of this order; they are not simply ambiguous or undefined terms. In "The Nature of Language" (1957), Heidegger says that "It is as much a property of language to sound and ring and vibrate, to hover and to tremble, as it is for what is spoken [*Gesprochenes*] to carry a meaning."[27] This is partly what Heidegger's famous expression, *Die Sprache spricht*, comes to. Language speaks, but not in the structuralist's sense that, whatever the surface variability of our speech, meaning remains a product of deep structure (grammar and ideology). Rather, for Heidegger our linguistic competence—our linguisticality—consists less in the monological ability to produce intelligible sentences than in the ear's ability to pick up on all the punning that is always going on in language. In our relation to *Worte*, for example, it is hard to distinguish between speaking and listening. It is this indeterminacy of speaking and listening that Heidegger talks about in "The Way of Language" (1959), where listening is said to be our mode of belonging to language: *gehören* is a pun where listening and belonging intersect.[28]

So (to the scandal of philosophy) in Heideggerian *délire* the infelicities of words are not repressed; on the contrary, they are what poetry and thinking must remain open to. This is why Heidegger's way with words is more Joyce-like than Husserlian; that is, his way is never to define them but to listen for the way other words—almost always strange or alien words, words from another language or words no longer in use—resonate in them. The famous example from *What is Called Thinking?* concerns the words for thinking itself. In *Denken, Gedachtes, Gedanke*, think, thinking, thought, Heidegger hears the echo or hint [*Wink; Hinweis*] of the Old German *Gedanc*, where thinking and thanking intersect: "We take the hint," he says, "that in the speaking of those words [*Denken, Gedachtes, Gedanke*] the decisively and originally telling word sounds [*das maßgebend und ursprunglich sagende Wort lautet*]: *der 'Gedanc'* " (WD91/139–40).[29] The upshot of Heidegger's listening to *Gedanc* is the idea or reflection that thinking has more to do with receptivity or openness than with reasoning in the sense of representational-calculative operations of description and explanation; it is, well, more like listening than, say, questioning or critique. Indeed, in "The Nature of Language" Heidegger says as much: "to think is above all to listen, to let a Saying happen to us and not to ask questions [*das Denken allem zuvor ein Hören ist, ein Sichsagenlassen und kein Fragen*]" (US180/76). As if thinking were, in some way yet to be understood, dialogical; that is, as if thinking presupposed a dialogical relation with language rather than a logical mastery of it.

This seems roughly the idea of Heidegger's *Gelassenheit*, letting-be or, as I prefer, letting-go.[30] This comes out in the essay on "The Word" (1958), where Heidegger explicates the word "renounce" [*verzichten*] from the final couplet of Stefan George's poem, "Das Wort": *So lernt ich traurig den verzicht:/ Kein ding sei wo das wort gebricht.* Renunciation, Heidegger says, means giving up language as logos, that is, as the power of framing representations. It means giving up signs as names that "rule over things" (US225/144). Renunciation is the poet's way with words. By means of renunciation, Heidegger says, the poet opens onto "a different rule of the word," one which is not based on signs of any kind and has nothing to do with the designation of objects or the making of representations. "The poet," he says, "must relinquish the claim to the assurance that he will on demand be supplied with a name for that which he has posited as what truly is [note the reference to positing: *das wahrhaft Seiende gesetzt hat*]. This positing and that claim he must now deny himself [*sich versagen*]. The poet must renounce having words under his control as the representational names [*darstellenden Namen*] for what is posited" (US227–28/146/47). Things are not, *pace* the philosophical tradition since Kant, logical posits; they are not constructions of any sort. Poetry does not connect up with things in the way of worldmaking; it does not connect up with things at all but simply lets them be in Heidegger's strong sense of letting them stand (like the work of art) in their otherness or strangeness, their difference or uncontainability, within the conceptual schemes by which we make sense of them. Heideggerian things are more events than objects; they "thing" rather than present themselves as entities in time and space.[31] Heidegger's word for letting things be (that is, "thing") is *Gelassenheit*. *Gelassenheit* is the mode of being with things that thinking must learn to get into. The poetic equivalent of *die Gelassenheit zu den Dingen* is called *Verzichten*: "Renunication [*Verzichten*]," Heidegger says, "commits itself to a higher rule of the word which first lets a thing be as thing [as against *res* or *ens* or Kantian object]; the word 'be-things' the thing. We should like to call this rule of the word 'bethinging' [*Bedingnis*]" (US232/151).

Now the interesting thing about *Bedingnis* is its obsolescence. "This old word," Heidegger says, "has disappeared from linguistic usage" (US232/151). Bakhtinians will appreciate why it turns up now in the context of thinging things (v. logical posits). For it is not just that Heidegger seeks in this old world a more true or proper meaning than the sense of current usage. Heidegger does not think of himself as playing an etymological game in order to recover a primitive sense. Listening is not a form of exegesis, or at all events it is not enough to think of it simply as a listening-for-meaning. For the meaning of *Bedingnis* is more parodistic than primordial or proper. Goethe, Heidegger says, still knew *Bedingnis,* but the word was subsequently superseded by Kant's lingo, *bedingen* and *Bedingung,* posit and condition. These are the basic terms of foundationalism. *Bedingnis* doesn't fit in with this vocabulary, nor is it a primitive version of it. Call it the game that language plays with philosophy; call it (and

Heidegger in the bargain) an eruption of *délire* within the unitary discourse of the philosophical tradition. "A condition [*Bedingung*]," Heidegger says, "is the existent ground for something that is. The condition gives reasons, and it grounds. It satisfies the principle of sufficient reason" (US232/151). *Bedingnis* is the sounding, ringing, vibrating of language that goes on in excess of explanation. Heidegger (parodistically) appropriates this excessive word as the word for what happens with the refusal to name things, that is, to posit things within the forms of time and space and the categories of explanation. It is the word for what happens with the poet's word—the poet who, like Blanchot, steps back from the moment of speech, speaks "in order to say nothing."

Letting go of language in this way means letting language speak, that is, letting it *language* in the manner of *Gelassenheit* and the *thinging* of things. There is no textual equivalent for the speaking of language, that is, when language speaks it is not productive in the sense of *poiesis*. So it would not be correct to think of *Finnegans Wake* as what happens when language speaks, only that in texts like the *Wake* (here a synecdoche for the history of poetry) we draw close to the strangeness of language, its otherness, its resistance to consciousness, its essential illegibility, its excessiveness before reason, it unusability, its irreducibility to meaning. When language speaks, its utterance can perhaps be traced in things like *Finnegans Wake*—or, not traced, but heard as if at an infinite distance. In the essay on "Language" (1950), Heidegger says, "Language speaks as the peal of stillness" (US30/207), that is, not as a naming in the sense of designation but as a calling in the sense of summoning. Heidegger has in mind the tolling of churchbells at vespers. Think of the speaking of language not as the empirical sound of the bells but of the disappearance of this sound into the silence, that is, as the resonance or vibration of the silence as the tolling dies away. "The peal of stillness," Heidegger says, "is not anything human" (US30/207). Think of *Finnegans Wake* as an echo of this other.

Chapter 8

POSTMODERNISM AND THEATER

Fred McGlynn

The theoretical announcement of a postmodern theater was given by Antonin Artaud in his seminal work, *The Theater and Its Double*, published in France in the 1930s. Artaud called for an end to all representation in the theater, the replacement of a dead theater of 'authors' and 'the word' ("no more masterpieces") with a sacred theater of gesture, the liberation of the actor enslaved to the text and therefore divided from himself, into a pure carnal presence "signaling through the flames,"[1] and the replacement of a passive theater of speculation with a sacred festive theater of participation. The radical interrogation of traditional theatrical practice implied in his 'theater of cruelty' and his recommendations for a new 'impossible' sacred theater have set the challenge to which all postmodern theater has responded, either by trying to overcome what in traditional representative theater was the subject of his criticism or by trying to institute his 'impossible' sacred theater. "If the public does not frequent our literary masterpieces it is because those masterpieces are literary, that is to say, fixed, and fixed in forms that no longer respond to the needs of the time."[2]

Artaud assaulted the theater of authors as the fundamental source of the death of theater. In this traditional theater the author dictated his 'text' to the enslaved actor, who could only perform the role of mouthpiece for the absent author. Such theater was then received by the passive audience within the closed space of the proscenium stage. The author functioned like an absent god, controlling the process from a distance, providing the illusion of a closure with meaning for both the actor and the audience. The classic drama of authors presumed to represent an essential reality founded in the meaning established by the absent author/father. "The theater of cruelty is not a *representation*. It is life itself, in the extent to which life is unrepresentable. Life is the nonrepresentable origin of representation."[3]

> Speech and its notation—phonetic speech, an element of classical theater—speech and *its* writing will be erased on the stage of cruelty only in the extent to which they were alleged *dictation:* at once citations or recitations and orders. . . . This is . . . the end of the *dictation* which made theater into an exercise in reading.[4]

Artaud called for the end of the theater of didactic content. This was the theater for 'readers' which defeated everything that was specifically theatrical, i.e., the plasticity of the *mise en scène*. In the place of such a theater both Artaud and Jacques Derrida call for a use of both speech and writing as gestures which subordinate or eliminate the notion of speech as a vehicle of "rational transparency."[5] Artaud's challenge could be understood as calling for a theater which could capture life in its full passionate presence without the remainder implied by a representation which points beyond itself.

I will examine three phases of the reaction to Artaud's challenge which has become postmodern theater. The first phase is best represented by the early work of Samuel Beckett, which marks a transitional phase between a modern theater that challenged the themes of traditional theater but did not undertake a fundamental rethinking of theatrical inscription, and a postmodern theater that does undertake this rethinking of the whole idea of theater. The second phase is found in the work of the Becks' "Living Theater," Richard Schechner's "Performance Group," and the French groups from the late 60s and early 70s, *Theatre du Soleil, Le Folidrome,* and *Theatre de la Salamandre,* which sought to replace the dead theater of representation with Artaud's "impossible" communal festive theater, either in a sacred form (the Becks and Schechner) or a secular form (the French groups). The final phase is found in the work of Daniel Mesguich in France and Herbert Blau in the United States who, recognizing the impossibility of Artaud's "Impossible Theater," sought to respond to Artaud's challenge with a thorough interrogation of both the text (primarily Mesguich) and its mode of presentation (both Mesguich and Blau). This last phase suggests that Artaud may not have had the last word to say about the possibilities of theater for a postmodern era.

I   Waiting for meaning

The theater of Samuel Beckett in the early 50s (*Godot* and *Endgame*) marks a transition from modernist theater to postmodern theater. Beckett acknowledges that tradition which Artaud would banish from the stage, but rather than employ it as the grounding subtext or masterword which would provide a closure with meaning, he begins a process of interrogation which opens a new era in theater. Unlike some other so-called 'absurdist' dramatists, Beckett does not merely interrogate the commanding ideas of the tradition or challenge them with absurdist or nihilist positions; he interrogates the whole idea of theater as a site for the appearance of meaning.

Who else is Godot, if not the absent 'God' or 'Author' of the Masterword of traditional theater whom Artaud wished to banish from the stage? Didi and Gogo, like the audience before them in the dark, await the coming of Godot to provide a resolution to the absurd confusion of their present existence. Didi and Gogo are not unlike Artaud's enslaved actors stuck on a stage without a text, awaiting the master director/author who will tell them what to do. Beckett has repeatedly denied that he knew who Godot was, saying that if he had known, he would have said. Despite much critical commentary which insists upon it, Godot *is not* the absent god of traditional bourgeois drama; it might be more accurate to say that he is the name for an unspecified absence. In the lacuna of this absence language loses its central role in the service of the master plot; it no longer uncovers for us any metaphysical or ideological center which might serve our understanding. Beckett decenters the 'Word' in the quest for a center which never appears, except through the reiteration of the promise of its occurrence (the coming of Godot). In the place of 'plot' and developed action we have stasis—Vladimir's memory of meaning and hope for its reoccurrence and Estragon's persistent presence, lacking both memory and possibility. Pozzo appears like a classic antagonist right on cue when the progress seems to flag, but his appearance is deceptive. His theatrical bluster provides only an interlude, not a key to the play. Lucky's great speech is a *reductio ad absurdum* of the traditional dramatic set speech, the Masterword. The response of 'the thinker,' the philosopher, is incomprehensible babble. The audience is confronted with the defeat of all of its traditional expectations of meaning. The tableau vivant at the end of the play does not provide emphasis to a resolution but rather an indication of a possibly endlessly recycled quest without closure.

Endgame continues this process of deconstruction of the theater, focusing particularly upon the theatrical site itself and the problem of the production of meaning by actors, authors, and directors. Hamm is producer, director, lead actor, and perhaps author of the grotesque domestic drama which is being played out. This is a long-running drama in which everyone is exhausted by the endless repetition of the same lines and the same actions day after day. Artaud spoke of the actor in traditional drama as a 'slave' to the master author. "All words, once spoken, are dead and function only at the moment when they are uttered,"[6] says Artaud. The representative drama of master authors reflects this death precisely to the degree that its 'text' exists as a dictation to be endlessly repeated by the enslaved actor.

Hamm is this actor provided by the author with a 'juicy' role which he will milk dry as a demonstration of his central importance to the play. He calls upon tradition from the Old Testament to Sophocles to Shakespeare to ground his self-importance, but this tradition no longer provides any grounding answers to his questions. Clov is the enslaved actor nearing the point of rebellion when he will break from the stage and begin his 'life,' which surely, if it exists at all, exists on the far side of this theatrical site. To Hamm's query, "What's happening?" Clov replies, "Something is taking its course." "We're not beginning to mean something?" says Hamm; to which Clove derisively replies, "Mean something! You and I mean something! Ah that's a good one!" Yet Hamm suggests that to a foreigner (the audience, perhaps), unfamiliar with the emptiness of their routine, the repetitive pattern of their movements and speech might begin to suggest that there was some purposeful order in this farce.

Confronted with the failure of the tradition to provide an answer for the absurdity of his existence, Hamm assumes the double role of author. He will write the subtext which will argue his case. But like his three-legged dog which cannot stand and thus provides only the illusion of comfort to him, his story is left uncompleted. He would argue that cruelty is kindness (perhaps an aside to Artaud's notion of the need for a 'theater of cruelty'); that life (theater, perhaps) should come to an end; but he is left at the end to continue to play out the last dregs of the moribund tradition to which he has been wed; a tradition where "something is taking its course," but no final resolution of meaning seems possible.

Beckett displays the enervation of a tradition which no longer grounds either art or action. He does not provide us with the liberation of Artaud's sacred theater, however, because there is as yet no site for the epiphany of such a theater. In the meantime he demonstrates what the old theater and its culture have become. In both of these plays the site of the theater seems to be a prison in which actors are trapped within the confines of a proscenium space and the audience is walled off within the illusion of its speculative security beyond the footlights. Inside this prison the drama of the attrition of representation is played out.

For Beckett the whole issue of pretending to create a work of art which would communicate some seminal meaning became more and more problematic. He probably accomplished the ultimate in deconstructive minimalist theater with his play *Breath*, which has no characters or actors, no dialogue or setting (except an empty stage) and consists entirely of one long sigh delivered right after the curtain rises and just before it falls. Artaud called for an "impossible" theater of pure festival. What Beckett seems to suggest with this sigh is that even the simplest theatrical gesture is rooted in a fundamental impossibility of communication.

II   The impossible theater: "The Sacred"

Modern theater does not exist—it does not take (a) place— and consequently, its semiology is a mirage; . . . Since no set or interplay of sets is able to hold up any longer faced with the crises of State, religion and family, it is impossible to prefer a discourse—to play out a discourse—on the basis of a scene, sign of recognition which would provide for the actor's and the audience's recognition of themselves in the same Author. . . . This is a failure to constitute a communal discourse of play (interplay).[7]

This famous account of Julia Kristeva's of the failure of modern theater may well be a response to the attempts in the 60s and early 70s by various American and French theatrical groups to institute Artaud's communal festive theater.

In America the experiments of the Becks' "Living Theater" and Richard Schechner's "Performance Group" were directed at creating the 'sacred theater' which Artaud argued should replace the dead theater of representation.

> The true purpose of the theater is to create Myths, to express life in its immense, universal aspect, and from that life to extract images in which we find pleasure in discovering ourselves. . . . May it free *us*, in a Myth in which we have sacrificed our little human individuality, like Personages out of the Past, with powers rediscovered in the Past.[8]

The problem these groups confronted in trying to institute Artaud's mythic theater, as Kristeva recognized, was "to constitute a communal discourse of interplay." They agreed with Artaud that a sacred theater should be a theater without texts, but in their most famous productions, the Becks' *Paradise Now* and Schechner's *Dionysus in 69* they appealed to some of the most ancient texts in our tradition: the Becks employing the *I Ching* and Buber's *Ten Rungs: Hasidic Sayings,* and Schechner using a free adaptation of Euripides's *The Bacchae* and birth rites from ancient tribes.

While these texts reflected a time of ritual practice and communal mythic consciousness, the transference of them into a faithless time, even with alterations which addressed the political and spiritual malaise of the present, could not miraculously accomplish the desire to create a new mythic consciousness or a new ritual practice. Both groups supplemented their appeal to mythic texts by a concerted effort to involve the audience in the ritual practice they were attempting to institute. They abandoned the proscenium stage as the site of theatrical presentation, trying to break down the infamous 'fourth wall' of bourgeois theater which divided the audience from the production, allowing only passive speculation rather than active participation. They invited the audience to join them in the playing area, to become active *participants* in this new festal theater. They instructed the actors no longer to be enslaved to the bourgeois idea of submitting themselves to characters, but rather to 'play themselves.' The actors were to function as shamans, the liberated knowing ones, who would now lead the audience to its own liberation so that all could be joined in festive unity.

The spacing which divides actor and audience, however, is not simply a function of proximity or distance. If the audience exists as spectator and the actor as performer, then both stand in a relation of absence to what transpires as the performance. The actor is absent behind the presence of the persona which is *represented* only to the degree that the actor is absent as a presence. The audience is absent as witness to the representation, exiled as anonymous *consciousness of*, so that the representation can be *present* to this consciousness. A resolution of this problem requires that the actor cease being an actor and that the audience cease being a witness: it requires a collapsing of the space of theater.

This is precisely the problem confronting Artaud's call for a sacred theater of holy actors; it is precisely the problem which the Becks and Schechner could not overcome. Artaud called for a theater of holy actors "signaling through the flames," actors who, liberated from the text of the master author, would become holy presences through their gesturing bodies. Such a strategy assumes that the problem of the division in the self can be overcome by simply casting off the oppressions of the dominant culture which repress the erotic body. Both *Paradise Now* and *Dionysus in 69* called for nudity as the central sign of this liberation. Nudity alone, however, does not restore the body to some primal unity with itself. The first *sign* of Adam's awakening to consciousness and the loss of primal unity was his recognition that he was naked. The human body is a conscious body still caught within the dispersion which is that of consciousness. Nudity, too, is a sign and as such is trapped within the dispersal of signs which is language. The nude body knows itself as nude only in opposition to the clothed body; it cannot simply recover a non-dispersed being by shedding its clothing. In addition the body, too, is a complex of social habituations, as every actor learns with difficulty. The dense layerings of cultural dispersion which imprison the self are not overcome simply by shedding one's clothing. Rather than indicating a holy presence 'signaling through the flames,' nudity in the theater of the Becks and Schechner became one more sign caught within the network of signs.[9]

"Ritual and liturgy in theater are either mockery or profanation."[10] The attempt of the Becks and Schechner to institute a new ritual consciousness may have been both mockery *and* profanation. In order for ritual to have a place within theatrical practice it would have to be sustained by a community bound within a ritual understanding of life outside the theater. The ritual theater of the Greeks, the Japanese, and Artaud's beloved Balinese was supported by a shared ceremonial cultural consciousness which is profoundly lacking in this postmodern era of dispersed meanings. Unless the audience is already immersed in ritual, an invitation to join the "shaman-actor" on the stage does not immediately overcome the audience's passive alienation.[11] Some reviews of both *Paradise Now* and *Dionysus in 69* suggest a desperate attempt to sustain the ritualistic nature of the productions even at the cost of open hostility towards the audience whom they wished to invite into participation.[12]

The problem is that the audience, lacking a sustaining ritual consciousness which they might bring to the theater, can only *witness* the *play* of ritual and *play* at being initiates; lacking a sustaining ritual consciousness, the actors can only *play* at being shamans. Contrary to their intent, "The Living Theater" and "The Performance Group" did not institute a new sacred site for communal festive play. Rather they found themselves only able to *represent* such a possibility.

III The impossible theater: "The Secular"

While the experiments of the French groups were directly influenced by the work of the Becks' 'Living Theater' in Europe, their work aimed not so much at total spiritual liberation implied in the Becks' and Schechner's programs as it aimed to develop a

theater of secular, communal, political action which would replace the more speculative political theater of Brecht. The *Theatre
du Soleil, Le Folidrome*, and the *Theatre de la Salamandre* all grew
out of the revolutionary situation in France in 1968. "Art is dead.
Let us create our daily lives" was a popular wall slogan during
the early days of the student and worker rebellion in '68. The
attempts of these groups to 'go beyond Brecht,' who they felt
still isolated his audience as mere spectators, led them to conceive
of a theater without preordained texts. They tried to involve the
workers directly in the composition of their productions. In order
to communicate with a mass audience of workers, they usually
chose broad and unsubtle means of producing the *mise en scène*.
They used clowns, puppets, large masks, and tableau vivants to
communicate their message to the people. "We wanted to create
a theatre of re-presentation where each gesture, each word, each
intonation, had importance and became a sign immediately perceived by the spectator."[13] The directness of the sign, however,
prevented them from accomplishing their goals of liberation and
festive community.

> The power that is set over us is composed of a conjunction
> of authorities who think . . . write, speak, decide for us
> and over us. This monopolization of the word . . . fixes our
> destinies immutably along the barbs of logic. To create
> collectively is to end our status as objects, it is to become
> effective subjects of our lives and of history being made
> and to make. . . . We seize the word and the stage so as to
> no longer be inert or passive, so as to no longer be
> spectators of our reality.[14]

The word they "seized," however, the "direct sign," while it
enabled Nicolas Domenach and others to find a ready means of
connecting with the workers and farmers, did not enable the
liberation they sought. Domenach was correct in asserting the
power of the word over their lives. But seeking liberation through
the corrective of a theater of spectacle with its simple "good
workers" and "bad capitalists" suggests the acceptance of a prole-
tarian consciousness as the meeting ground where these liberated consciousnesses could come together in community. But
establishing and not merely *assuming* this meeting ground was
precisely the task which confronted this type of theater. They

broke with the site of the proscenium stage of bourgeois theater, but there was no liberated social site available to them within which they could create their community. The participants in their experiments still lived and worked within the culture dominated by the word, and the very simplicity of their theatrical signs prevented them from accomplishing a thorough deconstruction of the complex power of sociopolitical space within which they sought to center their new theatrical site.

Artaud had warned against any theater of content or message, recognizing that such theater was precisely that theater enslaved to the absent Author. One must assume that the absent Author/Father of this theater was Marx. Political theater is inherently a theater of texts commanded by language, because politics is governed by language. There was no way the task of liberation could take place without coming to grips with the play of language within the sociopolitical matrix of French society. Kristeva recognized the failure of this theater to provide a demonstration of its life-affirmation which could be severed from its "intra-linguistic production."

> Theater no longer exists outside of the text. This is not a failure of representation (as is often said), because nothing represents better than language—that privileged fabric of identification and fantasy. Rather it is a failure of de-monstration, of the theater as de-monstration. Severed from its intra-linguistic production, this demonstration can do nothing but chain itself to the normative ideologies to which the failure of contemporary social sets, and perhaps, even the failure of the human race, affixes itself.[15]

The simple contrivances of spectacle were no substitute for the more difficult task of examining the reifications, simulations, and dissimulations of social space which are the reality of post-modern man.

This secular theater of spectacle, like the sacred theater of ritual of the Becks and Schechner, assumed the existence of the site of communal interplay which it was struggling to establish. Just as miming the ancient rites of passage in lost mythic cultures could not turn audiences into holy initiates, so focusing their social alienation in agitprop situations of puppets and direct signs could not liberate the consciousness of the workers and give them possession of their own lives. This theater had the illusion of success, as when Armand Gatti's *Thirteen Suns of St. Blaise Street* led to the temporary occupation of the streets, but more ambitious projects such as Gatti's Brabant Wallon Experience, which was a year in development, involved more than three thousand people from the region in its production, lasted for twenty-eight hours and covered more than twenty-five miles of the surrounding countryside, were not successful. Gatti was not able to engage the young people of the area in the production, and he bemoaned the fact that, despite the willing participation of the older local residents, this participation did not accomplish its goal of raising their political understanding. The *Theatre du Soleil* encountered the difficulty of even attracting that very worker audience to which they wished to appeal. Their production of *1789* ended in self-mockery as they performed a reenactment of the revolution of 1789 "for the amusement of a group of gaudy *nouveaux riches*" within the production, while at the same time the production "was performed for the amusement of an audience with a large bourgeois contingent."[16] Kristeva was correct in analyzing the dilemma of such a theater which found itself unable to "take (a) place."

IV   Rethinking the thought of theater

Fortunately, theater had not exhausted its resources in the face of this dilemma. Two recent practitioners of theater, Daniel Mesguich in France and Herbert Blau in the United States, attempted to come to grips with problems of representation, the text, and enactment without any strategy of avoidance.

> When the actor of a text enters the scene we have the monstrous division of a text by a body as well as that of a body by a text. This division doesn't quite fit. There is a remainder, infinite, in movement. All the operations which might have produced it, all the texts and all the bodies, invent themselves from this remainder. To posit this division is to construct a Theater.[17]

Mesguich explicitly acknowledges the power of the Master-word of the absent author in his staging of a play such as *Hamlet*.

For him, however, the text is not simply the "dead word" of the absent author, Shakespeare, composed in the seventeenth century and now condemned only to an endless, slavish repetition in the theater of representation. For him the *mise en scène* is an *écriture*. In staging *Hamlet,* the play is not only the fixed text of the absent author, but also the long history of its innumerable productions and all of the previous and still proliferating commentary that has been devoted to plumbing its depths and showing its relevance to the innumerable occasions of its production. It has interacted with Freud, Lacan, and the entire cultural history of the West which has transpired since its original inscription. Mesguich attempts to open up the text to the indefinite layering of its inscriptions in our culture, including his own production ("we have the monstrous division of a text by a body as well as that of a body by a text").

Artaud argued that the actor is enslaved to the dead word of the absent author; what Mesguich would argue is that the actor must acknowledge the tradition of that inscription and the inscriptions upon that inscription in playing the difference which is "the division of a text by a body"; this is the explicit recognition of the division "of a body by a text." You can kill the play "by 'playing' that 'written' writing and the 'spoken' writing are fused. . . . Then the actor, through spoken writing, possessed by the Writings, no longer plays; he is played. The actor is no longer an actor."[18]

> When the actor enters the scene he does not come upon planks but—even for a Theater without a text—upon the difficult difference between speech and writing. And this difference—the very subject of the Theater—is called play. Upon this play, a body: the actor. When the actor of a text enters the scene, it is perhaps—and everything is in play— into the locus of a double-play: that of the difference between "written" writing (from the fact that it has been: the past of printing) and the "spoken" writing (from the fact that it is in the process of being so: the present of presentation): that of the difference between direct and deferred (but directly), and into the very locus of the difference between writing and speech. A blank of sorts.

> Further in this double-play, the actor. The actor of the text. The one who must play out the text, produce its play.[19]

Such an activity does not "liberate" the actor in the sense which Artaud envisioned. Mesguich is not asserting the superiority of *la parole* against *la langue* in opposition to Derrida; the actor, as speaker, is not in command of some indubitable *presence*, but neither is the actor simply enslaved to the dead word of the absent author. Rather the actor and the creation of the *mise en scène* are now the central locus of the play of differences which is the multilayered inscription of the text in our time.

For *Hamlet* Mesguich used a double theater: a main stage and a small curtained stage within the main stage. He doubled the main characters: two Hamlets, two Ophelias, etc., partially to prevent an identification of the character with the particular psychology of only one actor, but also to take advantage of the internal mirroring of problems in the play. The small curtained theater within the larger theater is the theater where the ghost (the paternal father) reigns. Much of the play is played as a struggle between these two theaters. The text includes passages from Gide, Jean-Luc Godard, Mallarmé, and Stoppard. When the theatrical company within the play enters, they discuss contemporary theater, including Mesguich's *mise en scène* for the play which is occurring. When Hamlet enters reading "the book of himself," the book he is reading is *Hamlet;* the 'play within the play' by which Hamlet would "catch the conscience of the king" is, of course, *Hamlet.*

This production awakens a sense of the endless intertextual play of classic texts within our cultural history in such a way that Artaud's cry of "no more masterpieces" is stilled. What he explicitly acknowledges is that no text can be a master text within the historical matrix of its inscription and reinscription within the culture. "To interrogate the paternal function and what eternalizes it, to interrogate the meanings of a text and their history, to interrogate meanings, to interrogate the body with the text, and the text with the body, to interrogate interrogation: there can be no more profoundly political gesture today."[20] Mesguich sees theater, with its play between the text and production, between history and presentation, as the essential interrogative act of the artist today. Rather than being enslaved by the dead word of master authors, the theater is the very space where the critical play of cultural interrogation takes place. It is where the play of representations and simulations which is postmodern culture can be called into question. Both producer and actor must recognize the complex of inscriptions which is the text within our culture and which is our culture itself insofar as it embodies that text as part of its inscription. The challenge is to open the space where this intertextual play can occur. Mesguich's theater avoids the problem to which Kristeva points, because his theater does not assume the need for a site of communal understanding. His theater explicitly acknowledges the play of differences which is the site of both the theatrical and the cultural experience. This theater is, then, appropriately sited within our postmodern culture.

Where Mesguich approaches the problem of representation in terms of the dispersal of meaning through an intertextual, undecidable cultural history, Blau's KRAKEN group concentrates on the challenge of appearance itself as it is encountered by the actor. What concerns him is not so much the illusory character of representation as a closure with meaning, but the more fundamental struggle for meaning to appear at all. "If we could do it [theater] as we desire it, it would be as highly charged in the body as *the first thought* that separated itself from life or mere being or whatever—was there—before in order to become *the difference-from-life which appears to us as theater.*"[21] KRAKEN explored these problems in studies based upon classic texts: *Elsinore* from *Hamlet, Seeds of Atreus* from *The Oresteia,* and *Crooked Eclipses* from Shakespeare's *Sonnets.*

Artaud challenged representation as illusory and unfounded, as pointing beyond itself to the indication of a foundation which does not in fact exist. The theater of representation is thus an illusion separated from its source. Against this kind of theater Artaud dreamed of a theater of fullness and immediacy, a theater which, in the words of Derrida, "is finite and leaves behind it, behind its actual presence, no trace, no object to carry off. It is neither a book nor a work, but an energy, and in this sense it is the only art of life."[22] Blau rejects the notion that theater, insofar as it is embodied in the actor, or even if we were able successfully to imagine it embodied in the social person, can avoid the problem of the illusiveness of the *presentation* of the self. For him theater is condemned to language because language is the essential medium for the presentation of the self and thus of theater.

> If the theater models the world and the world is a shadow of theater, it is language which models them both. The self, we hear, is a construct of language, not an entity but an *appearance*. In our work, we turn the subject over and over. It is the mirroring of language, world and theater in the refractions of the performing self, a subject slipping away . . . the insufficiency of the autonomous subject, the vanishing enterprise of the self as a contingency of language.[23]

Artaud, the Becks, and Schechner seemed to assume that while the actor trapped within the *role* determined by the master author was a slave who could only mime the illusion of representative being, the liberated actor could *be* himself, could *be* a shaman leading the audience into authentic communion with the sacred. Blau, like Mesguich, understands the self of the actor to be no more nor less dispersed than the social self. The 'advantage' or perhaps 'curse' of the actor as against the social self is that the actor is forced to confront the problem of the apparency of the self.

> In the language of deconstruction truth is *undecidable*, for there is nothing to refer it to, only more language. The attachment is to the structure of thought. The same might be said of naturalness in acting. It has no decisive referent either. Not "life," not "experience," certainly not "Nature"—and after Hamlet and Pirandello, neither the Author nor an authoritative "text"; and only the merest fiction of "character." What we take to be natural, then, is a matter of *mediations*. . . . What we see in reality is (what actors are normally taught to avoid) an "unsupported" emotion—embodied sign of the insupportable in experience—whose path moves not through the (false) continuity of a "role" but from actor to actor (there are no roles, only actors) in *a constellation of prospective meanings* . . . . In the disjunct light, behavior is ruptured, reflexively

looped, *abstracted* (in a double sense); not-there, or too much so; stealing from the figure or no sooner seen, still, stolen away.[24]

Thus Blau would construct the postmodern theater from the very materials which led Artaud, Derrida, the Becks, Schechner, and so many others to call for a theater of sacred immediacy. Recognizing the failure of this possibility, Blau refuses to accept the notion that the only options are a return to an unreflective theater of representation or the death of theater. To him, theater, at its best, has always been aware of the problem of theater, its unfounded apparency. He finds evidence for this awareness in the tradition of theater from the watchman of Aeschylus's *Agamemnon*, through Hamlet's apprehension of the ghost to Hamm's anguish to be "right in the center" in *Endgame*. In all these cases there is an acknowledgment that what gets *seen*, what is enacted, is only an unsupportable appearance sustained by the *play* of the actors focussing our attention upon their own unsupportable being. The task of postmodern theater is to investigate this apparency, to recognize that "theater does not take (a) place," i.e., that it cannot establish its center by retreating from the problem into the impossibility of sacred or secular communal festival, but can only continue to pursue the illusive foundation of an unfounded appearance. Rather than stand in opposition to life, theater is the most accurate mirror of life; the unfounded apparency of the actor caught within the dispersions of the text and the playing space mirrors the unfounded apparency of the social self caught within the dispersions of culture and social space.

One of the primary issues of any acting technique [is] *Centering*. What is the center? for the actor? for the entire performance? again, approached as a limit, a matter of perception, not a given. The point is—*where–?* The core of technique, elsewhere in Kafka: "Two tasks on the threshold of life: To narrow your circle more and more, and constantly to make certain that you have not hidden yourself outside of it." He says nothing about locating a center, only the narrowing down to it, like Stanislavski's circle of attention. The entire pressure of performance is, however, toward the center, the truth hid there, exempt from seeming—the impossibility of it.[25]

V

Artaud recognized the decadence of a theater which had forgotten the unfounded nature of its appearance and smugly sought to dictate to both actors and audience the illusory representation of a fully constituted tyrannical meaning, the tyranny of a supposed *reality*. Both the sacred and the secular experimental groups we have discussed sought to resolve the problem by abjuring the 'mere' *apparency* of theater for the presumed *reality* of either a sacred or secular community which they could not succeed in founding. Beckett recognized the problem to which Artaud pointed, but also seemed to recognize the impossibility of resolution. So he created a theater out of the anguish of that impossibility, introducing the first stage of that crisis of consciousness of meaning and the means to meaning which has become postmodern theater. Mesguich and Blau have sought to pursue the problem, recognizing that the occurrence of theater within any time always involves "the division of a body by a text and the division of a text by a body," which creates that *play* of difference which is the space of the play of theater. Theater, thus understood, mirrors postmodern culture caught within the freeplay of its unfounded apparency.

> The strategies of theater over the next fifteen years will be conceived after the spacious model of *language*. Whatever the linchpin with the body, the body cannot think of the future, as only language does—which has the amplitude we long for, and the indeterminacy, in its precisions . . . there is still the theoretical suspicion that there would be no theatre without it, no future, and no theory. The etymological linchpin between theatre and theory is in the place and act of watching; that is *speculation*, even before the words were sounded, as with the basilisk in the garden reading the situation, that smooth talker, *hypocrite lecteur*— the first actor.[26]

Writers, directors, and actors must confront this task of rethinking the theater without the nostalgia for lost presence which

Derrida warned us against and which, in light of the reflections of Artaud, Mesguich, and Blau, may never have existed in theater at its best, even as an illusion of presence. Theater is the site where that difficult acknowledgement of the division of a body by the text and the division of a text by the body must open a space for its occurrence. In this it mirrors that site where the body of the social self is divided by the intertextual play of the culture and the intertextual play of the culture is divided by the body of the social self. If, as Blau argues, theater at its best has always been suspicious of its own apparency, it may not be 'dead'; rather it may be the ideal site for the postmodern era to rethink the density of its inscriptions and the ambiguity of its margins amidst the clamor of our time.

Chapter 9

LUCID INTERVALS: POSTMODERNISM AND PHOTOGRAPHY

Allen S. Weiss

> I will open a studio where you go to have your picture
> "taken." You bring with you any photograph you like.
> After a small deposit, the photographer takes the photo-
> graph from you, at which time the balance falls due.
> —Hollis Frampton

Michel Tournier's brilliant short story, "Veronica's Shrouds,"
is a reworking of Poe's "The Oval Portrait" in relation to the
photographic signifier.[1] This is the tale of the photographer Veronica and her model Hector. Struck by his beauty, she takes
him in charge so as to make him *photogenic,* thus surpassing the
mere physical beauty of the real object. Her cares to this end
result in the decline of his physical beauty and health. Yet Veronica is not satisfied with the results. Influenced by the deliberate
capture of eternity in the photographs of Edward Weston, she
notes that aesthetic advances in life studies were mainly due to
the discovery of the corpse as an anatomical model. She thus
wishes to photograph corpses in a morgue, desiring to produce
a true still life, a *nature morte,* images literally *taken from life.*
Morbidly, but coherently, she insists on the move from dissection
to vivisection as the guarantee of authenticity! From these observations she creates a new mode of photography: the *direct photo.*
Wishing to surpass the technical constraints of her art, she produces "photographs" without camera, film, or enlarger, by
exposing large sheets of photographic paper to the light, then
having her model, dipped in developing fluid, lie on the paper,

which when fixed creates life-size silhouettes—much like those left on the pavements at Hiroshima, projections of the bodies of people vaporized by the blast of the atomic bomb. Needless to say, this artistic progress severely accelerates the physical decline of Hector, whose body is covered with the worst erythema, lesions due to the chemical action of the developing fluid. The final step is not far away. Veronica finally surpasses photography itself by creating *Dermography:* linen made light-sensitive by impregnation with silver bromide is wrapped around her model's chemically soaked body; when fixed and unfolded this creates a sort of funeral frieze, similar to the famed Shroud of Turin— "Veronica's Shrouds." Her ultimate work coincides with her model's death: in her art she achieves her wish to change the object itself.

The death of the subject transforms the subject into object, and permits its assumption as sign. If, as Roland Barthes claims, photography is "the dead theater of Death, the foreclosure of the Tragic; it excludes all purification, all *catharsis*,"[2] the photograph is nevertheless but a sign of death; Veronica's shrouds, to the contrary, transform the simulacrum into the real. Death is not signified, but caused, by the artistic object. Veronica's shrouds become a bizarre instrument of Walter Benjamin's desire to politicize art, of Barthes's desire to change the object itself.

The metaphysical poignancy of this tale is well expressed by a remark about the photographic signifier made by Philippe Dubois: what is at stake is "the impossibility of having the real coincide with its representation."[3] In fact, every depth hermeneutic is bound to this pathos. This explains the extreme fascination with one's own portrait: as Barthes understands so well, the portrait is a sign of the inevitable death of the subject, thus the portrait is in fact a sort of *nature morte* which might well pass into eternity, while the sitter never will. Hence photography's depressing vampirism, and the hidden pathos of the family snapshot.

Such pathos is not an attribute of postmodernist art. Indeed, it is a sign of the continuation of the romantic—and even the classical—tradition within modernism itself. Thus the pathos of tragic modernist irony—which overdetermines the codes of postmodernism—is transfigured into parody in the postmodernist work. In a sense, postmodernism entails the ironization of irony, achieved by making explicit the rhetorical and iconic forms of modernist art. In postmodernism's ideal limit, tragedy and parody are conflated in a new form of criticism. But it would seem, ultimately, that even such criticism itself will be assimilated in a more general textuality and iconography where it will disappear into a "universal" magma of signs, lost in the flux of history.

In this context, the apparent tautologies, stating that the representation is not the real and the signifier is not the signified, take on critical importance. Postmodernist epistemology, especially in Jean Baudrillard's model which we will consider, entails precisely the conflation of representation and reality, resulting in the inherent loss of (political) pathos and the failure of the modernist utopian project. Perhaps utopia needs tragedy as its mainspring, and perhaps postmodernist irony, cynicism, and apathy indeed find a major precursor in Marcel Duchamp's "aesthetic indifference" and "ironic causality." But in any case, we must be prepared to include the postmodernist work itself in a *mise-en-abîme* of aesthetic signifiers, and avoid considering postmodernism as the telos of modernist art.

The photographic pathos or tragedy is determined by the hermeneutic incommensurability of signifier and signified, surface and depth, image and referent. Modernism searches for this coherence in the depths of hidden phantasms; postmodernism manifests this coherence on the very surface of the artwork, produced as the referential purity (emptiness) of the simulacrum. Veronica's shrouds thus present the tragic irony of modernism from which postmodernism arises: the creation of the artwork always entails the "death of the subject." If would be too much to hope that the death of the spectator is not close at hand. For photography, that popular art, is the universalization of *vanitas*, where only the sophistry of criticism will discover Utopia.

The theorization of the visual image within the postmodernist debate finds its ontological/epistemological foundation in the theory of simulacra, notably in the version presented by Baudrillard. We will contrast Baudrillard's version to the quite different theory of simulacra proposed by Pierre Klossowski, with the intent of distinguishing between surface and depth hermeneutics, so as to examine the aesthetic variations and incommensurabilities of these two positions, and discuss their implications for a theory of postmodernist photography.

Klossowski, citing Hermes Trismegistus, explains the ancient origins of the notion of the simulacrum by revealing its inherent aesthetic of fascination and visual pleasure, and the concommitant "bodily solicitation of the viewer by the picture."[4] This solicitation is effected because the idol is the *simulacrum* of a god, an object in which the soul of a god or angel is enclosed, giving these idols and images the power of good and evil. Klossowski deems himself a creator of such simulacra, explaining that in fact the demons invoked by his artworks are merely "hypostases of active obsessional forces."[5] In uneasy conformity with modern depth psychology, the ancient gods are homologous with modern obsessions—as when Artaud insists that "God is the monomaniac of the unconscious." On the psychological level, Klossowski explains that, "The simulacrum in its *imitative* sense is the actualization of something in itself incommunicable and unrepresentable: properly speaking, it is the phantasm in its obsessional constraint."[6] These obsessions, operating differently but simultaneously in the artist and the viewer (two differently coded systems, of production and reception respectively), are the origins of simulacra. The simulacrum as representation transforms the inner phantasms into conventional and institutional stereotypes. Following Nietzsche's definition of truth, Klossowski defines simulacra and stereotypes: "In effect, at the level of linguistic expression as well as plastic figuration, stereotypes are only the residues of phantasmatic simulacra fallen into current usage, abandoned to common interpretation."[7]

This is a fortiori true of the photographic image: we might remember that in French the word *cliché* means both photograph and stereotype. Klossowski, following received opinion, understands photography to be a causal factor in the rise of modernist art; the appropriation of the figurative process by photography motivated the abandonment of the subject in painting—"The painting ceases to be a simulacrum in order to become an [object] in-itself."[8] Echoing Benjamin's observations in the "The Work of Art in the Age of Mechanical Reproduction" (which, not coincidentally, was translated into French by Klossowski), Klossowski writes that, "After photography, the cinema will, all the more so, 'liberate painting from the need to imitate nature.'"[9] This would seem to obviate the cathartic effect of the simulacrum. Aesthetic catharsis, for Klossowski, consists in ridding the artist of the phantasm's obsessional constraint, only to instill it anew in the viewer. Thus the simulacrum is understood according to a depth hermeneutics of representation (phantasm/simulacra) which operates as a structure of exchange (artist/viewer). Catharsis, for Klossowski, operates on a psychological/theological model; despite his antimodernist fears of the loss of the subject in art, despite his figurative artistic production, and despite his other protestations to the contrary, his theoretical stance remains one of high modernism, even while his pictorial production attempts an anachronistic classicism. Klossowski's work, in all its manifestations, escapes the "postmodernist" temptation.

For Benjamin, the photographic image (or simulacrum) entails the dissolution of artistic "aura," and inaugurates the possibility of the political use of the image. As such, catharsis can no longer be understood according to a personalist psychological model, and must now be grasped in a political, revolutionary model. Discussing the relations between mechanical reproduction and mass movements, he explains that: "Their most powerful agent is the film. Its social significance, particularly in its most positive form, is inconceivable without its destructive, cathartic aspect, that is, the liquidation of the traditional value of the cultural heritage."[10] By releasing art from ritual and endowing it with a political usage, aesthetics now enters the realm of political ideal utopianism, veiled by Benjamin as dialectical materialism. Yet that one final, social catharsis is necessary for this effect; if this is to be a mass catharsis, it is no surprise that it will be effected through the most commonplace stereotypes, in the most appropriate medium for that end—the cinema. (Where Klossowski sees the end of cathartic possibilities, Benjamin sees the final transformation of catharsis in an apocalyptic political upheaval.) This new reign of photographic and cinematic simulacra entails a radical epistemological break: "Thus is manifested in the field of perception what in the theoretical sphere is noticeable in the increasing importance of statistics."[11]

This position is in marked contrast with Baudrillard's notion of simulacra, where catharsis no longer exists, and where the "euphoria of simulation" is free from the "anguish of the referential."[12] For Baudrillard, the generation of simulacra is no longer a function of referentiality or phantasmagoria: "It is the generation by models of a real without origin or reality: the hyperreal."[13] The simulacrum is thus opposed to representation; it is the radical negation of the sign as exchange value. Its ontological status is defined according to diverse (and, according to Baudrillard, historically successive) phases of the *image,* defined as that which,

(1) reflects a profound reality;
(2) masks and denatures a profound reality;
(3) masks the *absence* of any profound reality;
(4) is without relation to any reality whatsoever: it is its own pure simulacrum.[14]

What is of concern here, as the crucial ontological question of the simulacrum, is precisely where we are to establish the epistemological cut. To make it between phase (2) and phase (3) would be to remain within metaphysics; to make it between phase (3) and phase (4) would be to take the deconstructive position whereby metaphysics is not overcome, but is rather presented as a particular discursive possibility which happens to be at the foundations of our culture, according to which all else must be read, but which is nevertheless a fiction, a model of reality. As such, the simulacral entails the loss of reference in the media of a mass culture, and the absorption of the social into the statistical. Representation (on both the aesthetic and the political model) is no longer possible. Fascination is a function of neutralizing meaning in favor of the idol, and truth in favor of simulacra.[15] (Representational theory entails the generation of models by reality; simulacral theory entails the generation of reality by models.) Both rationality and meaningful dialectic (as well as any "master narrative") are rejected.

> They are given meaning: they want spectacle. No effort has been able to convert them to the seriousness of the content, nor even to the seriousness of the code. Messages are given to them, they only want some sign, they idolise the play of signs and stereotypes, they idolise any content so long as it resolves itself into a spectacular sequence.[16]

In an earlier work, Baudrillard describes the central structural features of hyperreal simulation (i.e. phase (4) of the image):[17]

(1) the deconstruction of the real in its details; the paradigmatic

declension of the object; the flattening, linearity, and seriality of partial objects;

(2) the doubling and multiplication of objects in a *vision-en-abîme*, which is ultimately another type of seriality, where the real is no longer reflected, but rather exhausted in its own involution;

(3) the abolition of both the syntagmatic and paradigmatic dimensions in a properly serial form, fully without reflexion; the infinite generation of forms by models; the infinite diffraction of the object within itself;

(4) the generative form is not of pure repetition, but rather of minimal differences which differentiate the various terms; hence this is a mode of digitality, not representation.

It is striking how these characteristics describe—in a markedly avant-garde mode—the photographic and especially the cinematic signifiers, those foundations of our age of mechanical reproduction. We cannot help seeing the "euphoria of simulation" as homologous with the visual pleasure generated by the cinematic apparatus.[18] Yet we must contrast the realist and the hyperrealist—the representational and the digital—models of cinema. André Bazin's *realist* ontology of the cinema—advocating the telos of cinema as the ultimate *Gesamtkunstwerk*, the ultimate representation of reality—saw film as the ontological closure of art, where the cinematic machine is dissimulated by the very illusion its produces, in order to heighten the impression of reality.[19] To the contrary, Baudrillard's *hyperrealist* ontology of simulacra—relying on a cybernetic model in which artwork and machine are interchangeable signs—is nothing less than a cinematic delusion of the real as an endless projection of copies, an "aesthetic hallucination of reality." We are accustomed to the commonplace notion that modernism was the result of the encroachment of photographic reproduction on the artistic field; we may now note another commonplace—also proclaimed by Benjamin and thematized by Baudrillard, among others—that cinema's encroachment on the artistic field, and especially the invasion of "high" art by "popular" art, is the foundational event of postmodernism.

Writing of the differences between modernism and postmodernism, Craig Owens explains: "Postmodernism neither brackets nor suspends the referent but works instead to problematize the activity of reference. When the postmodernist work speaks

of itself, it is no longer to proclaim its autonomy, its self-suffi-
ciency, its transcendence; rather, it is to narrate its own contingency, insufficiency, lack of transcendence."[20] According to this
definition of modernism in terms of autonomy and transcendence, we might consider Michael Snow's film *La régione centrale*
(1970–71) as a high point of modernist art. The scenario is of
minimal simplicity—approximately three hours of views of a
purely natural mountain scene, describing a day and night, with
the camera rotating on a special machine which permitted it any
possible camera angle, rotation movement, rotation speed and
focal length, making it a sort of truly panoptical cinematic device.
The sophistication of the cinematic machine belies the utter simplicity of the iconography, which varies from figurative to abstract according to the speed of camera movement and degree of
natural lighting. The result of this vacillation between figuration
and abstraction, caused by an excessive, unhuman (mechanical)
motion, is that of extreme vertigo, the metaphysical implications
of which are described by Annette Michelson: "Snow's infinitely
mobile framing, his mimesis of and gloss upon spatial exploration offer, most importantly, a fusion of primary scopophilic and
epistemophilic impulses in the cinematic rendering of the grand
metaphor of the transcendental subject."[21] It is precisely as a
hyperbolic instantiation emblematic of the transcendental ego
that this film is a prime example of modernist art, where the
transcendental ego—a metaphoric transformation of the cinematic apparatus—becomes the implied "*auteur*" of the filmic narrative. Yet *this* allegorical situation is hardly the case for the
postmodernist condition.

Stressing the explicit contingency and lack of transcendence
characteristic of postmodernist art, Owens ends the aforemen-
tioned article with a quotation from Barthes's seminal essay,
"Change the Object Itself." This title is clearly a paraphrase of
the eleventh of Marx's *Theses on Feuerbach*: "The philosophers
have only *interpreted* the world in various ways; the point, however, is to *change* it." Hence Barthes's observation that, "It is no
longer the myths which need to be unmasked . . . it is the sign
itself which must be shaken," in order to "fissure the very representation of meaning," to "challenge the symbolic itself."[22] In
fact, in regard to the problematic of the aesthetics of mechanical
reproduction and catharsis, the autonomy of a pure, transcen-

dental ego would have no need of catharsis; only the empirical, psychological ego, tainted by the impurities of contingent existence, needs catharsis to cleanse it of the anxieties wrought by history and the Other. The ideal(ist) spectator of modernist art is utopian; the ego of the postmodernist spectator is purely empirical: the previously utopian ideal is transformed into a dystopian parody. The wish to *change the object itself* evokes Benjamin's notion of the politicization of art; yet in Baudrillard's version of postmodernism, Benjamin's slight optimism is overcome by pessimism, or perhaps more correctly speaking by apathy, in which the very reality of the object itself is no longer of any concern, since all changes are on the level of the model which generates objects and reality. For Baudrillard, simulation is no longer a function of semiology. Yet if we are to investigate the transition from modernism to postmodernism, we must note how the semiological aspect of the object has been reworked and overcome; if the object as sign is to be changed, then semiology— the science of signs—must be evoked as the critical tool of such a task, as an objective leading to the postmodernist project of deconstructing semiology itself.

For Baudrillard, the ontological disparity between reality and representation, between signified and signifier, no longer obtains within the simulacrum. Simulacra are not, strictly speaking, signs. Thus we must investigate the ontological limits of signification, of signs, and determine precisely how simulacra can originate in a social field previously theorized as a nexus of signs and sign systems. The central question is whether the object of postmodern thought is a simulacrum whose operation is beyond signification—a sort of pure *pragma* without a determined task or goal; or whether it is an uncoded term within a vaster significative scene, a type of floating signifier generalized, universalized, made the norm instead of the exception. If the former is the case, then semiology itself becomes obsolete, just one more avatar of depth hermeneutics. If the latter case obtains, then the simulacrum may be understood as a new mutation in the significative field, a manifestation of an arational mode of production and communication. But perhaps both possibilities are simply theoretical constructs, and the simulacrum is merely the other side of the sign, apparent there where communication fails and where the social system cannot escape the stereotypes of its own ideology. Perhaps the simulacrum is the ironic reversal of the sign, just as postmodernism effects the appropriation and ironic—often carnivalesque—reversal of modernism.

Contemporary theory of the photographic sign (even within the context of postmodernism) relies heavily on C. S. Peirce's tripartate categorization of signs as *icon, symbol,* and *index.*[23] In relation to the aesthetic (photographic) modification of reality, these modes of signification correspond respectively to the *mirror* of the real, the *transformation* of the real, and the *trace* of the real. The photograph partakes of all three modalities of signification, and though it is usually praised for its extreme iconic (mimetic) possibilities, the iconic aspect is not essential to the photographic sign. Rather, its indexical nature (due to the chemical action of light on the film) is its essential characteristic. Peirce already noted the essentially indexical nature of the photograph in 1895; and it is this feature which grounds current theoretical research on the photographic sign—most notably the work of Rosalind Krauss and Philippe Dubois—in which a theoretical shift has occurred, from a theory of *mimesis* to a theory of *traces.*

Yet this pertains strictly to the *ontological* status of the photographic sign. Conversely, the *sociological* status of the photograph is that of a highly coded, indeed overcoded, entity. The photograph is caught in the intersection of two sets of codes: those of artistic composition and production *and* those of spectatorial aesthetic consumption, ruled by the systems of distribution and presentation. Only at the very instant of exposure can the photograph be deemed simply a pure trace; as a completed, presented work it is highly coded, and its meaning overdetermined by the multiple significative and social systems into which it is inserted or implicated. Hence Barthes's famous claim that the photograph is a "message without a code" is in fact inaccurate:[24] this condition obtains only at the split-second of exposure of the bare film, before the photograph exists as a visual entity. It is true of the latent image, never of the finished work. We must agree with Dubois that, as index, "the photographic image has no semantics other than its own pragmatics."[25] (This would almost seem to indicate that structurally the photograph is *a priori* a postmodernist aesthetic entity!). The photograph's pragmatics preceed its semantics, which is precisely the cause of what Barthes speaks of as its "Urdoxical" quality,[26] its peculiar mode of fascination, which in fact seems to reveal a new sort of aesthetic "aura." This quality is precisely the key to the "photographic impulse" (*pulsion photographique*[27]) which distinguishes photography from the other arts, be they mimetic, symbolic, or indexical. Yet as the photographic work is taken up into coded social systems, all three significative functions come into play in the constitution of its meaning. Thus to study this "change" in the photographic sign—to reveal its simulacral position within postmodern enunciation—we might consider several postmodernist works of photographic art which reveal the shifting emphases of iconic, symbolic, and indexical signification. This will disclose the very insufficiencies and ambiguities of the photographic signifier.

Perhaps the most radical work on the *indexical* function of the photographic sign is that of Sherrie Levine. Levine's most famous and controversial work consists in rephotographing the images of certain "modern masters" of photography. One example of this is the rephotography, off a Witkin Gallery poster, of an Edward Weston photographic portrait of his son's nude torso. Discussing the possible infringement on copyright laws, Douglas Crimp explains the rights at stake here:

> I think, to be fair, however, we might just as well give
> them to Praxiteles, for if it is the *image* that can be owned,
> then surely these belong to classical sculpture, which
> would put them in the public domain. Levine has said that,
> when she showed her photographs to a friend, he
> remarked that they only made him want to see the
> originals. "Of course," she replied, "and the originals make
> you want to see that little boy, but when you see the boy,
> the art is gone." For the desire that is initiated by that
> representation does not come to closure around that little
> boy, is not at all satisfied by him. The desire of
> representation exists only insofar as it never be fulfilled,
> insofar as the original always be deferred. It is only in the
> absence of the original that representation may take place.[28]

This work's counterfeit aspect is a function of its iconic perfection, while its representational aspect is a function of its indexical complexity. Its singular value lies precisely in the difference between counterfeit and representation. The photograph—a meta-image, since it is printed from a negative image—is a fortiori simulacral. Levine's photograph is thus at least a third-order simulacrum (Levine—Witkin poster—Weston—Weston's son), with the potential interposition of an indefinite number of stylistically generative models. (We must differentiate between model and simulacrum). The referent of this photograph is lost in the world history of images and forms, while the photograph itself remains a thing among things. What is lost within this intertextual series of references is the authorial reference: while the authorship of the photograph-as-physical-object is never in question (it is Levine's, with whatever consequences of copyright infringement it may entail), the authorship of the photograph-as-semiological-object is always ambiguous, and never resolvable. This work thus exemplifies the post-structuralist critique of transcendental ego-centric subjectivity by making explicit the manner in which authorship is a social fiction, dependent upon the interplay of rhetorical/narrative structure and significative reference. While the classical (and modernist) artwork entails the construction of an ideal spectator and authorial presence, Levine's work, in a postmodern mode, entails the loss of the author and a confused spectatorial position. It is perhaps the epitome of the "anxious" art object, since the very ontological status of its image remains in question.

Among the important critical works on the *iconic* aspect of the photographic sign is Cindy Sherman's series of untitled studies for film stills. In these photographs, invariably "self-portraits," Sherman presents herself made up as an always different "heroine" of '50s and '60s Hollywood B-grade movies. While there exists a perfect congruence between author and image, there is an endless shift of persona presented by these portraits. Hence these are the hyperbolic instances of images as simulacra, where the person becomes nothing but a projected image of a stereotyped personality. Yet this conundrum on the structure of simulacral iconography is offered with an ironic twist; if the self is a fiction structured by the desire of the Other, and if the cinematic (Hollywood) image of woman is structured by male desire, then Sherman's images are the parody, or deconstruction, of such desire. Her images are the female representation of the object of male desire, in a totally narcissistic framework. Sherman opposes her own epistemophilia to male scopophilia, in a significative system where the closure of reference (self-portraiture) is belied

FIGURE 2 Cindy Sherman (untitled film still)

by the openness of the simulacral system (stereotypicality). The arbitrariness of the icon is revealed in a duplicitous presentation of true-author-as-false-idol. The images of women (of *a woman*) serve as a series of tropes, where authorship is made explicit while the subject is revealed as fictional. Mimesis creates icons, always false, but hardly less desirable for that deception. And, though these be stills from films never in fact produced, they nevertheless refer to an entire genre of films and an entire mode of desire still very much in vogue.

The *symbolic* aspect of the photographic sign is investigated in Barbara Kruger's works, for example her untitled 1984 photograph of a book open to a page on Impressionism, on which there rests a pair of eyeglasses distorting part of the text while framing the words "my eye," and on which page are also collaged the words, "You are giving us the evil eye." The presence of linguistic text *as* photographic icon already achieves a disconcerting—anti-apotropaic—inmixing of different modes of signification, where it is impossible to determine whether image or text is the signifier or the signified, or even if they act together as one

FIGURE 3 Barbara Kruger, untitled (1984)

whole sign. And the confusion of text as meta-text *and* as icon establishes an equivocation between epistemophilia and scopophilia in the symbolic register. This situation is complicated by the use of the linguistic shifters "my," "you," and "us," which results in an ambiguous relation between image, author, photographer, and spectator/reader. The ambiguity of spectatorial/authorial position is even further complicated by an ambiguity in gender identification, contesting mainstream phallocentric subject construction in Western artistic imagery, thus attacking the core of the symbolic.

Yet however much we succeed in changing the object, however much we attempt to attack the symbolic, the photographic image will always consist of a subtle interplay of its iconic, symbolic, and indexical functions, just as the subject will always consist of the intertwining of the imaginary, symbolic, and real. All work on the object depends upon the formal structure of the signifier, and all criticism is but an explicitation of that structure, and of its sociological contextualization. In the postmodern realm, criticism differs from art in its sociological—and not semiological—function, now that photography has assumed the role of criticism.

Perhaps the most profound critical complication entailed by the postmodern condition is that it is no longer possible to determine unequivocally whether any given enunciation of image is a statement or a metastatement, while no enunciation (even, or especially, the metaphysical) may be deemed totally void of narrative content. This suggests a radical critique of the inherent Romantic expressionism of depth hermeneutics: signification is now realized as a *mise-en-abîme* of signifiers, where authorship and spectatorship are merely rhetorical/grammatical constructs; every signified is nothing but another signifier; literality is but another trope; depth a play of surfaces; the person is persona. A particularly complex example may delineate these differences.

In Toronto's Eaton Center (an ultra- or postmodernist enclosed shopping mall) is to be found Michael Snow's photographic sculpture *Flight Stop* (1979). This work consists of a flock of sixty fiberglass geese with applied black and white photographs, suspended from the malls's high ceiling, each formed in a different instance of flight posture. To examine the diffuse references of this work will disclose not only the very origins of modernism, but also the most contemporary simulacral productions of postmodernism.

(1) Most immediately, the presence of these geese—an emblem of Canada's vast wilderness, one of this country's remaining myths—within its most (post)modern architectural complex, surreptitiously creates the disquietude and ambiguity of the nature/culture distinction through the incongruity of the situation. Yet all the while this distinction is made manifest in the structure of the work itself, where the icon of a natural being is composed of artificial materials.

(2) The seemingly incongruous placement of this icon is perfectly coherent in relation to the iconography of Snow's previous photographic and cinematic works, in which the imagery of the Canadian wilderness is transformed into works of high modernism, a transformation exemplified by his now classic avant-garde film, *La régione centrale* (in whose wilderness regions the geese would certainly not be out of place).

(3) Yet the particular form of the icons of *Flight Stop* are not exclusively Snow's. We find the earliest, and most direct, precedents of *Flight Stop* in the nineteenth-century stop-action sequential photographic experiments of Étienne Jules Marey and Ead-

FIGURE 4 Michael Snow, *Flight Stop* (1979)

weard Muybridge, works which were to give rise to the cinema. Marey utilized his *chronophotography*—photographs composed of multiple exposures upon a single photographic plate—to study animal locomotion. In a work which serves as the formal origin of *Flight Stop,* Marey created three-dimensional models, derived from his photographs, of the positions of birds in flight. Thus the photographs which, according to common knowledge, were to give rise to the cinema first gave rise to sculpture. Interestingly enough, Muybridge's own proto-cinematic invention, the zoo-praxiscope—comprised of a magic-lantern which projected painted images derived from Muybridge's photographs—was one in which the photographs that were also to give rise to cinema first gave rise to drawings. We might note the major difference between Marey's and Muybridge's techniques, since it entails critical aesthetic and metaphysical differences. Marey's works were composed of numerous shots of minimal time lapse (sixty images per second) on a single photographic plate; Muybridge's works were composed of numerous plates of stop-action shots, juxtaposed for sequential viewing. Needless to say, Muybridge's technique vastly increased the possibility of introducing narrative into the temporal sequence, all the while breaking up the continuity of the depicted motion (since the time lapse between images is more variable).[29] It is perhaps within the false scientificity and the crypto-narratology of this latter project that we may discover the narrative intent of Snow's minimalist artworks, and effect our own entry into the narrative condition which we have termed postmodernism. The ambiguities and illusions which mark our experience of discrete visual differences are to be found both at the technical/optical origins of the cinema as well as at the theoretical foundations of postmodernist artistic and theoretical production.

(4) The postmodern aspect of *Flight Stop* is revealed in its most literal, immediate aspect: its ultimately simulacral quality. More than a few of the viewers of this work believed the geese to be "real," stuffed geese (taxidermy as art), and there was even some conservationist outcry at their presence! The artwork, the artifice, is taken for a real object, to be denied both its representational status and its status as art. The artwork as practical (and metaphysical) joke reveals the ridiculousness of critical and commonplace discourses, just as it evokes the sublimity of the wilderness

to which it refers. Its very ontological status is evanescent, depending on the frame of reference: photograph as sculpture as proto-cinema as reality. Modernist by heritage; postmodernist by situation. Representational in its circular play of reference; simulacral in its illusionistic play of *trompe l'oeil*.

This work reaches back to the origins of photographic and cinematic practice, all the while projecting forward into the precession/procession of simulacra which governs our postmodern condition.[30] It reveals the complexity of the simulacral as well as the transformative possibilities of representation, and may serve as an emblem of the articulation between modernism and postmodernism. As such, *Flight Stop* is a work which reveals the aporia that defines our existence, disclosing the major contemporary conditions of representability and simulacral production. These conditions, of course, are the forms of our consciousness.

Chapter 10

FILMING: INSCRIPTIONS OF *DENKEN*

Wilhelm S. Wurzer and Hugh J. Silverman

I Heidegger and filming

Filming—philosophy's new thesis? A radical trembling? Post-modern task of thinking? Let us suppose, provisionally, that filming is the beginning of the *Abbruch* from philosophy. From this point of view, what does filming signify? Perhaps, we should first ask, rather briefly, what filming does not signify. Filming, as it is named here, is not disclosed in Leonardo da Vinci's notion of *camera obscura*, not in Thomas Edison's invention of the first workable motion picture camera. Indeed, it may not be ascribed to anything that began to flourish when an archaeology of cinema revealed detailed studies of filmmaking. A definite historical and cultural theory concerning the very possibility of filming would certainly include these and many other cinematographic consid-erations. But our concern will be to expose filming within a zone of thinking that leads to a nonlogocentric, yet critically imagistic reading of the postmodern interplay between *Denken* and *Einbil-dungskraft*.

In modern metaphysics, we encounter the beginning of this kind of thinking, primarily in Kant's *Critique of Judgment*, in Nie-tzsche's *Birth of Tragedy*, and, more recently, in Heidegger's phi-losophy. From a genealogical perspective, we may also find the terrain of filming in the epistemic, ontologic, and aesthetic issues of a metaphysics of subjectivity. The hidden history of filming, however, goes back much further and may initially have been presented, mostly negatively, in the configurations of Plato's discourses on Eros in the *Symposium*. We can see, therefore, that the question of filming is one that has not been raised explicitly by the metaphysical text. In short, the history of philosophy, at least from Plato to Spinoza, has consistently repressed the notion of image and confined its limited significance to a logocentric view of reason. Even in the early part of the nineteenth century, after the invention of the camera, we find a philosopher complaining that his era "prefers the image to the thing, the copy to the original, representation to reality, appearance to being."[1] Apparently, Ludwig Feuerbach did not appreciate Kant's attempt to loosen the subject's dialectic dependency on rationality in order to free imagination for an aesthetic breaching (*Bahnung*) of subjectivity.

In retracing the philosophies of Kant, Nietzsche, Heidegger, and Derrida, in which the name of filming has not yet been received, an economy of filming, however, has already come into question. In particular, this can be delineated in the Heideggerian discourse in which the matter of philosophy concerns a thinking that can be neither metaphysics nor science. For us, filming is such a thinking. It addresses the *to pragma auto* of technology in its postmodern diffusion of images. Thus filming, today, challenges the event of the end of philosophy by examining technology's own ironic upheaval of the metaphysical text and by reinforcing Heidegger's unique claim of technology's dependence on metaphysics.

Let us dwell for a few moments on the mere thought that Heidegger's thinking may help to gain a deeper understanding of the postmodern era of filming. Let us therefore begin our account of filming by returning to the year 1938, when the world revealed one of its darkest historic images and Heidegger presented at Freiburg a compelling lecture, initially entitled, "The Grounding by Metaphysics of the Modern World Image."[2] In this text, Heidegger describes the modern age within a horizon of truth that comes to pass in what he calls *"imaginatio."* He remarks: *"Der Grundvorgang der Neuzeit ist die Eroberung der Welt als Bild."*[3] This thought, which will be examined within the larger context of what came to be known as the lecture on "Die Zeit des Weltbildes," will guide our disclosure of filming in postmodern culture. The phrase "postmodern culture" will here refer to the sociohistoric diversity of the late capitalist world as well as to the imaginative realm of difference in which filming may take place.

Let us briefly examine Heidegger's reading of world as image.

He claims that the modern age presents itself as a productive interweaving of world and man. Both events are described in their transformation into an "imagistic" realm of the Open in which man appears as *subjectum imaginum* and world as production and reproduction of images. At first glance this "anthropologic" reading of the decisive character of the modern age seems to suggest a subjective, metaphysical interpretation of *Dasein*. In Heidegger's own words: "Man becomes the representative of that which is . . . ,"[4] and "image means the formation [*Gebilde*], that is, the product of man's producing which represents and sets before."[5] Does this reading take recourse to a Cartesian formulation of being, or, perhaps, to a Nietzschean hermeneutic which is then transformed into an ontological analysis of modernity? Heidegger's *Auslegung* of man become subject in and through the world of images does not give priority to a "will to power" conception of man and "none at all to the I" of the Cartesian tradition.[6] Nonetheless, control, subjection, domination, in short representation still play an important role in his reflection of the modern era. Although Heidegger sees the image of world within representation, his lecture will also show that filming may be presented in connection with the Open which "extends itself out into a space withdrawn from representation."[7] Hence, his thinking is indicative of postmodernism without being essentially postmodern. For instance, his reference to the subject as self-presence is characterized by a representative interplay of images. On the other hand, later on in the text Heidegger delimits this reference by affirming *das Offene*, which is not antithetical to a postmodern dissemination of images wherein the self is invariably glimpsed as a "flickering" nonidentity.

Today, it seems that filming constitutes a process of thinking which affirms *écriture* so long as we understand writing as the possibility of *via rupta*, "the path that is broken, beaten, *fracta*,"[8] what Derrida calls "violent spacing." Filming may thus be conceived as the postmodern displacement of metaphysics in the continual attempt to free imagination *from* the transcendental constraints of *Verstand* and *for* a more privileged play of *Vernunft*. This suggests an "imagistic" mode of thinking that is not in any sense prerational, irrational, or philosophically bedraggled. On the contrary, at issue is a kind of *Besinnung* that has the courage to question the truth of its own presuppositions as well as the diverse directions of its interests.[9] Such a conception of filming is not an imagining without reflection; instead, it announces a critical unconcealment of "movement-images"[10] in a postanalytic Kantian sense.

In our proposal to address filming as thinking (i.e., as *"denkendes Wort"*), we are describing a "cultural" elevation of schematism from the transcendental realm of understanding to the opening (*"das Freie des Offenen"*) of reason. Although Kant limits the schematic activity of imagination to the empirical direction of understanding, he still claims that schematism is "an art concealed in the depths of the human soul, whose real modes of activity nature is hardly likely ever to allow us to discover and to have open to our gaze."[11] Furthermore, in the *Critique of Judgment* Kant strives to free imagination from the praxeological interests of transcendental representation by dislodging it from the epistemic interplay of *Verstand* and *Vernunft*. Two attempts which attend to the delimitations of the egocentric dominance of imagination are made within the horizon of the aesthetic idea and the sublime. It should be noted that in these attempts Kant wants to exceed the theoretical confinement of imagination to the schematism of understanding, thereby paving the way for a Heideggerian and postmodern disclosure of filming.

Let us briefly examine the Kantian endeavor. The aesthetic idea gives "imagination occasion to spread itself over a host of related representations"[12] without being constrained by spatial and temporal intuitions. This host of representations is represented by the "representation" of imagination. Indeed, in a vaguely postmodern sense Kant describes the aesthetic idea as "that representation of imagination which induces such a wealth of thought as would never admit comprehension in a definite concept."[13]

In his description of the sublime, Kant attempts to formulate a "discontinuous" relation between thinking and imagination. The sublime, lacking definite form, transcends the boundaries of imagination and emerges as a self (*Gemüt*) participating in imagination's play of presence and absence. Neither presence nor absence of self can ever be fully attained conceptually, or—and this may be the eventual aesthetic demise of Kant's *Critique of Judgment*—by means of the taste of reflection. Thus "free play" of imagination lies more in *apprehensio* than in *comprehensio aesthet-*

ica. And this suggests that the continuous play of imagination rests upon the discontinuity of aesthetic totality.[14] When aesthetic imagination, for example, creates a second nature and transcends experience, it is engaged in the reflective operation of aesthetic judgment in which a logocentric position is not forthcoming. In this operation, it is possible to encounter *promesse* of synthesis, i.e., an aesthetic gathering of the manifold of intuitions without attaining the unity that is anticipated in a cognitive, logical judgment.

In its aesthetic transition, imagination presents a fading onto-theologic subjectivity which is superseded by reason's sublime eros for totality. But is imagination wounded by its reflexive inability to attain a sensible realization, that is, a *comprehensio aesthetica*, much less a *comprehensio logica* of totality, when the transcendental dialectic has already shown that a conceptualization of ideas remains illusory? If it were not for Kant's own legitimation of an absolute teleology to which transcendental imagination is still subjected, no violence would be done to aesthetic imagination. In transgressing Kant's critique of judgment, imagination would then be free to embrace its maximum, i.e., the supersensible or the matter itself without having to surpass itself dialectically, or to sink back into itself aesthetically. Such a transgression, however, is inconceivable so long as the sublime—aligned with finality—is thought to be outside the "free play" of aesthetic imagination. Thus the displeasure that the sublime incurs on imagination is due not so much to the absence of a *comprehensio aesthetica* of totality, perhaps, as to the absence of a genuine comprehension of totality whatsoever.

What comes into question now is this: how does filming deconstruct the Kantian delimitations of imagination and the metaphysical domination of filming as such? For one, we find that the categories of the transcendental analytic are desolidified in filming and freed from the conceptual descent to a repressive aesthetic sensibility. This suggests that they are made free for imagination's transition to the aesthetic zone of reason's play. The realm of intuition is then no longer conceived in terms of an epistemic, logocentric operation, which eventually manifests itself in the production of objects of knowledge, but rather in terms of a post-ontological, genealogical, and epistemologically more disruptive terrain of difference. Since intuitions are no longer welded into the instrumentality of transcendental apperception, they may engage in a play of imagination that is liberated from discursive analytic actions as well as from an ineluctably moral extension into Kant's teleological order of reason.

As for the repression of filming: it surfaces not only in transcendental philosophy's failure to free imagination from the putative violence of the sublime, but also from Kant's ideational reduction of world to the problematic region of reason. This repression has only begun to be eluded by Heidegger's pursuit of an imagistic play of withdrawal and, more recently, by an American thinker's understanding of this play as one of occlusion,[15] i.e., the appropriation of *mundus intelligibilis* to *mundus sensibilis*. When Heidegger "dethrones" world from the metaphysical concept of idea to a play of images, he makes it possible for us to introduce filming as the *Besinnung* of *Einbildungskraft*'s new terrain by means of which we may then discern the hidden art of imaging within "the invisible shadow that is cast around all things everywhere."[16] Heidegger understands the schematic activity of imagination beyond the egophanic sphere of *Verstand* and teleology. In attempting to resolve the cosmic antinomy of pure reason, he inscribes a filmic mode of *Verstehen* within the free play of imagination without acknowledging dialectic representations of totality.[17] Inasmuch as Heidegger envisages the new age as one which frees man from himself to himself and as one which frees world from the antinomies of logocentrism, he already anticipates that imagination is not entirely subject to representational discourse *more metaphysico*. Thus, the relation of imagination to representation must now be seen differently.

In filming as *Besinnung*, representations of man and world do not emerge as concepts of objects but rather as images of increasingly diffuse beings-in-imagination. Heidegger exceeds the dialectic limitation of a teleologic closure insofar as thinking shows itself in a historic opening where world may variously appear as image. Hence filming denotes a reflective desire to disrupt the path of *logos* within the dispersed "movement-images" of contemporary technology. We are reminded here of Nietzsche's Apollinian comments on human existence: "We may assume that we are merely images. . . . For it is only as an *aesthetic phenomenon* that existence and world are eternally justified."[18] For Nietzsche, man's *consciousness* of his own being is merely an illusory *representation* of his being. Similarly, (*das denkende Wort*) filming underscores that thinking is no longer primarily determined by self-consciousness but rather by an aesthetic-historic occlusion of being. In its genealogical transformation to filming, thinking is disclosed as a "creative questioning and shaping out of the power of genuine reflection" upon the twilight of subjectivity in the postmodern age of images.[19]

Let us be more specific. Filming, in Heidegger's sense of *Besinnung*, disengages images of being from the hermeneutic power of establishing a new presence, i.e., images of *Ge-stell*. This suggests that filming must be differentiated from film-making, the showing of films, and the intercultural disclosure of electronic images in general. It must also be differentiated from the purely quantitative proliferation of images, negatively described by Heidegger as disclosing the modern age in its unlimited power-play of "calculating, planning, and molding of all things."[20] To the extent to which filming participates in the task of thinking, it must be accorded critical, discursive reflection within the play of occlusion itself. Such play need not be dominated by dialectical desires; instead, it will be inspired by a dialogical, Apollinian impulse whose creative images will make it possible to disrupt "the relational center" of man as *subjectum*. In conceiving the nature of world as image within representation, one may ask whether a Heideggerian reading of Dasein as *subjectum imaginum* is not in itself caught within the closure of metaphysics?

One might be tempted to think this, since his ontological reading of man as primary presence of being is still determined by the pervasive force of *hypokeimenon*. Nevertheless, one cannot fail to see that Heidegger's putative recognition of man as center belongs to the perspectival descriptions of possible postmodern reflections. With respect to that, one may also take note of Derrida's idea, anticipated by Heidegger, that a radical trembling can only come from *outside* as suggesting that it cannot be derived from the Greco-Western philosophical closure. If this is true, it may follow that *outside* emerges as filming, and in a twofold manner. One, filming as *Besinnung* of images, in short, as reflection of the commodity world and of a "self" culturally immersed, dispersed, and displaced in that system. Such reflection subverts the metaphysical immurement of representation and exceeds the presencing of man as *subjectum imaginum*. Two, filming appears in an ontic, intercultural, practical, social-political terrain whose ubiquitous "presence" inspires the very activity of filming as thinking, that is, as thinking of filming. Thus, a double play of occlusion suggests itself. And world as image discloses a postmodern play of diffuse images within "the recurrent appropriation" of filming as ontological thinking and filming as ontic doing. There occurs, if you will, an ontic-ontological interaction between the events of these two modes of filming. This interaction may be conceived as the theoretic-practical transformation of subjective and objective representations into a filmic dissemination of images wherein neither subject nor object are readily discernible. Both modes of filming will then interrelate with one another without becoming binary metaphysical forms. Within the occlusion of "movement-images," filming will reveal what Heidegger designates as "the event of withdrawal." In a postmodern aspect of his work, he remarks: "What withdraws may concern and claim man more essentially than anything present that strikes and touches him. The event of withdrawal could be what is most present in all our present, and so infinitely exceeds the actuality of everything actual."[21] Indeed, filming invites "the event of withdrawal" within a constellation of images that is neither alien to the Kantian problematic of imagination, nor to the particular, ontic-ontological crisis of self-identity in postmodern culture.

It may be appropriate now for us to return to a brief consideration of some transcendental, ontological, and cultural aspects of filming. Filming traces a discontinuous interplay of *Denken* and *Einbildungskraft* which, in its images of presence and absence, leads from Kant's conflict of imagination and reason in the transcendental analytic of the sublime to Heidegger's phenomenon of the "*gigantic*," and on to postmodernism's *glissement* of the subject.

When Kant suggests that the sublime does not encourage imagination to reach the *telos* of absolute synthesis, he announces the possibility of an unruly play of images that indicates the nihilistic absence of form and objectivity. "True sublimity," Kant writes, "must be sought only in the mind of the subject, not in the natural object."[22] The violence, however, which the sublime incurs on imagination, by means of the intense event of the absence of object, may evoke a subversive imaging in which man's center as subject is threatened too.

This threat concerns what Heidegger calls the *co-agitatio* of representation, which relates to man confirming himself as "the authoritative measure for all standards of measure with which whatever is can be accounted as certain, i.e., as true, i.e., as in being."[23] The certainty of this ontotheologic security, which lies in the way man has been conceived, is shattered in the play of occlusion which reveals imagination coming into appearance as *fantasia*. The "gigantic co-agitational" possibility of *fantasia* may transform the Kantian encounter of the sublime into an event of withdrawal which discloses "movement-images" of the absurd and the disruptively ob-scene. Thus, the ex-plosion of Western man may be seen from Heidegger's implosive reading of Kant's aesthetic turmoil: "Man as representing subject fantasizes, i.e., he moves in *imaginatio* in that his representing imagines, pictures forth, whatever is, as the objective, into world as image."[24]

Filming is a paradox. Yet, the coming-into-appearance of man (i.e., subject) as filming opens the scene in ob-scenity as a new freedom. Heidegger's initial description of subjective representation as self-presence does not touch upon the point of this new freedom. Nonetheless, the other Heideggerian projection of subject as *fantasia*, which can clearly be discerned in the text, invites imagination's disengagement from the co-agitation of representation. Within this transitional freedom, filming releases its images from the Kantian presence of the noumenal self *and* the Heideggerian anxiety of *co-agitatio* in order to crystallize Heidegger's hope of *Gelassenheit*. Accordingly, the shadow of the end of man will extend "itself out into a space withdrawn from representation."[25] As can readily be seen, the discontinuity of the Heideggerian text lies precisely in Heidegger's supplementary reading of the historic inscription of being: "But where danger is, grows the saving power also."[26]

Heidegger's discursive turning away from techno-ontological representation makes possible the *Lichtung* of "an as yet uncomprehended form of the gigantic,"[27] a radical trembling that can only come from filming. In its "Americanism," filming originates out of the commodity world, but not necessarily out of the metaphysical nature of Western thought.[28] But, by the same token, does what Heidegger calls "Americanism" belong to the future of filming as something that lies outside the metaphysical realm? If "Americanism" is thought to be the cultural ob-scenity of the subject, or the sociohistoric event of withdrawal, then it seems that it has not attenuated the unruly play of imagination which Kant's thinking of the sublime installs. In our view, filming and "Americanism" will hardly ever form a constellation. For "Americanism" already knows fundamentally what man is. Filming, however, will always ask about the dialectic "ends of man" and will want to show how imagination desires a certain alterity within its transition. Astonishingly, it will strive to attain this alterity in the "recurrent appropriation" of infinitely displaced "movement-images" of a self directed toward a "flowing" imagination,[29] which exceeds the subject's metaphysical presence and absence.

In short, we wish merely to note that Heidegger's lecture "Die Zeit des Weltbildes" suggests that what thinking (i.e., filming) is called upon to think ("film") can no longer be thought ("filmed") in a purely theoretical or practical vein, at least not to the extent to which thinking is related to a fading of presence and absence. Thus, in a postmodern era, the relation of thinking and filming may be conceived as a gathering of images that is not wedded to a representational *Erlebnis* of imagination's identity. The difference that filming evokes dissipates the self-presence of a dialectically confined imagination. The teleological images *more metaphysico* fade into the transitional movements of imagination's free play of occlusion.

What precisely is imaged in this play of occlusion? The self as dialectical presence in identity emerges as transcendental illusion. Man is seen as withdrawing into a time of filming in an ob-scene world of postmodern images. Image (*Bild*) may never again be what we are still calling—world. "And so we find philosophy falling asleep once more: this time not the sleep of dogmatism, but that of anthropology."[30] From the vantage of "the end of philosophy," it could be said that filming is dedicated to awaken thought from such sleep and that this awakening (i.e., filming) occurs in the very uprooting of anthropology and subjectivity. Such a disruption of the center is first discerned in the Nietzschean experience: "The point at which man and God belong to one another, at which the death of God is synonymous with the disappearance of man, and at which the promise of the superman signifies first and foremost the imminence of the death of man."[31] Foucault contends that the "violent spacing" of man's disappearance is the return of the beginning of philosophy. We would like to understand the unfolding of this spacing as something that is named filming, in which it is once more possible to think. Thus, filming might announce "an imminent new form of thought" by means of which an open voyage through "movement-images" may serve to bring our eyes beyond the disintegration of the subject to the Heideggerian hope of imagination's new *Heimat*. In *Les Mots et Les Choses*, Foucault describes the mood which characterizes thinking in its postmodern task of filming:

> To all those who still wish to talk about man, about his reign or his liberation, to all those who still ask themselves questions about what man is in his essence, to all those who wish to take him as their starting-point in their attempts to reach the truth, to all those who, on the other hand, refer all knowledge back to the truths of man himself, to all those who refuse to formalize without anthropologizing, who refuse to mythologize without demystifying, who refuse to think without immediately thinking that it is man who is thinking, to all these warped and twisted forms of reflection we can answer only with a philosophical laugh—which means, to a certain extent, a silent one.[32]

II Inscriptions of *Denken*

Is the age of filming the age of the modern *Weltbild*? In order to answer this question we need to examine the phenomenon of filming more deeply. The construction of this term establishes a place in the contemporary (postmodern) age where a certain activity occurs, an activity that designates the space in which alternative readings multiply and co-exist. Various readings will elaborate this space called "filming."

Let us ask again: what is filming? Filming cannot be ontic. It cannot be the celluloid, the screen, the projector. It cannot be the director, producer, costume designer, the photographer. It cannot be the movie-house manager, the theatre, the television, the VCR, the videocassette, the audience, or the spectator. Filming cannot even be a photograph, a picture, a portrait, or a sketch. Filming also cannot be ontological. It cannot be the Being that sets itself off from what is. It cannot be the general condition for the existence of celluloid, scenery, actors, photographers, cameras, theatres, televisions, and VCRs. Filming cannot as such be the ground for all picturing, representing, imaging, showing, etc. It cannot originate, nor found, nor establish, nor provide the basis for that which is pictured, represented, imaged, shown.

Filming operates between the scenery, actors, photographers, celluloid, cameras, theatres, televisions, VCRs, *and* the Being that establishes their identity (and difference from one another). Filming is that ontico-ontological activity and space that has no identity of its own. It is the coming into its own of an age in which a new set of technological equipment, human roles, and aesthetic functions establish themselves. Filming, then, arises, occurs, and happens in the place of difference, in the place where meaning takes shape.

In this curious, non-identified place, this context for meaning, filming can do its work. But filming can only begin to disclose itself here. In the pre-postmodern age which Heidegger announces and informs, traditional metaphysical oppositions set the stage for where filming can happen. Filming is neither transcendental nor empirical, neither subjective nor objective, neither a feature of the self nor a characteristic of the world, neither a reality nor an appearance, neither a thought nor a thing. Yet in the context of these oppositions the space for what will be called filming can be established. With Heidegger the space of opposition at the edge of a modern age, where the oppositions themselves still have meaning, announces itself as calling forth a closure. What comes to closure is both the modern age itself, the age in which polar identities delineate features of experience, and the type of meaning that circumscribes the context of such experience. When both the modern age and its meanings come to an end, the question of what will happen at its edges is set up by the Heideggerian enterprise. Heidegger makes room for a postmodern age by designating the places of difference—most notably ontico-ontological—in which "filming," for instance, can occur.

In "The Age of the World-Image," Heidegger states: "That the world becomes image is one and the same event with the event of man's becoming *subiectum* in the midst of that which is."[33] For Heidegger, the tendency to separate the self as subject and the world as object has come to an end in the modern age. They can no longer be thought as separate identities. They 'are' in that they fill the space of difference. The *subiectum*, Heidegger points out, is a translation of the Greek *hypokeimenon*. *Hypokeimenon* names "that-which-lies-before, which, as ground gathers everything onto itself."[34] Heidegger then indicates clearly and explicitly that this *hypokeimenon* is not to be identified with the "I". The *subiectum* is that which is thrown under, that which underlies, that which grounds by lying before and gathering into itself. What the *subiectum* gathers into itself by being "that-which-lies-before" is the world—in the form of image (*Bild*). The *subiectum* cannot stand in opposition to the world. It must gather into itself by lying before in the form of image. This *Weltbild* is neither of the world nor of the subject. It fills the space of difference (between *Zeit and Geist*) that stands at the edge of the modern age. "Filming" occupies this same space, but in a different way.

How does filming occupy this same space in a different way? It is not centering, focusing, identifying for the ontico-ontological difference. Filming does not gather together as world-image does. It does not render determinate what is multiple and indeterminate. It is not the specification of what is broad, disparate, and non-specific. Instead, filming is the activity which renders into film what is not film. It is not the machines (projectors, cameras, and video-editors) which technologically produce film. Filming is the making different of that which is not film into that which is film. In its spacing, differencing, textualizing, filming is the production of films in a filmic language that has become text. The filmic language (as Metz would call it) has no place in the world—except as a commodity, as an expression of viewpoints, as a representation of reality. The filmic language can be used in these various ways, but that is not what it is. Filmic language—the textualizing that makes other than what it is—is a set of differential codes, marks, and traces, a "filmic dissemination of images." It involves a tracing, leaving traces, marks, inscriptions. Filming not only renders that which is not film into film, but it also leaves a signature of a post-multi-authorial inscription.

Yet, filming does not reinscribe a new kind of *auteur* theory. It also does not announce itself as a theory to accompany an age of mechanical reproduction. Filming is a differencing whose very language textualizes by not reproducing, expressing, imaging, identifying. Filming sets its own limits, margins, and borders, temporally and spatially. What Deleuze calls the "image-mouvant" (moving image) gives action to the sequence of frames, but it also frames the framing. The only frame that filming reproduces is the frame of the modern age. Filming repeats the frame of the modern era by circumscribing it, limiting it, giving it content, meaning, form, character. The indeterminacy of what is postmodern is due to the fact that it has no style. The perplexity about post-modernism is that, like filming—among other spatial activities—it has no definite shape, no determinate form or content. Postmodernism itself frames and filming metonymically marks off the modernist outlook. Filming offers no content, style, or form of its own. What it offers is a content, style, or form for modernism, thinking modernism within its own frame. The modernist should be glad—its production of the new, the stylish, the colorful now has shape. Postmodernism is its difference. Filming is one of the ways that postmodernism performs this tracing, framing, marking off—textualizing—of the modernist age of which we are now *ex post facto* witnesses.

Chapter 11

THE TELEVISED
AND THE UNTELEVISED:
KEEPING AN EYE
ON/OFF THE TUBE

Brian Seitz

JB: "I don't deny history. It's an immense toy."

SL: "Yes, if you remain glued to the screen, or fascinated by the giddiness of commutations."[1]

I   TV guide

Television viewing opens on an image toward which it must continue to orient itself. The problem of the relation between the televised and the untelevised is a problem whose end is not a resolution, but an indefiniteness to be cultivated.[2] What is at stake is a decision currently situated at a crossroads in a labyrinth.

One of the paths intersecting this crossroads is the traditional metaphysical line, which bifurcates and hierarchizes the True (Reality) and the false (television), and which refuses to take the play between the televised and the untelevised seriously (which refuses, that is, to recognize the productive power of TV).

Another path, a distinctly postmodern one, is characterized by the philosophy of Jean Baudrillard, which narrates the advance of a "hyperreality" constituted by the collapse of all "real" distinctions into the play of floating signifiers; the difference between the televised and the untelevised finally vanishes on this flat surface or screen.

But the truth must be different from either of these polar

positions, something in between. Our aim here is not to clarify or name it (there is no truth to name), but to emphasize the insistence of the truth, which is the insistence of the difference between the televised and the untelevised, as well as the insistence of their inseparability.

However, while the difference between the televised and the untelevised is a problem requiring articulation—a basic one, the sort philosophers cannot resist—it is also a problem that could lead us into affirming an oscillating network of lies, a problem likely to channel television into a dangerously self-contained box, a problem bound to create problems. Pursuit of this difference might generate another hierarchizing and thus overly partial account of the opposition between reality and appearance, or between fact and fiction, reflection and distortion, information and propaganda, literal and metaphorical, object(ive) and subject(ive), true and false "modes of consciousness," truth and ideology, active and passive, immediate (present) and mediate (a transformative detour, a negotiation of the remote/*fern*), and speech and writing, not to mention vigilance and somnambulance and all the other dyadic cuttings which serve to repeat and constitute the most dazzling tropes of the philosophic tradition.[3] But we should affirm two preliminary points before following this line further.

First, and despite the danger of these dyadic possibilities, the problem of confronting the difference between the televised and the untelevised is one that cannot be avoided, not without risking a lapse into an isolated discourse, a discourse that might wind up alone in a closed room, talking to the boob tube. A television viewer is never alone (not even when no one else is in the room) until s/he starts talking to the machine. It is worth noting here that the absurdity of the prospect of talking to the TV provides an image which affirms that television is not simply an inherently neutral instrument or system of *communication*.[4] If it is a system of communication at all, it is one that radically transforms what *communication* is. Or, possibly (a Derridean perception), it shows in a new way that "communication" never was (a self-identical thing, a self-evident positivity, a clear, interference-free channel).

On the other hand, a discourse that presumably engages and intersects other discourses, other *people*, is obliged to consider the relationship between the televised and the untelevised. This relationship is not an arbitrary, accidental or even chosen one—we did not and do not "choose" TV—and we live in a time when the televised and the untelevised have and will have become inseparable, which is not the same as indistinguishable, a distinction that will continue to assert itself.

Besides, *this*, which is "about television," is itself untelevised, and the difference is in operation, then, from the very outset, as usual. This superficial but decisive point would have been impossible to make fifty years ago, but it cannot be avoided now.

Second, setting this relation up in terms of the televised and the untelevised—instead of "television versus Reality"—opens up a discursive breach, a different philosophical site of intersection and exchange which, once established, cannot be closed off or its terms given the fixed, determinate value essential to identificative enterprises. In fact, and flying in the face of common sense and traditional wisdom, this transmission tends to skew the picture nicely by insinuating the processes of television everywhere from the outset, thereby extending the range of TV, and granting it a kind of priority that cannot be affirmed in the end, but which may nevertheless be strategically exploited.

Most generally, this strategy aims to problematize the metaphysical priority traditionally associated with discursive complexes such as "Reality" (over against, for example, "TV," or any other errant appearance network). At the same time, though, and equally important, its use helps ensure recognition that the untelevised will always disturb and disrupt the univocity and self-identity of TV—as well as vice versa—which means that the untelevised will prevent "the televised" from congealing into a discrete or monolithic technological singularity or source,[5] and also that the economy constituted by their relationship will serve less to separate than to bind them. Put plainly, this strategy emphasizes that the televised and the untelevised are co-constitutive and even, in many respects, coextensive with each other.

In other words, articulating the difference in these terms instead of beginning with an opposition between "television and Reality" may help interfere with some of our own heliotropic receptions. From the moment we turn the TV on and enter into a relationship with it, we must remain sensitive; 1) to the way that the light of a television cannot be traced to an original sun or referred to an originary transcendental signified—cosmological and ontological continuity have limited power here—and 2) to the way that this light is as *real* and as formative (in contrast with illuminating) or as giving or withholding as any other. The first point implies that we cannot confine television to a single identity or account,[6] since its origins are multiple and do not dissolve into a masterable, finally single or singular (or "dialectically" split, i.e. Unified) source. The second point invites philosophy to take television as seriously as any other light that has ever found passage into the archive(s) (and—here, have a seat on the couch—this light's less effort to see than most; you just turn it on; it's "free," and you—numero uno!—are always "free" to change the channel!).

II   And now we pause for station identification: Writing and the scene of television

As soon as we begin to put into question the notion that the televised simply records or amplifies the untelevised (whether poorly or well), we invoke the relation of television and writing. In fact, a viewing of television may underscore one of the important ramifications of Jacques Derrida's deconstruction of the speech/writing dyad, since the power of television has been linked to the privileged power of speech (which is the power of immediate presence, the making-present of that which is (true, self-identical)) as opposed to writing.

Although, to its credit, it is not entirely consistent in this move, Fiske and Hartley's *Reading Television*, which offers many strong insights into television, associates television with an "oral" ("bardic") voice as opposed to a "literate" one.[7] Despite the range of both traditional and current identification patterns that *RT* and the notion of "the bardic" serve to question and disrupt this particular association resurrects the traditional opposition between speech and writing. This opposition is hierarchical and (in)decisive because television's alleged alliance with orality automatically and explicitly devalues the literate component ("the abstract, elaborated codes of literacy") of the semiotechnics of television. In short, the "concreteness" of the oral that is counterposed to the "abstractness" of the literate is synonymous with *presence*. Interestingly enough, *RT* achieves this devaluation of the literate even while it associates a literate bias with those who *produce* television; here, the speech/writing opposition gets overtly transposed (e.g., *RT*, p. 145) onto the "dialectical" opposition between the (oral) proletariat (the audience) and the (literate) bourgeoisie (the producers), a risky and overly straightforward opposition in this age of circulating "information."[8]

But even more interesting—and leaving aside the obvious empirical fact that most TV voicings have actually been written in advance—this association obscures a reading of television as a form of writing or, to put it less logocentrically and to avoid misunderstandings, as a form of markmaking.[9]

While the power of television has been linked to and made dependent on the power of speech or *immediate presence* (as opposed to writing), it should also be seen that television is not speech—it is audiovisual, which is not the same as oral—and the power of televised speech is an effect or dimension of the power of this complex, electronic system of "writing" or markmaking, not the other way around. If reversal were our game here, it could even be argued that radio is a "form of writing" rather than a "form of speech"; most crucial, the radio is not just a neutral technological network serving to amplify and expand the "natural" range of the human voice, and television is not just a fancier version of such a value-free amplification. The point is that television and radio are both formative and transformative, and not just (neutrally) amplificative technologies. Television does have a bardic function insofar as it not only repeats but also generates powerful mythologies of our times. Its "essence" is not that of direct speech or immediate presence(/truth); in this sense, television may not express so much as it weaves or *makes* stories(/"realities").

Finally (Derrida rejoins the discourse), what would Plato have thought of the electronic "media" which (doubly) bind "postmodern" culture? He probably would not have approved of them, since he would have seen them as forms of writing, forms bound to lead us astray (Plato was someone who understood writing [and television] as transformative and deviant); a literate idiot can sound smart reading a speech, and a persuasive actor can woo a nation on TV. This is not even to mention the directions the production/editorial process necessarily makes a televised storyline "turn" (as if it were possible for a story to do anything other than turn, as if there were some independent standard, some *straight* story!).

But we must admit that TV is as undecideable as the philosophical medicine(/poison) that Plato wants to feed us. Among other things, this admission forces us to hesitate and observe that Plato, who clearly had plenty of use for writing, might also have had uses for television after all. The recent recruiting advertisement in which the dominant image is an engraved officer's sabre—a highly polished phallus, shining with meaning—and which concludes, "We're looking for a few good men with the metal to be Marines," might be just the right edge for shaping Plato's auxiliaries, who will defend and preserve the Unity of the State. (In considering the kinds of techniques it takes to produce a sword and its bearer, remember also Michel Foucault's *Discipline and Punish*, which explores the productive effects of earlier and not unrelated regulative—"dividing"—practices and disciplinary technologies.)

However, more to the point, we must contest the way Plato writes or writes off television in the end, and we must refuse to reduce or align television (or other electronic media) to or with either writing or speech. Among other factors, television is not just a conduit for speech or a housing for writing (or Being). Television is a new discursive element (as water is an element) and a new "system of production," the likes of which has never existed in all of history until just now.

It may be true in the domain of the untelevised that "Dow lets you do great things" (with ziplock bags or napalm), that "Toyota is looking out for number one" (guess who that is!), and that "Ford has a better idea" (although not better than some "ideas" from Japan). But television is doing something powerful, basic, and formative, too, something situated in the fold between the "Dow" and the "you," not to mention something somewhere between Vietnam, the first full-scale televised war, and *Tour of Duty*, the first prime-time series "about" Vietnam, which CBS deployed as a counteroffensive maneuver in the ratings battle against NBC's immensely popular *The Cosby Show*.

So, what is (not "written" but nevertheless) marked out and transmitted here? Do we accept that the box is there primarily to communicate that "At McDonald's, we do it all for you," that "Coke is the real thing," or that Shearson Lehman Brothers is synonymous with "Minds over money," with "Capitalism at its best"? Are these communications duplicitous, false, or are they as equivalent to the "truth" as any other "communication" these days? For those who live in its sphere of "informational" influence—i.e. within a broadcasting range made indefinitely broad by cable and satellite technology, by the technology of *channels*—it seems necessarily true (i.e. part of life) not only that "At Macy's we're part of your life," but also that the drama of *Dallas* continues (i.e., is aired regularly) in Paris, as well as in East Berlin. And now, thanks to decoders that pick up Soviet satellite signals, academics at American universities look for elements of the truth about "the U.S.S.R., Inc." by watching the "educationally" oriented Soviet television right in the comfort of the home institution.

Speaking of education, what about the unforgettable truth of the televised news image (since effaced by the famous photograph) of General Loan shooting the Vietcong suspect pointblank in the head? Editorial surgery made the televised image possible by excising unacceptably gory portions of the shot.[10] Can we not marvel, for example, at how effectively periods of silence are used in interviews to reinforce an aesthetic of realism in the service of investigative journalism? *60 Minutes* has used this silence and deployed this aesthetic every week for the last twenty years.

The realism of such an aesthetics is that "the look" marked out by TV both changes and does not change, "reflects" change and embodies repetition. For example, women newscasters are no longer such a rarity, and the drama of women (e.g., *Designing Women*) is no longer confined to the domestic sphere, and this is a change, a liberative and possibly even liberating effect; think back to that perfect domestic creature, Donna Reed.[11] Back in the days of *Perry Mason* and *Dragnet*, Cagney and Lacey would have been secretaries, not police detectives, and the significance of this change cannot be underestimated.[12] However, neither then nor now would a show about a male private investigator have been named *Leg Work*. Even as it admits women, then, TV, too, continues to push very traditional associations into the foreground (such as the privileged connection between woman and body, set against that of man and mind), clearly the foreplay, liberating the flow of images of T and A. Dolly Parton's general

193

success— and her crossover "from the Smoky Mountains to the Beverly Hills"—has always been linked to a high profile on TV, from the old Nashville days with Porter Wagoner to, more recently, her own prime-time variety show. (Dolly's voice, however, has never been contained by television.)

III   Telling the truth on TV:

"Will the real Montana please stand up?"[13]

Let us now approach the relationship between the televised and the untelevised from a different standpoint: how does TV in the United States refer to "America," an untelevised domain that is subject to television, to both its advertising and its shows? More likely, it refers to or is "America," an epic (epochal) saga[14] and anti-saga[15] which is the *subject* of most television shows, shows of every variety, including advertisements, as well as international news, and entertainment programs, such as *Amerika* (the ABC miniseries about an America conquered by the Soviet Union— without rival the most vapid forty-million-dollar movie ever made—a program which suffers even further when compared with *Berlin Alexanderplatz*, the remarkable epic that Fassbinder made for German TV). But what is "America"? Maybe something like geography can help provide an answer.

If we are to talk geography, consider the Concorde jet as a standard image for determining scale (and for traversing the distance between certain Parisian postmodernists and the North American intellectual scene); compare it to a Viking ship or the *Niña*, the *Pinta*, and the *Santa María* for contrast, or to a covered wagon or a pony or a dog travois. Or compare it to one of the pirogues that floated Lewis and Clark's "voyage of discovery" up the upper Missouri River in 1805. If the Concorde is our standard, watching TV in Montana now means watching on a "postmodern" plain, a site where the underground architecture of prairie-dog towns get mixed in with the also underground architecture of missile silos (there are over two hundred of them in Montana), which are never too far from the TV and which may, in fact, be part of the same network of the technologies of speed.[16]

From the standpoint of *white* culture and "the rest of the

world," Montana is a territory that used to be remote, far, at least, from big cities, isolated from the kinds of Cultural things that happen there, a wild sort of place. For example, in 1876, the year Nietzsche was finishing his *Untimely Meditations*, a heterogeneous group of plains tribes marked and counted a splendid (if also untimely) war coup at Little Big Horn, and the following year—the year art enthusiasts were admiring Monet's new paintings of the Gare Saint-Lazare—Joseph's exhausted Nez Perce surrendered to the United States Army near Chinook, just shy of the Canadian border, after a fifteen-hundred-mile chase scene that began in Idaho. The newspapers tracked the Nez Perce tribe's remarkable and desperate adventure. The Eastern media, too, were still a long way from Montana, but, thanks to the train and the telegraph—thanks to the technologies of accelerated exchange—they were absorbing the distance and narrowing the gap all the time.

Nothing was televised in those days, and Montana was out of the way (of everywhere else). But it was before the use of airwaves for instantaneous remote transmission and reception, and the big sky country has changed a lot since then. It is different because of all of the technologies of speed, transportation, and efficiency—which include Burger King and K-Mart as well as personal computers, automobiles, interstate highways, telephones, short connecting flights to international destinations, and those missile silos—but it is different perhaps most of all because of the mundane and pervasive quasi-presence of television, which in a peculiar way annihilates territory or circumnavigates the problem presented by space, and upsets the play between that which is near (local) and that which is far (remote), and between that which is regional and that which is unlocated or general and generalizing. In relation to the question of territory, this upset changes the landscape, and keeps Missoula as "on top of things" as in-the-know New York is. The citizens of Havre—near where the Nez Perce lost their independence, not just a "semiotic" event[17]—may continue to dress, speak, and live somewhat differently from the citizens of Houston, Seattle, or Memphis, but Dan Rather, Peter Jennings, and Tom Brokaw[18]— not to mention Charlayne Hunter-Gault, *L. A. Law*, *People's Court*, *Wide World of Sports*, "Heeeeere's Johnny . . . ," *Monday Night Football: Special Thursday Edition*, MTV, *St. Elsewhere*, Julia Child,

Jimmy Swaggart (televised confessions of a sinner), Ted Koppel, *Honeymooner* reruns, *Star Trek* reruns, *Star Trek: The Next Generation*, and ("this Bud's for you") that bulldog party animal extraordinaire, Spuds McKenzie, not to forget the lovely Vanna White, *One Life to Live*, and *As the World Turns*—all significantly in-form (and determine) Americans and America now. They expose and *make* or contribute to making the epic (epochal) "America" what it is, in Montana and Massachusetts (and Iowa and New Hampshire), as well as in the Persian Gulf and Latin America, and in Japan and Korea, where so many televisions are manufactured.

Mentioning Montana here, then, is a move to geography in the attempt to get at the relation of the televised and the untelevised, but it is also a move away from geography, since the possibilities of remote transception displace important dimensions of the gap traditionally associated with spatial, geographical differences.[19] With the advent of cable television and home satellite dishes, the location of not only the receiver but the transmitter (or broadcasting source) becomes practically irrelevant, as Great Falls watches an Atlanta or Spokane station.[20] This displacement says a lot about the relation between the televised and the untelevised; watching *CBS Evening News* in Montana is "the same" as watching it anywhere else, which means that Montanans receive just about as much instantaneous "information" as the rest of Amerika.

But Montana is Montana. This means not that Montana is some self-identical thing (and cannot be made into one), but that it remains different from London, San Francisco, and Toronto (and from Ho Chi Minh City, Mexico City, Vladivostok, Milan, Soweto, Thule, and Damascus), as well as from its neighbor, Alberta, across the border (a border that does not constrain air signals). The insistence of the difference between the televised and the untelevised reinstalls itself in Montana, as it does wherever there either is or is not television reception. Television changes everything, and it overcomes the distance between Montana and the rest of the world. But even as its transmissions are picked up by Montana, TV does not close the gap between the televised and the untelevised. TV complicates and makes, for example, geographical or cultural differences increasingly ambiguous, but it does not eliminate them. Montana is still different (and, within it, the cabled city of Billings remains different from Rocky Boy's Reservation, where the Chippewa-Cree are tuned in to satellite dishes, and from the Bob Marshall Wilderness, where, so far, there are neither televisions nor TV). The *Wheel of Fortune* turns everywhere, but Montana remains Montana, unique, although never absolutely so, thanks in part to the play between the televised and the untelevised, a relation indefinitely in *Jeopardy*.

IV The subject of TV

"The heartbeat of America"[21]; "Be all that you can be. . ."[22]

"Children between the ages of 2 and 12 watch an average of 25 hours of television a week. By the time they graduate from high school, American children each will have spent 15,000 hours in front of a television set, compared with only 11,000 hours in the classroom."[23]

If we take numbers seriously,[24] which does not have to mean reductively, these statistics indicate a critical transgression of the centrality and integrity of the classroom as the privileged site of "education" in our culture. If what Heidegger might call the "objective world time" suggested by units of hours can be considered important (even "fundamental"?), these numbers suggest, for example, that the process of education—of in-forming the subject—must revolve around television at least as much as school. Standing alongside and woven into the value of arithmetic and the pledge of allegiance ("to the flag of the United States of America, and to the republic for which it stands, one nation, under God, indivisible, with liberty and justice for all") are the never-ending battle of good and evil offered by She-Ra (so many of the bad guys in this genre have foreign accents; it makes it easier to identify them), the pervasive jeering attitude that is even part of *Sesame Street* (see Miller, *WT*, p. 221), and the perpetual, more generalized repetition of the value of consumerism—consume, consume, consume—which, clearly, is not just a matter of *buying*, but a whole way of life, with the music and special effects now provided by MTV (generationmood by Pepsi).[25] The numbers speak loudly, and it would above all be a mistake to dissociate these two spheres of "learning" too strongly, since they feed and reinforce each other, and since, apparently, what they share in common is the function of *transmission*.

We could derive from this observation another traditional, hierarchical account of power as something that gets applied to subjects from the beginning of their lives. Here, television (and, perhaps, "education") is in the service of the dominant, sovereign power—a medium and weapon of rule—and citizens and proto-citizens (children) are in a position of subordination. In this account, citizens are subjugated by means of the media; the citizen(-consumer) is the identity of the subject of TV, and, in television cultures, the "self" is a false consciousness, a subject that has fundamentally deviated from its possibilities or is deceived,[26] having fallen prey to "ideological" discourse, to "chatter," or even to "that trash they show on TV." This implies, of course, that there is some Real Identity independent of television, an identity that this subject must either have lost or surrendered. Television is a, or perhaps *the*, coercive medium through which power is exercised on subjects now.

This account is not "false," but it offers a far too partial story, one that does not go far enough in getting at the relation between the televised and the untelevised. The televised is articulated here as essentially a "slanted" version of the untelevised, while the untelevised—the Real untelevised—is reduced to being the exclusive domain of the few who really know the whole story, i.e., either to an enlightened elite (or, alternatively, vanguard) that knows what's *really* going on, or to those shades and spooks who spin the tale and turn the wheel of fortune. Again, this picture is not "wrong," but it is too simple and too neat, and it remains solidly within the confines of metaphysics in its repetition of the central binary image of an appearance network used to manipulate the masses, to conceal from them (who exist independently of the TV (?)) the way things Really Are. It is obvious that television is often and in a variety of ways used and used effectively to deceive and manipulate—arguing otherwise would be sheer lunacy—but is that what it is really *about*? Is it fundamentally just a(n in itself neutral or masterable) conduit used to relay the backroom power plans of those on the top, or a way to cover up or paint a false picture of Reality, to fool the subjects?

An alternative suggestion might help upset a traditional metaphysical discourse about television here;[27] if television is a medium, it is not, mainly, one in the form of a (possibly bad) communications conduit between the elite and the masses, not a one-way line for sending (control) messages from point A to B. If TV has become or is a *medium*, it is so in the form of an adhesive, a binding agent that holds a culture together.[28] Not a medium of rule so much as rule of medium (to echo a familiar message). What this means is that what "we" are as a culture is not just put across or communicated on the TV, but that we are in part produced by it. In other words, TV is a basic dimension of what and "who" we are, a basic aspect of our *identity*. It embodies, shapes, *constitutes, and transmits* ("postmodern") cultural values, and becomes one of the glues that binds a culture together. Twenty-five viewing hours a week is the necessary time of initiation, a rite of passage into a culture that has become televisual and thus wholly different from any culture or civilization that has come before it (without question a mark of the site of one of Foucault's "discontinuities"). As an adhesive, though, television is not *about* something outside of itself; what television is about is transmission and reception, but what this process of transception is or is about is "itself" (*which can never sever itself from the untelevised*).

The "subject" of TV may be the subject of self-reference, the main or consistent reference of the televised, which at the same time permeates the untelevised and is an active factor in determining what the untelevised, too, is. While this system of self-reference cannot be independent of those who are involved with the production of TV, it would nevertheless be inadequate to see the self-referential network constituted by television as finally masterable by any commercial or noncommercial network, since, in an important sense, it generates this self-referential system blindly, despite itself or despite the intentions of the elements that program the TV. For one thing, the very hardware determines or at least limits what sort of emissions are possible, and what sorts of "applications," uses, and aesthetic possibilities are available; this is just one instance of the sense in which technology is not just a neutral instrument in the service of (master) reason. The TV does have (not a life but) an indefinite existence of its own.

On the other hand, the self-referential subject of TV lends

itself to powerful political (and, of course, economic) uses and strategies, strategies which have displaced most traditional methods of, for example, campaigning, or of *producing* and maintaining an image.[29] It is worth observing that,

> Nobody, of course, can talk back to a screen. The situation has deteriorated so far that Robert M. Schrum, a political analyst, described a rally in California as three people around a TV set. Linda Douglas, political editor of KNBC-TV, Los Angeles, says: "The primary form of communication in the campaign has been the television commercial. The candidates are able to avoid less safe situations where reporters can ask questions."[30]

One side of televisual campaigning, which is certainly a form of warfare—war in the form of a popularity contest—is that politics has become more of a *show* (rather than a communicative process of exchange) than it has ever been. Reagan, of course, was the epitome or extreme product of this process. He was no doubt "the real C.E.O." in the White House. As media image, he helped consolidate a power network that has always and continues to extend far beyond him. The "Reagan" character was a role acted out by Ronald Reagan, an identity probably little or not different from the actor. Reagan was prone to asserting embarrassing misinformation when there was not a script in front of him or when his lines ran out (e.g., his grasp of history was rather imaginative without a script, an extension of Plato's reasons for concern about the danger of writing), and it sometimes seemed difficult for him to construct an accurate or even articulate sentence on his own. "Reagan" was a televisually produced identity surface, a *product* of the television, so well seasoned by movies and radio. As the president, Ronald Reagan was a television personality as much as a "real man" (and the one was the identity of the other). In part, this means that he could not contain or entirely control what the TV made out of him, and what "worked" about him was the role he played on television, and what didn't work about him was clear when the role conflicted with his established television identity or simply ran out. What was amazing about his presidency is that whenever he did not play the role well, the country tended simply to shut him off (while the scandals in his administration began early on, they did not seem to bother Amerika much for a long time). Viewers simply awaited the next installment of the Reagan Show, a show in which the Soviet Union was less a nation, society, or place than a televisual trope, and the cast of Central America included "freedom fighters," practically blood-relatives of the freedom-fighter heroes of America's grand, technicolor past. Reagan never grew out of the Golden Age of Television, and he never stopped starring in *Death Valley Days*, never abandoned those oneiric days. He chopped wood for the camera. He eulogized a dead hombre (Commerce Secretary Baldrige, who died [7/25/87] practicing steer-roping for a rodeo) in the no-nonsense kind of terms that they understand in Death Valley; when Reagan phoned to invite him to join the administration, "he was out on his horse roping and couldn't come to the phone. Right then, I knew he was the kind of man I wanted." A key aspect of the Reagan identity was that he continued to talk like you have to talk in Death Valley (that decisive, dusty moment under the hot sun, when you'd better sound like you mean it when you say, "There ain't no smoking gun,"[31] because it could be your last line, and if you don't deliver it right, you could be going down, and maybe not in the glorious flames you had in mind).

Even in the field of politics, then, the primary "subject" of TV seems to be TV, and Reagan's presidency made this clearer that it had been before. But that is just part of the picture, part of the picture of Reagan shown on TV, and it does not mean that the world is "outside" of television (or vice versa), or that television is basically sealed off from it. In fact, the moments of vertigo and anxiety in the Reagan presidency grew out of the breaks between the televised and the untelevised, in the folds constituted by their relation, breaks that caused anxiety *in the very process of being televised*, as, in the final year, when he sounded phony and nervous and stumbled and hesitated through responses to questions about Oliver North, Ed Meese, and Nancy's astrological signs, all things *intended* to remain untelevised. Television continues to determine that which is "on" it and that which is "off" it; the transmissions of the televised are never separate from the transmissions of

201

the untelevised. The subject of the TV is the televised and the untelevised.

V   The untelevised televised: Keeping the lines open

"Trinity Broadcasting Network is God's network . . . Call (714) 731-1000" "Call the AIDS hotline, (212) 496-5156"; "Citicorp: Because Americans want to succeed, not just survive."

What I am broadcasting (but not televising) here is the return of the untelevised (and the televised). We need to find or cultivate a route somewhere between traditional metaphysical viewings of television, on the one hand, and postmodern viewings of the variety exemplified by Baudrillard, on the other.

Traditional metaphysical viewings, which present TV as a network of nothing more than appearances—which present TV as *not real*—generate hierarchically organized discourses, which are hazardous because they reduce television to the status of *mere image*, a tin echo of the True Form of Being ("Plato commented to reporters today in Athens"), a deviation from a Reality that is rendered fundamental. The first danger here is the reliance on a conception of reality as self-identical, self-present, and ultimately self-evident. The second danger—the danger that follows an affirmation of this privileged Reality—is the refusal to recognize television's productive capacities. That is, the danger is in underestimating the powerful way in which the televised informs and contributes to the untelevised (to what the untelevised is). Of course there is a "reality," but television is certainly a significant and determinative part of what it is these days; TV makes and does not just reflect reality (and the material of its production is no more false than any other aspect of this culture). At the moment of truth, the traditional metaphysical viewing of television will necessarily miss the power of this point, and will thus miss the power of television (reducing it, possibly, to laziness, ignorance, or even stupidity on the part of viewers).

But an equally hazardous viewing is the committedly nihilistic, *polar mate* to the traditional one; this is the sort sketched out by Baudrillard. Here, all distinctions vanish into the tube, and television "is" reality, or equivalent to reality, since equivalencies, commutations, and simulacra are all that is left on this planet, according to the axioms of this discourse. This species of postmodernism—which translates some astute sociological observations into outlandish philosophical claims—is dangerous primarily because a lot of people are taking it seriously, buying into this conflation of differences. It might be easy and perhaps appropriately cynical to say that there is no *danger* in this diversion, since it is only harmless intellectuals and academics who pay this mode any mind. However, this theory is reactionary all the way around; it fits just a bit too comfortably into the milieu it seeks to describe or even criticize; if only harmless intellectuals engage in the discourse of "hyperreality," this engagement renders them harmless, glued, as they may be, to the tube.

Yes, always in Heraclitean flux, "TV is reality" these days. But meanwhile, for example, the Central Intelligence Agency remains a (power) network that operates, for the most part, untelevised. The televised Iran-Contra hearings—a drama in which the C.I.A. was repeatedly mentioned, a televised and untelevised narrative in which it clearly played a major role—made this observation no less true, but more obvious and more true than ever. Is it possible that some clever postmodernism expert at the C.I.A. (or the K.G.B.) invented "Baudrillard"?[32] Certainly, the C.I.A., which no doubt keeps track of such trends, must welcome the circulation of a theory forced to argue that *intelligence agencies* are also simulacra, just like everything else, equivalent to everything else, nothing more than flat, infinitely repeatable signifiers, nothing more than floating "signs." Why would the police be an exception to this fundamental insight?[33] And perhaps the Israeli army consulted Baudrillard before declaring areas of the West Bank and the Gaza strip off-limits to journalists, on the grounds that the presence of camera crews causes Palestinians to riot, on the grounds that Television causes (hyper)reality. At any rate, we may reasonably doubt that Baudrillard's theories are very popular with the direct victims and combatants of police logic and police power on this planet,[34] with those whose experience and understanding of this powerful logic is *not identical* with its profile on TV. If "power is dead" (*FF*, p. 11), it is at least less dead than the academic theory that announces its demise. Here, the power is not in the discourse that either thematizes or denies power, but in what has indeed become Eisenhower's *Death Valley Days* military-industrial complex (a complex of which the university if part), televised and untelevised.

But we need not remain so serious, since, at the same time, Baudrillard generates some keen jokes, or provides some borders open to deconstruction, a couple of sites of which I will only generally suggest here. A careful reading might find that Baudrillard's simulated critique (of metaphysics) or recasting of the sign generates and hinges on a hyperbolic valorization of the (autonomous) sign (and a reinscription of metaphysics), and that the accompanying simulated critique of the subject might depend upon or produce a radical subjectivism (specifically, this subject might be the image of the shopping mall consumer as seen on TV), one additionally characterized by the overt repetition of European ethnocentrism; television in Moscow or Monrovia is different from television in Paris, and that difference is *not viewable* on TV in Paris or in New York; whether Baudrillard is interested in it or not, this difference—difference "within" the vast and multiple networks of television (see n. 5)—informs and helps determine the difference between the televised and the untelevised. Furthermore, by pushing his important insights into the productive capacities of "the media" as far as he does, Baudrillard *reduces* the increasing difficulty in distinguishing between image and world (e.g. televised news and event) to the absence of distinction (to the absence of difference, a metaphysical move *par excellence*). "The weather" (numbers, arrows, maps, satellite images, and other predictive indexes) may eclipse or merge with the weather sometimes, but it is not identical with it; this becomes most obvious when the weather turns out differently from the forecast provided by "the weather."

This world's surface is dotted with cities (and deserts and oilfields and oceans and farms and waste dump sites and rivers) and other developments (and places to watch TV)—not just with sound stages, oscillating images, and television-viewing couches. While they might not be "subjects" as the subject has come to be articulated in the last several hundred years, and although I necessarily hesitate to be more specific here, the occupants of these places are *people* (active television viewers, among other things!), not just actors. The hyperreality is—precisely—

in Baudrillard's theory. While not separate, the televised and the untelevised are different from each other. Different. By no means equivalent, certainly not interchangeable. Emphasizing this difference does not have to depend on granting one of these two terms some ultimate priority, because neither has priority. Both are productive, both inform, constitute, and determine each other.

Perhaps the point of this emphasis on the televised and the untelevised, then, is to affirm the limitations of dividing them and deciding between them, to affirm that the strategy of favoring the one over the other—positioning the one in the service of the other—misses the strength of their relation. By privileging Reality, traditional metaphysics underestimates the productive capacities of television, and misses its power as a generating and binding agent (Fiske and Hartley's "bardic mediator"), something more than and different from the mirror that will always remain restricted to a faithful or distortive reflection. And by privileging TV—the screen and network—Baudrillard loses the world, which has not become just a simulacrum. (As others have asked, is Baudrillard nostalgic for some mythical time when signs "really meant something"?) The traditional metaphysical route reduces differences to the reassuring clarity, distinctness, and predictability of what have become necessarily hierarchical, objectifying categories. Baudrillard's route seems to lead to *a denial of difference* altogether (and what could be more metaphysical than that?). Both lose the truth in the process.[35]

To repeat, the question of the relation between the televised and the untelevised is a philosophical question that cannot be ignored, even if and perhaps because it remains itself untelevised. Television is not a "communications" technology that presents itself as a *choice*, as just one more possible human activity, just another way of using or using up time. Whether *we choose* to view it or not, the TV is there and on, not just in the simple binary sense of on/off, but on in the sense that it continually in-forms (i.e. contributes to the formation of) the untelevised. Whether we choose it or not, the television (and the general technology of "communication" and "information") is here and here to stay, and we are the first generation to live with its indefinite but determinative and disturbing as well as vital, "informative," and fun (!) co-presence.[36]

We must continue to watch the relationship between the televised and the untelevised, and to keep sight of their differences, which (as Fiske, Hartley, Baudrillard, and many others have emphasized) are not the simple, polarized, metaphysical differences between appearance and Reality. The relation between the televised and the untelevised exceeds and upsets the domain governed by metaphysics, as this domain has always been upset (by the possibility of the relation between the televised and the untelevised). The difference between them remains unresolved, as always, and still turned on, on the air.

Chapter 12

POSTMODERNISM IN DANCE: DANCE, DISCOURSE, DEMOCRACY

David Michael Levin

Art fights reification by making the petrified world speak,
sing, perhaps dance. Forgetting past suffering and past joy
alleviates life under a repressive reality principle. In contrast, remembrance spurs the drive for the conquest of suffering and the permanence of joy.

—Herbert Marcuse[1]

To win the energies of intoxication for the revolution . . .
an ecstatic component lives in every revolutionary act. This
component is identical with the anarchic. But to place the
accent exclusively on it would be to subordinate the method-
ical and disciplinary preparation for revolution entirely to a
praxis oscillating between fitness exercises and celebration
in advance. . . . Nevertheless . . . after such dialectical anni-
hilation—this will still be a sphere of images and, more
concretely, of bodies. . . . Only when in technology body
and image so interpenetrate that all revolutionary tension
becomes bodily collective innervation, and all the bodily
innervations of the collective become revolutionary discharge, has reality transcended itself to the extent demanded by the *Communist Manifesto*. For the moment, only
the Surrealists have understood its present commands.

—Walter Benjamin[2]

. . . if art concerns itself with life, if philosophy seeks out
truth, and religion inquires into the meaning of God (or

what is the same, the meaning of God for us: salvation), then criticism, beginning with art as its object and by way of the mediation of philosophical insight, establishes the ultimate link with that realm with which mere life in its immediacy can have no contact: the realm of redeemed life. . . .

—Richard Wolin[3]

On a primary level, art is recollection: it appeals to a preconceptual experience and understanding which re-emerges in and against the context of the social functioning of experience and understanding—against instrumental reasoning and sensibility.

—Marcuse[4]

There is no limit to the capacity of immediate sensuous experience to absorb into itself meanings and values that, in and of themselves, . . . would be designated *ideal* and *spiritual*.

—John Dewey[5]

There is perhaps no better definition of culture than that it is the capacity for constantly expanding the range and accuracy of one's perception of meanings.

—Dewey[6]

. . . sense, as meaning so directly embodied in experience as its own illuminated meanings, is the only signification that expresses the function of sense organs when they are carried to full realization.

—Dewey[7]

Philosophy is not a particular body of knowledge; it is a vigilance which does not let us forget the source of all knowledge.

—Maurice Merleau-Ponty[8]

In 1968, at the moment when I first entered into the critical discourse on dance, I could find, much to my surprise, nothing at all corresponding to the movement which, in the critical discourse on painting and sculpture, was already being called "modernism." This realization provoked me to think—and eventually, after I had completed extensive research, to write. My first contribution to the discourse of the time was an essay on the work of George Balanchine.[9] In this essay, "Balanchine's formalism," I attempted to demonstrate that, in such works as *Agon* (1957), *Monumentum pro Gesualdo* (1960), *Violin Concerto* (1970), *Duo Concertant* (1970), and *Symphony in Three Movements* (1972), the historical significance of Balanchine's formalist, minimalist choreographic display emerges into visibility when interpreted in the light of "modernist" aesthetics.

Since the analysis of postmodernism in dance presupposes an understanding of the concept of modernism, I would like to begin the present study with a definition of "modernism." The definition I will suggest here is based on the clarification towards which I was moving in my essay on Balanchine.

Clear definitions of "modernism" and "postmodernism" are imperative here, because there is at the present time a confusion of interpretations: a situation in which the existence of essentially conflicting conceptions is further problematized by inadequate definitions, the same terms denoting different historical phases, and failures to recognize the points of difference. In fact, after having read the critical literature on "postmodernism," I think it would not be an exaggeration to speak of a "riot" of interpretations. Adding to this conceptual chaos, different authors take different normative and political stands: some, for example, condemn the postmodern aesthetic, having defined it, in effect, as "neoconservative," while others see in it a utopian, emancipatory potential, a celebration of democracy. There really is no way to define these aesthetic movements without in some sense taking sides. I do not want to claim objective neutrality for my interpretive definitions, as if I could somehow stand outside history-in-the-making and observe the procession of aesthetic movements with a universal consciousness.

So far as I can tell, on the basis of considerable research, there was no recognition of the modernist aesthetic in the critical discourse on dance prior to the publication of my study on Balanchine. But it was not long thereafter that this critical discourse "caught up" with the discourse on painting and sculpture and was giving a very lively reception to the modernist aesthetic, the modernist grammatology. Although the earlier critical discourse certainly could illuminate important elements in the Balanchine style, I would argue that *only* an interpretation in terms of the modernist aesthetic can adequately account for the revolutionary works in question.

What I introduced into the critical discourse on dance through my interpretation of Balanchine's choreographic innovations was basically the theory of modernism that I had found brilliantly articulated in the essays of Clement Greenberg and Michael Fried.[10] These essays, interpreting the paintings of Stella, Olitski, Noland, and Newman (among others), and the sculptural 'constructions' of David Smith, Donald Judd, and Robert Morris (among others), gradually formulated the principles of a compelling 'modernist' aesthetic. Moving in the direction suggested by their theoretical thinking, I defined this aesthetic—modernism—as a Kantian revolution. Thus, works of art exemplify the modernist aesthetic insofar as they instantiate the self-referential, self-reflective, rigorously transcendental turn, making present the conditions of possibility constitutive of their genre-being.

The Dutch masters—van Eyck, for example—already hinted at the possibility demonstrated later by modernist painting. Their strategic use of mirrors could certainly be said to inaugurate a self-referential moment, though of course the reference is (not yet) to the painting *as* painting. Velasquez pushed this strategy somewhat further. The painting represented "within" *Las Meninas*, for example, begins to function self-referentially in the modernist way, signifying the signifier. It is not until Manet's *Déjeuner sur l'herbe* and the *Olympia*, however, that we see paintings painted in self-conscious relation to earlier paintings and to texts on painting: paintings proclaiming their freedom, as well as their indebtedness, to what Foucault called "the archive." But, in modernist art, the defining conditions of the work finally become the sole *subject* of the presentation. Because of their essentially constitutive function, however, these conditions cannot be "made present" as the subject of traditional techniques of representation. They can only be made present indirectly or obliquely: brought to presence, demonstrated, in the objects that betray them, performing their disclosure and their eventual deconstruction. In modernist painting, the traditional frame, the canonical shape of the canvas, the flatness of the painted surface, the classical legibility of the brush stroke, and even the traditional painterly commitment to representationalism, a requirement of the correspondence theory of truth, are revealed—revealed *as* the traditional essence of the art—and implicitly called into question. In the elegant steel constructions of David Smith, the modernist aesthetic took hold by revealing the fact, through its refusal to obey the prevailing principle of closed sculptural volume, that the enclosure of sculpted, shaped volume has been absolutely crucial in the historical definition of that art.[11]

In literature, the modernist aesthetic is at work, though in different ways, in the shaped poetry of Apollinaire, the grammatical anarchies of Mallarmé, the paradoxical stories-within-stories crafted by Borges, and the later novels—*Ulysses* and *Finnegans Wake*—of Joyce. It is also at work, as I have argued at length in "The Novelhood of the Novel," in the peculiarly self-reductive surfaces of Vladimir Nabokov's shimmering prose.[12] But this modernist aesthetic was already foreshadowed much earlier by the narrative strategies operative in Sterne's *Tristram Shandy*, self-referential, but not yet thoroughly self-reflective in relation to its essence, and in Flaubert's *The Temptation of Saint Anthony*, the first literary work whose exclusive subject is books and the reading of books.

In theater, I see the modernist aesthetic in the productions of the late 1960s and early 1970s, in New York, of Richard Foreman's work. Foreman's performance space was articulated by the use of strings connecting props with other props, objects with stage settings, and floor areas with performance spaces, disclosing the spectatorial epistemology—viewing angles, privileged positions, significant relationships—it presupposed.

Works of art in the modernist aesthetic *make explicit* the constitutive conditions of possibility, the perceptual and ontological commitments, that *have been* definitive for their historical kind— dance, painting, sculpture, theater, music, the novel; but they do so in a mode of disclosure that is self-reflective and self-referential *without* being strictly representational: the conditions are displayed in the play of their deconstruction. Such works of art implicitly *call into question* their traditionally definitive conditions, but they do so in nontraditional ways: indirectly and without representation, by *being* the deconstruction which calls attention to those very conditions it is subverting. Modernist works of art defy the classical law of identity: they are what they are not and are not what they are. They structurally *instance* the implicit possibilities of being-different that have been inherited with the traditional forms and kinds. Modernist works of art are therefore implicitly subversive, not "innovative" or "original" in the traditional way—the way, for example, that Mozart or Beethoven were in music, Bournonville in dance, Fielding and Flaubert in the novel, and Shakespeare in theater.

These men unquestionably changed the prevailing conventions. But neither the changes they wrought nor the historical conventions they were in the process of challenging constituted, as such, i.e., as historical essences to be examined, the sole "subject matter," the only "substance," of their art. In modernist art, however, the "substance" of the work, what used to be called the "content," has become an implicitly subversive process of self-reflection and self-disclosure, a process in which the historical essence of the art is instanced and displayed, revealed by an "object" which plays with the functioning of its defining conditions. The artwork as aesthetic object, the artwork in its aesthetically constituted objecthood, becomes the "subject" of the work. The "subject" is thus the work of art *as* the constituted "object" or "matter" of aesthetic experience.

The structure of the modernist work is rigorously determined by, and consequently simply *is*, its self-reflective self-disclosure, the display, or performance, of the epistemic and ontological conditions that have ruled over its (contingent) historical essence. In brief, then, the modernist work of art is an object explicitly created to disclose the workings and unfolding logic of its historical essence. And it is the process of this disclosure, together with the conditions necessary for its performance, which structure the modernist work. As I have argued elsewhere, the modernist work of art *performs* what it is and *is* this performance.

If the above account suggestively interprets the modernist work, and the aesthetic of modernism, what is postmodernism? Before we can begin to reflect on "postmodernism" in relation to dance, we need a shared understanding—a clear understanding—of the terms we will be using in our critical discourse. At this point, therefore, I would like to introduce some conceptual clarity into the prevailing nomenclatural chaos. The interpretive power of the schema may not be immediately apparent; but I trust that, as we proceed, its usefulness will become increasingly evident.

If we think historiographically about our terminology, it makes sense to construe -*ism* and -*ist* as endings which make the "modernist" works of "modernism" a metanarrative, a style or genre or category of art *following* the modern in historical time and commenting in some way on it, rather than understand them as forming words that *describe* the modern. Keeping to this same strategy, we should also give the prefix *post-* its due, construing "postmodern" to designate what *follows* the modern: all the genuinely innovative works of art, together with their aesthetic, which come *after* the modern, the works and aesthetic of "modernity." We will, then, let the ending -*ist* mean what to the ear of my grammatical sense it wants to mean, and construe the term "postmodernist," together with the term "postmodernism," to refer specifically, and more narrowly, to the innovative artworks and aesthetic which come after, and contribute a commentary (metanarrative) on, distinctively modernist works and the aesthetic of "modernism." In other words, "postmodernist" and "postmodernism" will designate only those innovative works, together with their aesthetic, which come after (*post*), and comment on, the (modernist) works and the (modernist) aesthetic that followed, and commented on, the art and aesthetic we are calling "modern."

What I am suggesting, then, is that "postmodernism" may be divided into *two* distinct phases, both coming after (*post*) the modern, and that "modernism," the aesthetic of "modernist" art, be assigned to its *first* phase. The schema we will be using accordingly organizes the history of art into three major periods: (i) a traditional period, i.e., art through the middle of the nineteenth century, (ii) a "modern" *avant-garde* period, i.e., art from the mid-nineteenth century almost to the middle of the 1960s; and (iii) a "post-modern" period, i.e., art from the mid-1960s up to the present. The "post-modern" period needs to be divided, however, into two distinct phases: (a) a "modern-*ist*" period, "modernism," extending from the early 1960s through the 1970s, in which the still-traditional essence of the "modern" work was brought to appearance in self-reflective structures of self-disclosure, and (b) a "post-modernist" phase, "postmodernism," beginning in the 1980s, in which the residual essence of the "modern" work, initially explored by the modernists, is finally being exploded, radically called into question, explicitly and overtly challenged, deconstructed. Among the different arts, of course, these historical periods begin and end with slightly different dates. The above schema, making no claims to be the only possible, or even the only useful interpretation, should be productive as a general historiographic guide.

I will argue that later, in what I will call the *second* phase of the postmodern aesthetic, the inherently critical, implicitly subversive character of the modernist disclosure (the modernist performance of the historical essence) becomes increasingly more pronounced, more overt, and more radically deconstructive: whereas, in the "modernist" art of the *first* phase, a performative disclosing of the traditional essence is primary, it seems that, in the *second* phase of the postmodern movement, i.e., in "postmodernist" art, the disclosing becomes *explicitly* deconstructive. In other words, the structure of the disclosive process becomes *overtly* deconstructive; it becomes a performance of the traditional conditions, which appear as constitutive of the work's essence (as dance, theater, novel, painting, sculpture, music), and displays them in the process of their deconstruction. Thus, in the *first* phase of postmodernism, the phase belonging to the "modernist" work, the critical function is strictly immanent and transcendental, taking place *within*, and more or less reaffirming, the hegemony of the prevailing practices and cultural institutions; but, in the *second* phase, the "postmodernist" work, the critical function becomes more radical, increasingly calling into question the supporting institutions themselves.

In a recently published book called *Has Modernism Failed?*, Suzi Gablik holds that "modernism" is "the term that has been used to describe the art and culture of the past hundred years."[13] Considered as a historical account, I think this is needlessly inaccurate; moreover, considered as a nomenclatural recommendation, I think it is unwise. In the scheme I am proposing, the "modern" and the "modernist" are profoundly different and must be distinguished. And since "modernism" is a term that goes together with the art called "modernist," I would urge that "modernity" be associated with the art called "modern."

In his book on Walter Benjamin, Richard Wolin says: "The fact that [Baudelaire] consciously incorporated the often grotesque images of mid-nineteenth century city life into his poetry qualifies him as the first 'modernist,' the first true poet of urbanism."[14] Baudelaire's "modernism" consists, for Wolin, in the fact that he "attempted to destroy from within the affirmative values of bourgeois aestheticism" and "to incorporate the contingencies of everyday life into the hitherto sacred preserve of autonomous art"—an approach, he argues, "which would henceforth become paradigmatic for the entirety of modernism." Wolin's choice of terminology is unfortunate. Baudelaire precipitated the *end* of modernity; he was one of the first to revolt against the modern aesthetic. His revolt began the *avant-garde* movement that eventually turned modernist. For Wolin, "modernism" is a term that denotes what I would call the modern *avant garde*, the last phase in the art and aesthetic of modernity; cubism, expressionism, and surrealism, the "de-aestheticized" art, *l'art engagé*, that followed, in a dialectical opposition, the earlier aesthetic of *l'art pour l'art*, art encapsulated in an "aura" of spiritualized cultural value, esoteric, accessible only to the privileged few, the collectors, critics, and artists themselves.

For Wolin, "modernism" refers above all to the shocking works of such artists as Breton, Aragon, and Baudelaire, and to the epic theater of Brecht. As an art and an aesthetic, it repudiates the "aura" of naturalism, the illusions of traditional art, although we may infer from his exemplars that "modernism" is not antagonistic to representationalism as such. Wolin does not consider any works of dance; nor does he define very precisely the denotative class of his category. Is Manet's *Déjeuner sur l'herbe* a "modernist" painting? He offers no evidence that would exclude from his category the danceworks of Duncan, Graham, and Humphrey, or even the later productions of Diaghilev, in which the marvelous Nijinsky danced. The problem with Wolin's narrative, though, is that it cannot differentiate the works of this modern *avant garde* from the works of a later period, in which there is a structural self-disclosure that calls attention to the continuing authority of the traditional essence in the structure of "modern" art. Nor can his narrative take into account the "postmodernist" art and aesthetic that have radicalized the process of self-disclosure and turned it into a process of deconstruction, making objects whose principal structure *is* the performance of this deconstruction.

The concept of "modernism" at work in Wolin's thinking was derived from the aesthetic theories which originated in the critical analyses of the Frankfurt School philosophers: in particular, Adorno, Horkheimer, Benjamin, and Marcuse.[15] For all these thinkers, "modernism" designated an art and an aesthetic in revolt against *l'art pour l'art*: the esoteric art of pure formalism, narcissistically self-contained, arrogantly autonomous, and politically disengaged, protecting itself from the realities of social life by its creation of what Benjamin called an "aura." Jürgen Habermas has unfortunately continued to make use of the Frankfurt School nomenclature in his own contributions to the critical discourse on art.[16]

The nomenclature I am proposing also diverges, then, from the many interpretations that fail to articulate the two distinct phases of "postmodernism," i.e., the "modernist," which is critical of the tradition of *modern* art, and the "postmodernist", which is critical of the *modernist continuation* of essentialism. These other interpretations see only a "modern" period, culminating in such *avant garde* movements as cubism, dada, and surrealism, and followed by a "postmodern" period, supposed to begin in the 1950s or 1960s. Since such interpretations do not see the logic of phases and transitions that I have noted in the historical unfolding of the "postmodern" period, they often add to the confusion by using the terms "modernist" and "modernism" to describe all the art of modernity, all the art of the modern period. This adds to the confusion, because it appropriates a term first introduced into the critical discourse by Greenberg and then uses it in a sense that directly contradicts its very precise original signification. It seems to me that Greenberg's lucid sense of this term, a sense that Fried later assumed in his own equally definitive studies, should now be taken as paradigmatic for subsequent discourse.

The terminological problems to which I appeal are not semantic niceties we can disregard without penalty, and sweeping them aside with a gesture of impatience will not make them disappear. Let us then continue the task of clarifying and defining the principal concepts in our discourse. The more successful we are in this task, the more perceptive we will be in interpreting the dance of our time.

In her new Preface to the forthcoming, revised second edition of *Terpsichore in Sneakers*, Sally Banes proposes a nomenclatural schema for dance in which the "modernist" and "postmodernist" aesthetics are clearly differentiated from one another and both set apart from the modern tradition and the *avant-garde* revolt that tradition generated in the late nineteenth-century. She is the only critical theorist writing on dance today who has clearly perceived and understood these phases. And although her contributions to the critical historiography of dance are extremely important, she nevertheless refrains from introducing into her schema a terminology that would mark the differentiations she has recognized and so carefully spelled out by reference to specific dance works.

In the terminology of her schema, "postmodern" dance began with an "analytic" phase, ruled by an aesthetic emphasizing reduction, minimalism, and formalism, and abolishing the expression of meaning in order to reveal the essential structure of the art. This phase has been followed, however, by a new phase—a "metaphoric" phase, she calls it—in which there has been a "return" to meaning, a "retrieval" of meaning. As she says, in the beautifully lucid new Preface,

> The current generation of post-modern choreographers
> (and the current work of the older generation) reopens
> some of the issues that concerned historical modern dance.
> Thus it seems to depart from the concerns of its immediate
> predecessors [i.e., the modernists]. But it would be
> ahistorical to call the current generation "modern
> dance.". . . The views and practices of the current
> generation are not simply a return to an older style or
> method. They build on and, in their turn, depart from the
> redefinitions and analyses, as well as the techniques and
> anti-techniques, of the post-modern inquiry into the nature
> and function of dance. The shift is an obvious reaction by
> the new generation of choreographers to the concerns of
> their elders; by the end of the 1970s, the clarity and
> simplicity of analytic post-modern dance has served its
> purpose and threatened to become so short of meaning

(other than reflexive) that for a younger generation of choreographers and spectators it was beginning to be regarded as almost meaningless. The response was to look for ways to reinstall meaning in dance.[17]

In modernist art, the *first phase* of postmodernism, we see that the disclosure of essence required a reduction: the work had to be reduced to its absolutely necessary elements and conditions. The modernist aesthetic is therefore, in a certain sense, methodologically committed to the achievement of minimalism. In modernist dance, there is an unwavering attention to the nature of the movement as such, movement pure and simple. The "meaningfulness" that infused earlier forms of dance—not only the illusions, the representational "meaningfulness" of traditional, classical ballets, but also the symbolic "meaningfulness" of the modern, avant-garde expressionist dances of Isadora Duncan, Martha Graham, and Doris Humphrey—must be totally excluded. In the modernist dance of Merce Cunningham, George Balanchine, Yvonne Rainer, Trisha Brown, Steve Paxton, Laura Dean, Meredith Monk, and Lucinda Childs, the traditional ideals of accurate representation and aesthetic illusion are strictly suspended, making way for disclosive explorations of the 'more basic' questions: "What is dance?" "Where, when, and how is it (to be) performed?" and "Who should perform it?" Modernist dance avoids making character dances and dances with narrative structures: dances such as Bournonville produced in Kierkegaard's Copenhagen, and Frederick Ashton's *Enigma Variations*, created for the renewal of the English Royal Ballet's traditional repertory. Character, narrative, representation, and expressionism were all sacrificed, in order to display performatively the essentials, the basic syntax, of the art: postures, positions, attitudes, steps, glides, leaps, gestures, turns, twists, shifts in weight, balance and imbalance, weight and weightlessness, the vertical and horizontal axes, the constitution of time through rhythm and pacing, the shaping of space through movement. Instead of showing meaning, modernist dance showed the *birth* of meaning: the existence of meaning already immanent in the very presence of the moving body as such.

Now, in the *second* phase of postmodernism, meaning has been reintroduced into dance. Now, it is no longer captive to essentialisms, transcendentalisms, historicisms of genre and style, cultural imperialisms, and the exclusionary principles of traditional bourgeois society—principles dictating matters of gender, race, and class. Since the modernist negation of meaning succeeded in releasing it from these historically arbitrary conditions, it could now be reintroduced without foreclosing creative explorations of the potential, the resources, newly disclosed by the preceding modernist reduction. The performative presence of meaning *after*, and in the *light* of, the modernist questioning of meaning is entirely different from the presence of meaning *before*, when meaningfulness was taken for granted and worked, therefore, dogmatically.

Aware of the terminological problems I have been addressing in this essay, Banes observes that,

> In dance, the confusion the term *post-modern* creates is further complicated by the fact that historical modern dance was never really *modernist*. Often it has been precisely in the arena of postmodern dance that issues of modernism in the other arts have arisen: the acknowledgement of the medium's materials, the revealing of dance's essential qualities as an art form, the separation of formal elements, the abstraction of forms, and the elimination of external references as subjects. Thus, in many respects it is *post-modern* dance that functions as *modernist* art. That is, post-modern dance came *after* modern dance (hence it is post-), and was, like the post-modernism of the other arts, an anti-modern dance. But since *modern* in dance did not mean "modernist," to be anti-modern dance was not at all to be anti-modernist. In fact, quite the opposite. The analytic post-modern dance of the Seventies in particular displayed these modernist preoccupations, and it aligned itself with that consummately modernist visual art, minimalist sculpture. And yet, there are also aspects of post-modern dance that do fit with the [second-phase] post-modernist notions (in the other arts) of pastiche, irony, playfulness, historical reference, the use of vernacular materials, the continuity of cultures, an interest in process over product, breakdowns of boundaries between art forms and between art and life, and new relationships between artist and audience.[18]

Banes summarizes very accurately, here, the major elements in the aesthetic of the second period of postmodern dance. Noting that "Some of the new directions of dance in the 1980s are even more closely allied to the concerns and techniques, especially that of pastiche, of [second-phase] postmodernism in the other arts," she argues:

> But if we were to call Sixties and Seventies post-modern dance *post-modern* and dub Eighties new dance *post-modernist*, the confusion would probably not be worth the scrupulous accuracy. Further, . . . I believe that the avant-garde dances of all three decades [i.e., the Sixties, the Seventies and the Eighties] are united and can be embraced by a single term. And I continue to recommend the term *post-modern.*[19]

I concur that the art and aesthetic of the last three decades exhibit a coherence that may be recognized by using the term "post-modern." And I also agree that the postmodern should be divided into two phases: in her terminology, the "analytic" and the "metaphoric." But I do not agree that we can avoid confusion by avoiding the terminology that Greenberg introduced for the analysis of painting and sculpture, for it was this terminology which inaugurated the critical discourse into which dance criticism and historiography only very recently chose to enter.

There is a reason for using the term "modernist" to designate the "analytical" dance of the first postmodern phase, i.e., the dance of the sixties and seventies. The reason is that the art of this period was committed to an aesthetic defined by its concern to reflect upon, and bring to disclosure, the essence of the traditional style—an essence that persisted in modern dance until the "avant-garde" revolt in the choreographic equivalents of cubism, dada, and surrealism. *A fortiori*, there is good reason to use the term "postmodernist" to designate the *second phase* of postmodern dance, because, in this second period, with a style of dance which Banes characterizes as "metaphoric," dance *breaks away* from the modernist aesthetic: it is not totally new, appearing *ex nihilo*, but defines itself in *dialectical* opposition to the modernist aesthetic, radically deconstructing the essential structures and conditions the functioning of which modernism was satisfied merely to disclose. Thus, in its second phase, postmodern dance could "return" to dances with meaning. But, as Banes notes, this return is not a return to the old modern; rather, it signifies a radicalization, or extension, of the modernist critique: a deconstruction of the meaning/no meaning difference, the binary logic, accepted and perpetuated in the modernist aesthetic.

The terminology for which I have been arguing has the advantage that it generates a nomenclatural schematism that enables us to see at a glance the dialectical relationships which constitute the immanent critical historiography of the dance. We can see at a glance that each aesthetic moment constitutes itself as a critical commentary on the preceding aesthetic moment. Thus, the modernist (modernism) is a disclosure of the essence of the modern (modernity), and the postmodernist is a critical deconstruction of the essence still at work in the modernist.

Sally Banes is particularly helpful in formulating the aesthetic implicit in the second phase of the postmodern period. Let me quote again from her new Preface:

> Where analytic post-modern dance [i.e., modernist dance] is exclusive of such elements [as images, the use of texts, stage settings and allusions to earlier historical styles], metaphoric post-modern dance [i.e., the second, or postmodernist phase of post-modern dance] is inclusive of theatrical elements of all kinds, such as costume, lighting, music, props, character, and mood. In this way, and in its making of expressive metaphors and representations, this strand of avant-garde dance resembles historical modern dance. But it also differs from historical modern dance in such important, basic ways that it seems more useful to include it as another category of post-modern dance than to consider it modern dance. These dances draw on post-modern processes and techniques. The key post-modern choreographic technique is radical juxtaposition. But also, these dances often use ordinary movements and objects; they propose new relationships between performer and spectator; articulate new experiences of space, time, and the body; incorporate language and film; [and] employ structures of stillness and repetition.[20]

And she concludes this description with a point to which I will return in discussing the political significance of postmodern

| Modern Dance | | Postmodern Dance | |
Traditional	Avant-Garde	Modernist	Postmodernist
Swan Lake	Duncan	Balanchine	Twyla Tharp
Les Sylphides	Humphreys	(*Agon, Apollo,*	Robert Wilson
The Nutcracker	Graham	*Duo Concertante*)	recent Rainer
Romeo and Juliet	Margaret Gage	Cunningham	Jim Self
Bournonville	Mary Wigman	early Rainer	David Gordon
Coppelia	Elizabeth Selden	recent Robbins	Kenneth King
Sleeping Beauty	Diaghilev/	Trisha Brown	Lucinda Childs
Giselle	Nijinsky	Steve Paxton	Trisha Brown
Enigma	Kurt Jooss	Laura Dean	Marta Renzi
Variations	Fred Astair	Meredith Monk	Gail Conrad
	Joffrey	Lucinda Childs	Karole Armitage
	Taylor		Remy Charlip
	Nikolais		Douglas Dunn
	Jerome Robbins		Simone Forti
	(*Fancy Free*)		Laura Dean
	Antony Tudor		Andy deGroat
	(*Jardin aux*		recent Joffrey
	lilas)		recent Nikolais
			"Men Together"
			(a gay dance
			festival)
			Saturday Night
			Fever
			Fame
			Break-dancing
			Dancing for the
			top hits video

dance and its aesthetic: "Metaphoric post-modern dance also counts as post-modern because it participates in the distribution system—the lofts, galleries, and other venues—that has become the arena for post-modern dance."[21] Defending her schematism, Banes contends that,

> Since 1978 or so, avant-garde dance has taken a number of new directions. Some of these directions stand apparently in direct opposition to the values of analytic post-modern dance [i.e., "modernist" dance], making the very use of the term *post-modern* problematic for current dancing. Perhaps we should reserve the term for use only in reference to the analytic mode of the 1970s, just as the strictest definition of

"modern dance" restricts us to the late 1920s through the 1950s. Then the breakaway choreographers of the 60s could be called the *forerunners* of post-modern dance, just as Isadora Duncan, Loie Fuller, and Ruth St. Denis are sometimes called the forerunners of modern dance. And the new dance of the 1980s could be called post-modern*ist*. But . . . I want to argue for an inclusive use of the term *post-modern*, one that applies to the breakaway dances of the 60s, the analytic and metaphoric dances of the 70s, and the new dances of the 80s, because all these currents are related, in large part because they set themselves apart from mainstream theatrical dance in ways that are not simply chronological.[22]

I want to argue that the schematism proposed in this chapter achieves the inclusiveness and integration Banes justifiably requires—but without sacrificing the historiographic power of a terminology which clearly reflects the immanent logic, the dialectical relationships, constitutive of the different periods in an ever-changing dance aesthetic.

In the first phase of postmodernism, the "modernist," the structural essentialism of the tradition that modernity continued to accept and legitimate was brought to light, made visible. This visibility, however, implicitly inaugurated the first stage of a critical challenge. Calling attention to something unconsciously accepted and continued already marks it for change. As Sartre pointed out in *Being and Nothingness*, consciousness is inherently critical: to know is to be separate from, to negate a hitherto unrecognized influence. Thus, the transcendental critique of the modernist work made possible the more radical critique, the deconstructive critique, effectuated by works in the second, post-modernist phase.

According to Stephen Toulmin, it was Frederick Ferré who introduced the term "postmodern science" into the philosophical discourse on the sciences, using it to designate scientific practices associated with a philosophical position not entangled in the modern dogmas of positivism, empiricism, realism, and transcendental idealism.[23] If it be reasonable to regard Jacques Derrida, Richard Rorty, Michel Foucault, and Paul Feyerabend as pre-eminently postmodernist thinkers, then, by extrapolation, we may perhaps approximate an equivalent of the philosophical movement in the second phase of the postmodern aesthetic.

Postmodern philosophy is a "family" of deconstructive strategies, questions, and suspicions, instigating playful provocations that subvert our prevailing logocentrism, a cognitivism which excludes all feeling. Postmodern philosophies subvert both realism and idealism; subvert both positivism and metaphysical speculation; subvert the quest for origins and absolute certainty and programs of foundationalism; subvert privileged standpoints and viewpoints; subvert hierarchies; subvert universalism in accounts of method, evidence, norms, and ideals; subvert totalisms; subvert essentialism; subvert the traditional models of objectivity; and subvert all schools of thought which proclaim the primacy or self-evidence of subjectivity. Indeed, they question all the traditional binary oppositions, insofar as they constitute fixed, independent, reciprocally exclusive positions: presence/ absence, subject/object, mind/body, self/other, individual/society, nature/culture, inside/outside, action/inaction, backwards/ forwards, regression/progress, science/ideology, reason/madness, observer/observed, form/content, structure/process, sameness/difference.

Postmodern thinking embraces relativities, conflicts, and competitions in interpretation, ruptures and discontinuities, the proliferation of differences, multiplicities, ambiguities, complexities; it acknowledges contingencies and accidents; it accepts the unfinished, the open, the fragmentary, the aleatory; it appreciates spontaneity, gives ready attention to the local, the regional, the specific, the unique; and it recognizes the existence of microprocesses.

In its second phase, postmodernist dance, like postmodernist art in general, has returned, in a sense, to the aesthetic of the modern *avant garde* which prevailed in the years *prior* to modernism—prior, that is, to the first phase of the postmodern period; because it, too, attempts to "incorporate the contingencies of everyday life into the sacred preserve of autonomous art." (These words, quoted earlier, are Wolin's, and refer, in his book on Benjamin, to Baudelaire.) In its second phase, now happening, postmodern dance rejects the introverted formalism, the "autonomy," of its earlier, modernist phase; it embodies an aesthetic which radically deconstructs the structural oppositions assumed or reinforced by the disciplinary reductions and restrictions of the modernist aesthetic. Whereas the modernist aesthetic ultimately continued essentialism, the postmodernist rejected it. Whereas the modernist aesthetic embraced formalism and strictly excluded all content, the expression of meaning, the postmodernist proclaims itself open to meaning. Whereas the modernist aesthetic required an introverted autonomy, the postmodernist aesthetic "incorporates the contingencies of everyday life."

The modernist aesthetic ultimately retained the binary logic of subject/object, observer/observed, and inside/outside, despite the fact that it also began to problematize such oppositions. In the danceworks that embody the postmodernist aesthetic, the structures constituted by this logic are deconstructed: costumes, sets, props, and all the elements of theatricality are reintroduced; nothing is essentially, necessarily excluded. The various media are mixed together; styles and genres are mixed together; written texts, speech, graffiti may be given a critical interpretive function; idioms of the vernacular, elements taken from mass culture, are not automatically excluded on the basis of an aesthetic which opposes high and low culture.

In some works, there is no pre-established, predetermined groundplan, no already fixed choreography. There may even be no ultimate choreographic authority, an ultimately responsible Master Choreographer, originating and orchestrating every gesture and movement like an absolute sovereign or god. There will be no privileged standpoint or viewpoint for experiencing and interpreting the work; nor will there necessarily be any fixed, clear and distinct, or absolutely certain boundary-line, separating the "spectator" from the "dancer" in the space of the performance. The "dancers" may at times be motionless, inert, object-like, incarnating and performing the deconstruction of a binary logic which opposes motion to rest, activity to inertia, life to objecthood, and assigns normative priority to one of these conditions. And there may be everyday movements, like walking and running; there may be references to life outside the spectacle, outside the theater, outside the work of dance, for the worlds of politics and dance are both different and the same. Indeed, the dancework may take itself *outside* the traditional places and spaces conventionally reserved for it: it may, for example, take to the streets. The dance is potentially as capable as theater and painting of communicating new representations of social reality.

One of the most exciting manifestations of the vitality of (second-phase) postmodern dance today is to be seen in the phenomenal legitimation and spread of break-dancing. (See the 1985 publication called *Fresh, hip hop don't stop*.)[24] Break-dancing originated in the Bronx, Brooklyn, and Manhattan—in the street-culture of the Black and Hispanic ghettoes. It was originally a stylized, ritualized form of aggressive male display, a way for the teenage boys in rival street gangs to show off their physical skill and acrobatic prowess. Being a form of competition, break-dancing was a combination of sport and fight, adjudicating male rivalries. Gradually, however, as it became more popular, more stylized, and more ritualized, it began to assume some of the qualities we associate with improvisatory virtuoso dancing. Eventually, it was "discovered" by the white mass media, and some of the most talented b-boys were catapulted, like some of the graffiti artists who ornamented the New York subways, into the stardom, the fame and fortune, of the showbiz world.

In "Postmodernism, or The Cultural Logic of Late Capitalism," Frederic Jameson asserts that "postmodern culture is the internal and superstructural expression of a whole new wave of American military and economic domination throughout the world. . . ."[25] This sweeping condemnation of postmodernism, of its art and its aesthetic, seems to be shared by Hal Foster in his book, *Recodings*,[26] and by Habermas, for example, in his essay on "Modernity versus Postmodernity,"[27] in the chapter on "Neoconservative Culture Criticism in the United States and West Germany"[28] and in "Questions and Counterquestions," a reply to critics published in Richard Bernstein's anthology, *Habermas and Modernity*.[29] Is postmodern art inherently reactionary? Is it necessarily neoconservative? Or can it serve a more progressive, emancipatory function, channeling critical social analysis or retrieving a utopian potential implicit within prevailing social conditions? Is it inevitable that postmodern dance be an instrument of political conservatism? Or is there a possibility, in dance, of a redeeming political significance?

Answers to such questions are dependent on the way the principal terms are understood. I will answer them in relation to the definitions I have spelled out earlier in this essay. In the first phase of postmodernism, the phase of "modernist" art, an aesthetic of strict formalism ruled: works of art turned self-reflective, introverted; they were exclusively concerned with the disclosure of their own essential structures of possibility. Like the traditional works of art of modernity *prior* to the *avant-garde* revolt (surrealism, dada, cubism, expressionism), and for some of the same reasons, modernist art detached itself from the concerns of everyday life; in the modernist phase of postmodernism, formalist, *essentialist* preoccupations required the isolation of art: separation of art from its world, art made self-referential. In the second phase, however—the phase we are now living—the structural boundaries that separated an esoteric art from social life have been radically deconstructed, and the independence, the indifference or neutrality of the realm of art discontinued. An aesthetic of *l'art pour l'art* not altogether unlike the aesthetic against which the *art engagé* of the modern *avant garde* rebelled has been replaced, once again, by an aesthetic of engagement.

Of course, as Wolin observes in his book on Benjamin, a "mobilization of aesthetic powers alone" cannot transform the world.[30] Moreover, the reintegration of art into everyday life constitutes a complex, ambiguous situation. As Wolin argues very cogently, echoing the analysis Habermas outlines in *Legitimation Crisis*,

> as history has demonstrated only too brutally in recent times, the political instrumentalization of the aesthetic faculty has deprived many "successful" revolutions of a vital source of self-knowledge. . . . The distance between art and life must be preserved. . . . In truth, once art and politics become fused . . . art threatens to become a matter of indifference.[31]

In this regard, Peter Bürger contends that works of art are inevitably caught within a dilemma: they can be critical of society only if they are free of its ideology; but, to the extent that they are autonomous, are independent, are also too detached, too isolated, too marginal to assume a critical function.[32] Abstractly considered, the impossibility of overcoming this dilemma does seem compelling. It is certainly true that total fusion, a complete absorption in every day life, would make it virtually impossible for art to function in a critical way. Insofar as postmodern art has gone too far in this direction, it has become commodified, fetishized, reduced to an object of capital investment and capital legitimation. And yet it is equally true, surely, that total detachment, the position of art produced during the hegemony of the *l'art pour l'art* aesthetic of the nineteenth century, encourages art to cultivate an arrogant indifference to the sufferings and needs of social life. By itself, moreover, social marginality does not ensure that art will assume a critical, effectively subversive function. Nor does a political solution worked out exclusively in aesthetic terms necessarily contribute to the critical transformation of political institutions.

In *Legitimation Crisis*, Habermas continues the critical discourse on art which Benjamin set in motion, particularly through his analysis of surrealism and his historiography of the "postauratic" revolution in "The Work of Art in the Age of Mechanical Reproduction."[33] Habermas concedes that the surrealist revolt against aestheticism—formalism, art with an "aura" that separated it from the profane world—was well-intentioned; but he points out that the surrealist attempt to put art back into everyday life failed to effectuate any significant changes in the structures of social life and the institutions of political power. Thus he warns against the two related dangers in such visions of integration; one is that art can become instrumentalized as propaganda; the other is that art can become thoroughly commercialized, accommodating, and ultimately legitimating the dominant political economy.

I would argue that both excessive independence (distance from life) and excessive integration (absorption in life) can encourage art to function as an "aesthetic consolation" rather than as critique or redemption. Art must exist in a situation where it can function freely in a responsive, dialectical mediation. It must be marginal enough to preserve its integrity, but close enough to avoid the kind of self-referentiality, self-absorption, and self-containedness that eventuates in an arrogant indifference to the world around it. Even when art is not *directly* critical or subversive, it *can* be genuinely redeeming. We do not have to choose between art that proposes a critique of ideology—Theodor Adorno's theory—and art that serves to redeem existential meaning—Walter Benjamin's theory.

The dilemmas of total independence and total integration—the dangers of aestheticism and commodification—require that we *distinguish* the modernist and postmodernist phases in postmodern art. The distinction for which I have been arguing is crucial and imperative here, because modernist art *is* "introverted" and marginal, whereas postmodernist art, performing the deconstruction of "inside" and "outside," is much more open to the world of its other. We will not get past these dilemmas and the problems they present until we have clarified *which* phase we are considering, for each of the phases constitutes a different problematic. The first generates the problem of indifference; the second generates the problem of commodification. Unfortunately, neither Wolin nor Habermas make the necessary historiographic differentiation.

In his essays on art, Benjamin articulated an aesthetic of redemption: an aesthetic committed to retrieving a forgotten or suppressed emancipatory potential. Adorno, however, argued for an anesthetic fulfilled in the critique of ideology. Must these aesthetics exclude one another? Can an art, can dance, be diagnostic and critical, but also utopian and emancipatory, communicating images of transcendence, images that redeem and transform social life?

I am going to answer the second question in the affirmative and indicate very briefly what can be said in support of this position. But I want to emphasize at the outset that I see most of the events in postmodern dance today—including the phenomenon of break-dancing—being turned very easily and very quickly into commodities, capital fetishes: new historical manifestations of an old reactionary aestheticism.[34] Thus, at the same time that I see in the events of postmodernist dance a certain emancipatory potential, and to this extent disagree with the analyses expounded by Habermas, Wolin, Hal Foster and others, I also see cultural conditions that make it difficult for even the most creative, most politically subtle choreographers, dancers, and danceworks *not* to be appropriated by "neoconservative" forces.

According to a schema proposed by Habermas, our postmodern world has been sectored into three often antagonistic spheres of life: a sphere that is primarily "expressive," "aesthetic," and "mimetic"; a sphere dominated by cognitive-instrumental rationality; and a sphere of life committed to moral-practical rationality. Habermas argues that the character of life *within* these three spheres needs to change. He also argues that these spheres of life need to be integrated and differently co-ordinated, so that they will constitute a just and fulfilling society. Thus, for him, the "progressive" or "emancipatory" character of an action (event) must be interpreted by considering whether or not, and in what way, these spheres of life are integrated, brought into balance, and transformed. But, although Habermas never turns his thought to dance, it can be argued that in many of the events announcing the second phase of postmodern dance, there is an explicitly acknowledged and explicitly deployed potential for the performative integration of these three spheres; and, in this process, a potential also for contesting the hegemony, the violence, of cognitive-instrumental rationality—the claim of technocratic reason to represent and express the *whole* of life's meaning and value. Dance can also articulate and celebrate necessary aesthetic relationships to nature, society, and individual experience; and it can express and interpret our present historical needs and collective dreams. It can even contribute to the attempt "to test the limits of the realizability of the utopian contents of cultural tradition."[35] However, I must reiterate the point which Habermas makes in *Legitimation Crisis*, viz., that works of art cannot effectively contribute to emancipatory or utopian projects unless they take part in, and contribute to, the *integration* of the three spheres of social life. Beautiful and edifying reconciliations—between art and life, science and culture, individual and society, democracy and class hierarchies, happiness and utilitarian rationality, war and peace—cannot take place only within the time and space of the performance, without tacitly legitimating the existence of unreconciled life.

Perhaps critique is never enough; perhaps it must always strive to be redemptive, if it is not going to surrender to despair or render itself ineffective. But how can dance be critical, how redemptive, without betraying itself as art? How can it be subversive or utopian, without becoming propaganda, a mere instrument for political action?

Foucault sites microprocesses of power in the human body. For him, the body is a crucial site for the application of power. For this reason, he would like to see it as the agent of resistance. And yet, the body he sees is "a body totally imprinted by history."[36] Is there nothing in our experience of embodiment to contradict what he calls "the process of history's destruction of the body?"[37] Why could the dancing body not constitute itself as a *challenge* to the ideology of the passive, docile, subjugated body and the ideology of a body driven by irrational, chaotic urges, lacking any inherent organization of its own and incapable of generating any order from within itself?

I suggest that experiences with dance can provide and demonstrate the existence of what John Dewey calls "organized fruitful channels of activity."[38] We are, as Dewey says, "very easily trained to be content with a minimum of meaning, and to fail to note how restricted is our perception of the relationships which confer significance."[39] Moreover, as a rule, "the senses and muscles are used not as organic participants in having an instructive experience, but as external inlets and outlets of mind."[40] Dance, I think, and perhaps most especially postmodernist dance, can show all of us something different: an active, inherently organized body, capable of developing its immanent potential of experiential meaning, a body capable of creating new kinds of order, new channels of perception, new structures of time, space, and sociality.

In "The Indirect Language," Maurice Merleau-Ponty observed that "it is characteristic of cultural gestures to awaken in all others at least an echo, if not a consonance."[41] Since dance can display cultural gestures with exceptional clarity, intensity, and conviction, it can be a communicative practice of great value—provided its aesthetic integrity is not violated by political dogmatics. Twyla Tharp's early work *Deuce Coupe*, for example, can perhaps be seen in this light. Her use of historiographic "quotations" from earlier styles of dancing, gesturing, and moving was not inherently sentimental. I saw it, rather, as ironic, or reflective. Her more recent work, however, does seem to be more fetishized. Break-dancing, too, was originally able to awaken in people, people *outside* the world of the Black and Hispanic ghettoes, at least an echo, if not a consonance: a visceral recognition, a momentary muscular communion, an image, perhaps of an as yet unachieved democracy. For the dancers themselves, the phenomenon of break-dancing suddenly created a channel responsive to some local situations and needs, a channel altering the "microphysics of power," if only very slightly, and making it possible for some disadvantaged ghetto kids to dance their way into recognition and meaningful careers. B-boys, boys used to hanging out on the streets, gangboys, could suddenly make themselves visible to the white bourgeoisie: visible not as criminals, but as people—young people with talents, abilities, dreams. But many kids, even kids who will never make a career of their prowess, will henceforth begin to develop some self-esteem, some motivation to achieve, seeing themselves for the first time, seeing their dreams, and the opportunities intersecting their world, in a constructive light.

In his essay on "Surrealism," Benjamin wrote that "The collective is a body, too. And the *physis* that is being organized for it in technology can, through all its political and factual reality, only be produced in that image sphere to which profane illumination initiates us."[42] Unlike painting and sculpture, dance has never existed solely inside museum walls. But postmodernist dance—and by this I do not mean only the break-dancing phenomenon—has further democratized the art, opening its values to masses of people who had been excluded from the experience; it has brought the *art* of dance into the ghettoes and onto the streets; it has also *redeemed* the dancing of the streets, and redeemed some lives which might otherwise have been wasted, lost, or destroyed there. Postmodern dance has abolished the theatrical walls that kept it inside, apart from the life of the political body.

But postmodern dance has also celebrated the body as subject, the body refusing to be made into an object: the joyful, aesthetically organized, creative body, the body whose hedonism—needs, desires, experiences of fulfilled meaning—resists the instrumentalization of contemporary society, transgresses the historical limits of the reality principle and seduces reason itself into an acceptance of its primordial wisdom. If the body is the preconceptual source of all knowledge (see the quote from Merleau-Ponty at the beginning of this paper), then the dance can be an "art of recollection" in Herbert Marcuse's sense (see the opening quote from *Counter-revolution and Revolt*), winning for our future not only "the energies of intoxication" (Benjamin), but the ideal meanings and values carried by our collective flesh (Dewey). The dance can be the body's speech. Through dance, the body can *speak* its pain, its oppression, its needs and dreams. Through dance, the body can *create* speech for its felt sense of present life, its vividly present sense of the present historical moment. Through dance, we can connect body and soul to a speech of liberation—and develop insight into the processes of commodity fetishization and violence that today control the socialized, well-tempered body. In a society such as ours, the dance's legitimation of the body, of its creativity and its intelligence, its inherent order and its capacity to generate new orders of social meaning, constitutes not only a critique of the traditional ideology even now prevailing, but a possible retrieval and redemption of those human capacities about whose spiritual cultivation Marx spoke so eloquently in the *1844 Manuscripts*, and which otherwise, perhaps, would be lost forever in the future of our civilization.

In "The Indirect Language," Merleau-Ponty suggested that "To choose history means to devote ourselves body and soul to the advent of a future humanity."[43] In the postmodernist phase as I see it, there are dance events which have made this choice, celebrating the wisdom of the body, exploring channels of communication between the individual body and the body politic, and redeeming the spirit of our historical democracy for the advent of a future humanity.[44]

Chapter 13

OBSOLESCENCE AND DESIRE: FASHION AND THE COMMODITY FORM

Gail Faurschou

> The spectacle, grasped in its totality, is both the result
> and the project of the existing mode of production. It is not
> a supplement to the real world, an additional decoration.
> —Guy Debord[1]

Introduction

In the first pages of *Capital*, Marx observes that "the commodity appears at first sight a very trivial thing." Three volumes later there can be no doubt that the commodity, as the desanctified, disengaged, abstract, quantifiably equivalent "object" of consumption, lies at the heart of capitalist society and is the point of departure for elaborating the complex matrices of capitalism's development.

Today, of all commodities, the fashion object initially appears the most superfluous, transitory, and especially trivial—infinitely distanced from its historical origins in the magic and mystic of ceremonial costume and bodily adornment. I would argue, however, that it is not in spite of, but precisely because fashion has this ephemeral, volatile existence that it becomes the exemplary site for exploring the dominant tendencies and contradictions of our late capitalist, consumer, or postmodern society. Indeed, fashion, when viewed from the perspective of its formal character as a system, discloses a pervasive and enveloping logic, a logic that circulates at the center or, rather, endlessly dissimulates the absent center of postmodernity and postmodern subjectivity.

That is to say, if postmodernity is here understood as a new phase of intensification and reorganization in the mode of production of late capitalism such that production, having surpassed its earlier rationale of satisfying the needs of a modernizing society, is now compelled to drive consumption to new extremes of insatiability, then *fashion* is what has become the propelling momentum, the dominant MODE of consumption itself, the infinite and indefinite extension of its modalities. As both the *organizational thematic and fluctuating dynamic* of consumption, fashion is rapidly instituting itself as the universal code under which all other previous cultural codes are subsumed, contained but not transcended, reiterated, re-dressed, seemingly forever "re-consumed" in a perpetual, circular semiosis of stylistic variation.

Understood in this way, fashion can be seen to exceed all other cultural logics at the same time that it recuperates or revitalizes them. Under the abstract sign of pure contemporaneity, fashion is able to recycle any and every object that was once endowed with cultural value, reintroducing it as a stylized simulation of itself. Hence, the success of the totalizing logic of fashion signals what Fredric Jameson has referred to as the end of the historical subject and the sense of history as development or progress; a finality all the more certain the more it is endlessly and urgently dissimulated in fashion's vertigo of historical references.[2] In the spectacular world of fashion, history is frantically and fantastically restaged in any, or in all its moments, all at once, as the now de-temporalized past ever immediately and instantaneously present.

Far from signalling the end of capitalism, postmodernity then can be seen as its purest stage, one in which fashion now increasingly represents the dominant expression and widening extension of the logic of the commodity form. By virtue of its indifference to the material content of social life, fashion cannot only transform any or every one of its aspects into so many successive "objects" of consumption, but intensifies the abstract systematization and accelerated logic of the obsolescence of value itself.

This is not to say that the "natural," "moral," or "utilitarian,"— "alibis" for production, as Jean Baudrillard characterizes them—

have disappeared, but rather that they exist now only as a few (particularly modern) possibilities in the infinite variety of signs that will wait to succeed each other in the order fashion sees fit. Following Baudrillard, who is discussed in greater detail below, we might say that having long since exhausted the catharsis of the symbolic world, the dead world of signs relives it as the endless procession of glamorized simulacra. Postmodernism is the dead world of objects become fashion-conscious.

Symbols and signs

But what does it mean to say that fashion parades objects as a reification of what they once were, or a simulation of what they imagined themselves to be? What is presumed in this trajectory of birth, death, and spectacular resurrection?

As far as objects go, we do know that there has never been a society satisfied with their sheer instrumentality. Just as we expect more from our bodies than labor, we also expect more from objects than utility. We tell stories with objects, endow them with meaning, become attached to them, sometimes deliberately destroy them. They can appear powerful and even magically autonomous. But since Marx at least, we know that all value is social and objects acquire it on the basis of the relations through which we exchange them and which they then express.

The precise designation of socially symbolic vs. signifying practices will always need some theoretical clarification, due to the diversity of the use of these terms across the disciplines of the social sciences and humanities. For my purposes, the logical (and generally historical) distinction between symbolic and sign exchange, developed by the earlier Baudrillard (but schematically adopted by the tradition of cultural Marxism at least since the Situationists) will serve adequately enough to develop an analysis of the social logic of fashion.[3] In what follows, the symbolic order generally refers to social relations of the "concrete," "organic" community, where relations of power are transparent, and meaning and value are not yet fully subordinated to the rationalization of capitalist societies in which the commodity form of value dominates social exchange. With respect to the abstracted relationships of the latter, Baudrillard's *Le Système des objets* and *For a Critique of the Political Economy of the Sign* offer an analysis of sign exchange through commodity consumption that becomes particularly helpful for the following discussion of the fashion system, providing a point of departure beyond the more basic accounts of commodity reification.

Drawing on the anthropological works of Claude Lévi-Strauss and Marcel Mauss, Baudrillard defines symbolic exchange as follows:

> In symbolic exchange, of which the gift is our most proximate illustration, the object is not an object: it is inseparable from the concrete relation in which it is exchanged, the transferational pact it seals between two persons. . . .
>
> This is the paradox of the gift: it is on the one hand (relatively) arbitrary: it matters little what object is involved. Provided it is given, it can fully signify the relation. On the other hand, once it has been given—and *because* of this—it is *this* object and not another. The gift is unique, specified by the people exchanging and the unique moment of the exchange.[4]

Baudrillard's example of a symbolic object that we are familiar with today is the wedding ring. One does not wear several, nor think of substituting one for another. This is because the ring, mutually exchanged in a ceremony that seals relations of obligation and commitment (the counter-gift, according to Mauss) is thus intended to be as unsubstitutable and permanent as the relationship itself.

The commodity, however, is a different sort of thing. With the separation of the spheres of production and consumption, the exchange of commodities in capitalism, now mediated through the market, can only take place on the basis of exchange value, i.e., the ratio of abstract, quantifiably equivalent units of socially necessary labor time (calculable only because generalized within the economic "unity" of a rationalized division of labor). Because of this, the exchange relation, which is a strictly quantitative one (usually taking place at the checkout counter), hardly allows for symbolic investment or the generation of meaning.[5] According to textbook versions of capitalism, however, this is of no consequence, for it is only in the celebrated moment of consumption, finally the consumption of "use" values (or in this discourse, "satisfaction of demands") that the teleology of the whole economic process is meant to find its conclusion and *raison d'être*.

If we were concerned here only with the most basic utility of objects, that is to say if we proposed for a moment that there existed some universally accepted notion of essential need—let us take for this example the need for food (although this is already problematic because we know people may starve themselves for symbolic reasons)—then the problems posed by the separation of the moments of exchange and consumption would not give rise to the complexities that it does when we ask how symbolic value or meaning is generated.[6] For here, the "meaning" or rather the rationale for the consumption of food is presupposed, anterior to the economy that is now only set in motion to fulfill it. Of course, as Marx pointed out, even if capitalism limited itself to satisfying a set of "given" needs this in no way alters the fact that 1) it does so inefficiently, 2) it extracts surplus value from labor under the guise of equivalent exchange,[7] and 3) it denies or destroys its social basis by atomizing human beings and requiring them to treat each other and their social bond as an instrument, as a mere means to acquire objects.

This latter contradiction, as we shall see, is a crucial one, and constitutes the point of departure for grasping the cultural contradictions in all phases or stages of capital's development. What does distinguish late capitalism, however, is the degree to which it renders entirely obsolete any explanation of consumption in terms of some anthropological "structure of needs," locating us now in the midst of a hitherto unimaginable proliferation of consumer goods. Moreover, as most theoreticians of advertising tell us, this expansion has become possible to the extent that commodities are now marketed first and foremost as "symbolic" goods and only secondarily as utilitarian objects.

The paradox of value in the circuit of consumption

All of this then leads to the question of how we can understand the basis on which this "symbolic" consumption (including the consumption of advertising[8]) not only takes place, but is continually generated, sustained, and further intensified. That is to say, if Baudrillard is correct, if it is the social relation, the *act* of exchange which symbolically invests the object and not vice versa, then can we say that anything at all is established, gratified, or completed in this celebrated moment of consumption? For the paradox of capitalist ideology is that the whole production and reproduction of use value (symbolic as well as utilitarian) is deferred from production, distribution, and exchange to *consumption*—yet in consumption it is just such values that are *presupposed*.

Moreover, if capitalism is a society in which objects have now become the goal, the end for which all exchange is merely a means, and if this necessitates that individuals treat each other as objects and treat objects as subjects of the process, then not only must the commodity find its symbolism from somewhere entirely outside the production-distribution-exchange-consumption circuit, but it must do so in a way that hides the sheer instrumentality of all these social relations of capitalist society, relations that are inherently antagonistic, relations that we might say constitute a *symbolic divestment* rather than investment.[9]

What all this means, of course, is that the commodity must import from some other source—*a source necessarily outside capitalism's exchange relation*— what can now only be the idea, or specifically what Baudrillard refers to as the *sign* of a symbolic relation. Thus, as we shall see, fashion excavates history, non-capitalist or "exotic" societies, marginal or oppositional social groups, etc., for the sign of a relationship whose meaning appears to be generated outside of the logic of equivalence. Within capitalism those relations that appear to resist the most obvious forms of this reduction to equivalence, e.g., the family, friendships, sexuality, resistant artistic and cultural practices, etc., are obsessively mined (and undermined) by this drive for signification.[10]

What should be emphasized here is that the process of obscuring symbolic divestment by reappropriating the symbol as a sign should not be thought of as strictly a patchwork solution to an unfortunate side-effect of capitalism's economic logic. The death of the symbol is the precondition for its birth as a sign commodity. Just as Marx pointed out how all concrete connections, blood ties, etc., must be dissolved or excluded from the production process to create the "free," "autonomous" laborer, likewise it is *only* by liberating itself from the specificity and concreteness of symbolic exchange that the sign can become the true object of consumption, that is to say a commodity—available to anyone (for a price), infinitely substitutable and, of course, ultimately disposable. As Baudrillard explains,

> The traditional object symbol (tools, furniture, even the house), mediator of a real relation or of a lived situation, clearly bears the trace, in its substance and in its form, of the conscious and unconscious dynamics of this relation, and is therefore not arbitrary. This object, which is bound, impregnated, and heavy with connotation, yet actualized through its relation of interiority and transitivity with the human gesture or fact (collective or individual), is not consumed. *In order to become the object of consumption, the object must become a sign,* that is, in some way external to a relation which it now only signifies. . . .[11]

What is important here for Baudrillard, as we have already argued, is that we understand consumption not as the consumption of objects as such, but as the idea of the symbolic relation that is supposedly expressed by the object. Thus it follows that in consumption

> ". . . objects are (not) mechanically substituted for an absent relation, to fill a void, no: they describe the void, the locus of the relation, in a development which is actually a way of not experiencing it, while always referring to the possibility of experience."[12]

As a consequence, no sign can become particularly powerful. And that is just the point. Unlike the symbolic object which was as unique as the moment of exchange in which it was constituted, and expected to endure as long as it remained meaningful, the sign object, it is hoped by those who produce it, will find its power quickly evaporate, become properly consumed, so that another, and yet another, will be required to replace it.

In late capitalism then, the collective, indebted, and obligatory world of symbols appears to reach its antithesis in the abstract universe of free-floating and forever fluctuating signs. Indeed, Marx's description of commodity society as one in which "all that is solid melts into air" seems particularly apt today. However, not only is this abstract freedom merely that of formal unrestricted exchange and substitution, replacing the now dissolved restrictions of the symbolic order, but it is a freedom immediately usurped by the imperative of this code of substitution itself.

The universe of consumption and the logic of fashion

If the preceding analysis described the preconditions for the exchange and consumption of sign commodities, we have yet to explore the dynamic of this process of commodification and the cumulative effects of its developmental logic in late capitalism. This means going beyond the individual analysis of this or that symbol/sign relation as it can be observed, for example, in a specific advertisement, object, or clothing design, to a perspective that allows us to grasp 1) the horizontal, systematic incorporation of signs under increasingly universal codes of consumption (which, as we will see later, can include "parallel universes" of individualized consumer totalities), and 2) the temporal (but no longer even seasonal) cycles of variation and substitution of these codes themselves as they are rapidly constructed and dismantled under what has become the most abstract and omnipresent of all signifying codes—that of fashion itself.

In other words, while the markets of late capitalism present immense selections of differentiated commodities that appear to compete on the basis of ever more minute distinctions, in fact, the more effective strategy to increase consumption (an imperative for the survival of late capitalism) is to create ever more elaborate and expansive categories of signs that can be consumed systematically, and *systematically rendered obsolete*, at an increasingly accelerated pace. The greater the integration of consumer universes and the more quickly they are rendered obsolete, the more fashion asserts itself as the totalizing logic of commodity consumption in late capitalism.

The system of objects

The first of these dual strategies of late capital, that of the integration of consumption, was already developed and visibly pervasive by the time Baudrillard began to theorize its social dynamic in the 1960s.

> The display window, the advertisement, the manufacturer, and the brand name here play an essential role in imposing a coherent and collective vision, like an almost indissociable totality. . . . We can observe that objects are never offered to consumption in an absolute disorder. In certain cases they can mimic disorder to better seduce, but they are always arranged to trace out directive paths. The arrangement directs the purchasing impulse towards networks of objects in order to seduce and elicit, in accordance with its own logic, a maximal investment, reaching the limits of economic potential.[13]

In *Le Système des objets* Baudrillard focused particularly on the coordination and integration of the activity of consumption not only to demonstrate its success in expanding the market for consumer goods, but to show how "consumption is an active mode of relations (not only to objects, but to the collectivity and to the world), a systematic mode of activity and a global response on which our whole cultural system is founded.[14] While in this early work Baudrillard moves awkwardly between psychological, psychoanalytic, structural, and class analyses of this phenomenon, his main polemic is directed against the oversimplified critique of consumption as manipulation, as the creation of false needs that prevented the satisfaction of "natural" or truly "human" desires. Such a critique fails to grasp that the power and seduction of consumption lies in the degree to which it establishes itself as the only form of collective activity in which the atomized individual of bourgeois society can participate. As the universal code of contemporary socialization, this abstract order and formal systematization of the consumption of sign objects becomes the substitute for all previous forms of symbolic unity and of its collective elaboration.[15] As Baudrillard summarizes it in *Les Système des objets*, consumption becomes "a collective and active behavior, a constraint, a morality, and an institution. It is a complete system of values."[16] The collection of objects thus dissimulates the disappearance of the collectivity of subjects. Indeed, as Baudrillard states, "the system of objects . . . imposes its own coherence and thus acquires the capacity to fashion an entire society."[17]

But to the extent that the system of objects is gaining coherence, its imposing strategy is also growing more complex. For the second imperative of late capitalism is to ensure that, to the degree such a formal integration is achieved, it never becomes permanent or substantive. Nevertheless, at any one moment such a system of objects must *appear* both absolutely substantive (one must be compelled to buy *these* objects, not others, and buy them now, not later) and in the next moment, equally expendable, disposable and obsolete, to make way for the ever fresh, new waves of consumer goods. Only an analysis of this modulation of consumption as it is propelled by the logic of fashion demonstrates how this process is managed and, more importantly, intensified in late capitalism. In *The Political Economy of the Sign*, Baudrillard does occasionally speculate on the increasing significance of this role of fashion:

> Fashion is one of the more inexplicable phenomena . . .
> its compulsion to innovate signs, its apparently arbitrary
> and perpetual production of meaning—a kind of meaning
> drive—and the logical mystery of its cycle are all in fact of
> the essence of what is sociological. The logical processes of
> fashion might be extrapolated to the dimension of "culture"
> in general—to all social production of signs, values, and
> relations.[18]

Having already drafted an outline of these logical processes of fashion, the following pages will explore the extent to which we can observe the pervasiveness of fashion as it increasingly extends to the exterior and interior dimensions of social life.

Fashion landscapes

> . . . everything belongs to design, everything springs from
> it whether it says so or not: the body is designed, sexuality
> is designed, political, social, human relations are designed.
> . . . This "designed universe" is what properly constitutes
> the environment.
>
> —Baudrillard[19]

243

Today, fashion as a signifying system increasingly dominates what John Berger would call our contemporary field of visibility. No longer limiting itself to designing and shaping the human body, fashion is now the overriding stylistic code that is configuring our whole environment and mannerisms of habitation. On the one hand, the windows of shops, boutiques, and department stores with their rotating fashion thematics are a daily encounter for the urban pedestrian, as are billboards and mediascreens for the commuter, transforming the city landscape into a virtual fashionscape of image competition. On the other hand, designers such as Ralph Lauren have moved beyond their humble origins in neckties, clothing, accessories, and perfumes, to nothing less than the design of the "total home environment." Lauren, not content to lend his name to merely a few household objects, has taken over a floor of Bloomingdale's to market this perfect self-contained universe. As one observer noted, a visitor to the Lauren interiors will initially be 'greeted' by the designer himself appearing on his own 'furnishings video' reciting the Lauren motto for the decade: "fashion is a function of lifestyle"—a tautological slogan which could easily and more appropriately be reversed to "lifestyle is a function of fashion."

> The collection is meant to be, in the words of Lauren's publicists, a *total home environment*. You can now put on a Lauren dressing gown, slip on a pair of Lauren slippers, shower with Lauren soap, dry with a Lauren towel, walk across a Lauren rug, glance at the Lauren wall paper, and slip between Lauren sheets, beneath a Lauren comforter, to sip milk from a Lauren glass. *You can now be part of the ad.*[20]

Gone, it seems, are the days when fashion success was simply a matter of putting together and perfecting the "total look." Today, the properly postmodern consumer's clothing will match his or her furniture, which in turn will be coordinated with all other living accessories to complete the "total environment"—a virtual total (specular) experience.

With the popularity and financial success of the Lauren campaign, the following conclusion drawn by Baudrillard a few decades earlier no longer seems particularly extreme: "We have reached the point where consumption has grasped the whole of life; where all activities are sequenced on the same combinatorial;

where the channel of satisfaction is traced in advance one hour at a time; and where the 'environment' is complete, completely climatized, furnished, and culturalized."[21] Nevertheless, in Baudrillard's analysis, this totalizing logic was still an essentially implicit rather than explicit characteristic of consumer society in the 1960s—a time when advertisers had to draw on their ideological ingenuity in order to appeal to, and indeed capitalize upon, the then youthful symbols of nonconformism, rebellion, and anti-authoritarianism. Today, in an era when the critical tensions of modernity have become just so much more raw material for the shifting signs of postmodern consumerism, and where this consumerism cannot seem to celebrate itself enough, the veil of ideology need not be so opaque. At least for the growing Lauren empire of signs, the aestheticization of the total consumer environment is not only unabashedly advertised, but the very essence of its appeal.

Lauren, however, goes even further. If Baudrillard warned that the "system of objects" was rapidly coming to dominate and displace any system of subjects, Lauren has moved beyond all this by incorporating the subject as object within the Lauren universe. For if we read Lauren's environment ad closely, we find that his team of professionals are developing not only the "collection," but the "clientele" for his creations. Presumably, the Lauren family of objects has evolved to a level of such sophistication that it has become choosy about who will be allowed to be its animate accessories.

In an earlier decade, this "challenge" to coordinate one's world with such a degree of perfection in a marketplace of overwhelming diversity may have seemed an impossible demand even for the wealthier consumer, a task which only a class such as the leisured aristocracy of previous centuries could perform (and there is no question that Lauren, with his Polo logo, plays on this aristocratic reference). But if Lauren's demand for perfection proves intimidating for the consumer, so much the better, for this is what allows Lauren and his team of professionals to become indispensable. In figure (5), the visual and conceptual absence of any concrete object, let alone "collection," in this discreet black and white "invitation" to the Lauren world clearly implies that it is not the method of selection, much less the specific products themselves, that need concern us any more—only the label they

245

FIGURE 5

will bear. Fashion literacy thus becomes as easy as matching Lauren labels, and indeed it is soon apparent that it is the label itself which comes to produce the coordinating effect.

The Lauren universe can thus expand indefinitely, incorporating ever more diverse objects to the extent that it abstracts itself from any one object in particular. The appeal is that the more the system is systematized, the more seductive becomes the system. The effect is that the consumer must acquire not just one object, but a system of objects which must be consumed *as a system,* as a complete collection.

The world of Lauren is thus completely self-contained, tautological, and total. But like the world of fashion it is, at the same time, necessarily paradoxical. For at any one moment this abstract collection, like that of any designer, must become definitively concrete, absolute in its uniqueness, specific in its detail. It must become *the* authoritative fashion statement. Yet, in the next instance, with the same abstract authority, it must just as quickly be overturned, "outdated," and replaced. Since Lauren began marketing his concept of the "total environment" in 1984, he has presented us with several such "perfect worlds": "New England," "Jamaica," "Thoroughbred," "Log Cabin," "Safari," and "Marina," to name his earliest projects. Each is meticulous in its detail, complete unto itself. Nearly all of these discrete totalities reflect Lauren's nostalgia for aristocratic "old world elegance," and genteel colonial leisure. Even "Log Cabin" has been described as the look of "moneyed rusticity, the furnishings equivalent of designer jeans."[22] All of Lauren's environments (or one might say "parallel universes," since Lauren often displays several at once) are rife with historical allusions, even if none reflects a great deal of concern for historical authenticity. "Thoroughbred," for example, is described by Witold Rybczynski as

a country gentleman's room of dark colors highlighted by the polished brass of the bedstead and the gleaming mahogany wall paneling. Pheasant and hunting motifs abound, as do paisley prints and tartans. Wall coverings are checks, tattersalls, and foulards. . . . "Thoroughbred" includes a distinctly anglophile table setting: teapots, egg cups, and a covered muffin dish as well as plates ornamented with scenes of mounted polo players. "A dream England filtered through preppy America," an uncharitable British journalist called it.[23]

While Baudrillard did not witness this latest trend in environmental fashion at the time he wrote *Le Système des objets*, his analysis of an interior in Georges Perec's novel *Les Choses: A Story of the Sixties* would have been just as "fitting" for Lauren:

> Clearly nothing here has any symbolic value, despite the dense and voluptuous nostalgia of the "interior" decor. . . . human relations are not inscribed in things: everything is sign, pure sign. Nothing has presence nor history, and yet everything is full of reference: Oriental, Scottish, early American, etc. All these objects merely possess a characteristic singularity: in difference (their mode of referentiality) they are abstract, and are combined precisely by virtue of this abstraction. We are in the domain of consumption.[24]

Before exploring the wider implications of this encroaching, systematizing tendency of fashion culture, I would first like to look at a few other examples of its pervasiveness. For despite Lauren's considerable efforts to convince us to the contrary, he has by no means exhausted the possibilities of fashion's totalizing capabilities.

Cosmetic cybernetics

In 1984 an article appeared in *Vogue* announcing that the cosmetic industry was in crisis; too many products were creating too much confusion for consumers who could no longer figure out which ones were 'right' to get the results they 'wanted.' But the industry, we are told, was already responding to this cosmetic chaos with a full-scale revolution in information marketing, research, and technology that would not only generate specialized beauty products coordinated and *programmed* to fit the needs of each individual, but would also greatly *expand and diversify* the range of such products that, in the words of its promoters, could now be "'custom fit' for your genes/lifestyle/environment."[25] If Lauren's team of professionals offered a master plan for consumption to anyone who could afford it, the cosmetics industry has gone one step beyond this. With the aid not only of a cosmetic professional, but of the latest in "space age" beauty technology, each consumer can now be provided with her (and increasingly his) own personalized, uniquely tailored, "individualized" universe of beauty products—a universe that contains more of such products, of course, than was hitherto imaginable. *Vogue*'s report on the development of this marketing campaign is worth noting in some detail, not only because this strategy has proven dramatically successful in boosting the profits of the cosmetics industry, but because it represents, perhaps, the clearest example of how this calculated expansion/specialization logic is put into effect.

While the point of this promotional campaign is to increase the scope of what can be defined as a beauty product, I will limit my description here to only those products that generally seem to fall within the category of skin care. According to *Vogue*, research specialists employed by the major cosmetic manufacturers now admit that no one any longer has (nor ever did have, apparently) simply dry, normal, or oily skin, nor even mere combinations of these types. This outdated vocabulary, it seems, was never taken seriously by cosmetic scientists but was developed as a strategy to simplify complexities for the (now outdated) consumer. Today, however, the introduction of cybernetic information processing via computers, video makeup simulators, and skin imaging systems employing all kinds of "microanalytic equipment," have made available to consumers a fantastic array of products to the extent that consumers themselves no longer need to make any choices (nor fear making any "mistakes," as *Vogue* puts it).

This revolutionary cosmetic-computer technology that is able to process cybernetically and chart a coordinated schema of products for each individual made its debut at Bloomingdale's in 1984 in the form of Pola's Intelligent Skincare Computer from Japan. As each customer lines up for assessment;

> . . . a video camera magnifies the skin 30 times on a television screen, which the advisor studies, then enters information on a keyboard. This data appears on a second screen, and a printout is made with information directing the consumer to the correct Intelligent Skincare products. Another computer plots hair color choices through an

instrument held close to the face to monitor skin color and tone.[26]

Following Pola, Elizabeth Arden's Makeover Computer advanced the process even further with the introduction of a specially designed, full-color, four-quadrant video screen that allows one to view four possible variations of one's image. Each simulation can be altered feature by feature so that the customer is able not only to compare, for example, four hair colors and styles at once, but any other cosmetic alteration that Arden products may potentially effect. Most importantly, once satisfied with your screen image, the computer prints out exactly what products are needed to match your video simulation.

Interestingly enough, *Vogue*'s "Beauty Report '84" describes how the field of cosmetic "intelligence" developed out of research and technology adapted from the U.S. space and military programs. The article ends with a "New Beauty Glossary" that is meant to testify to the scientific sophistication of the world of cosmetics.

> Surfometry—originally designed for metallurgy to measure smoothness of metal—now "traces" skin surface with a stylus hooked up to a computer to measure roughness/smoothness in twenty different parameters.
>
> Image Analysis—originally designed for use in military evaluation of "enemy land" and to study planetary surfaces—can deal with sixteen different images at once on a T. V. monitor, "breaking" the picture up into individual small dots that can be "graded" for brightness/greyness, used to grade the light-reflective properties of skin, particularly after treatment with a product.
>
> The Pixe—originally developed to search for atmospheric pollutants and used in forensic medicine—is now a source of diagnostic information for the skin allowing precise measurement of chemicals on a cellular level.[27]

The effect of this information technology on streamlining and speeding product choice is, of course, to allow an increasingly complex proliferation of these products in general. Research efforts are coordinated to develop both new needs and categories at the same time that products are created to match them. In an interview with *Vogue* John Levy, president of Cosmair, stated that "today 70% of our new products come from research, not from marketing demands." So successful has been this approach that *L'Oreal* spent an astounding 43 million dollars in 1983 on product development alone.

According to cosmetic professionals, then, as opposed to the "dry, normal, and oily" skin of the past, this new research has revealed that skin types apparently are infinitely more complicated than was previously believed. Skin conditions cannot only vary over the topography of the body but in relation to geographical region, climate, season, altitude, age (chronological or 'actual'), one's mode of activity, the time of day, etc. Taking into account the last of these, for example, requires "chrono-therapy," using products designed for specific times of the day to work with the body's "clocks." If this is not intimidating enough for the consumer, product "synergy" (a term borrowed from medicine) must now be taken into account. Skin products, like drugs, can apparently react positively or negatively in combination, hence must be chemically coordinated to complement each other if they are to achieve the right effect. Allan Mottus, described by *Vogue* as a leading industry consultant, sums up all this in a strikingly candid way:

> The cosmetics industry is finding the richest market comes
> from "dismembering" people. Except for the earlobe they
> have a product to cover just about everything. The beauty
> of this kind of segmentation is that after the parts are
> analyzed for lip, eye, neck creams, wrinkle preventers,
> moisturizers, astringents, masks, sunscreens, sunblocks,
> they can be reassembled and sold as a unit. The customer
> is given a prescribed regimen of four or five products each
> requiring the synergy of others for the best results.[28]

We have already discussed how this individuating/systematizing marketing strategy succeeds in expanding and accelerating consumption. What is also worth noting in Mottus's statement is the peculiar aestheticization of this process itself, one similar to Lauren's celebration of the totality of consumption. The way in which Mottus speaks not just of the segmentation of beauty but of the "beauty of this kind of segmentation" brings to mind Foucault's description of the pleasure involved in the exercise of

FIGURE 6

power over sexuality invoked by "contacting bodies, intensifying areas, electrifying surfaces. . . ." As Foucault theorizes, "There was undoubtedly an increase in effectiveness and an extension of the domain controlled; but also a sensualization of power and a gain of pleasure."[29]

If Lauren's designer "environments" demonstrate the extent to which the exterior dimensions of social life can be incorporated and coordinated as fashion landscapes, the cosmetic industry, employing the same logic, has moved in the opposite direction, intensifying the surface of the body in all its detail as an intimate landscape of infinite appropriation and variation. The field of skin care is particularily interesting in this regard. Bordering on the distinction between beauty and health, it exemplifies most clearly the increasing incorporation/abstraction of regions of the body's raw materiality into the singular plane of appearance, and the absorption of values from previously distinct dimensions (health, fitness, comfort, etc.) into the formal, stylized codes of fashion. (I will return to the phenomenon of this specular logic in the last section.) Again the cosmetics industry is explicit about its strategy. As Robert Miller, president of Charles of the Ritz, puts it,

> As in any fashion business, the cosmetics industry will always be in a state of change. Today, physical fitness is the major thrust. Two years ago, we signed an agreement with Fila, an Italian sportswear company, to develop a line of therapeutic treatment, fragrance, and other items related to physical fitness. Available in 1986, the Fila line will create a whole new category, a fitness system that will include specially designed equipment and topical skin-fitness products.[30]

The phantasmagoria of fashion

> The new is a quality independent of the use value of the commodity. It is a source of that illusion which is inseparable from the dream-images of the collective. It is the quintessence of false consciousness, whose agent is fashion. This illusion of the new is reflected like one mirror in another, in the appearance of the always-again-the-same. The product

of this reflection is the phantasmagoria of that "cultural history" in which the bourgeoisie thoroughly enjoys its false consciousness.

—Walter Benjamin[31]

The concept of style, as both Raymond Williams and Henri Lefebvre have reminded us, once characterized the concreteness and distinctiveness of a way of life: "Style gave significance to the slightest object, to actions and activities, to gestures; it was a concrete significance, not an abstraction taken piecemeal from a system of symbols."[32] Today its reversal (one now thinks of *mere* stylistic changes) parallels the reversal of what was once meant by tradition, not only as the wealth of a body of cultural knowledge inherited, reinterpreted, and contested through generations, but of the sense of the historical *passage* of time. In fashion, the re-presentation of the ever "new" erases the record of growth, maturation, and decay that history inscribes on material objects and bodies—what Benjamin has called their "testimony" to a history that has been lived through.[33] In the cycles of fashion, the dimensions of lived space and time are eclipsed (not only the material limits of an embodied or even technologically mediated subject, but also the existential journey of memory and imagination) and replaced with a digitalized image culture that flashes for us its own alternating versions of the "present" or the "past," the "familiar" or the "foreign," the "exotic" or the "far-away," etc. In this sense, fashion collapses the coordinates of space, geography, place, into a variety of equivalent marketable environments that now, like Ralph Lauren's, can be bought in or out of season on the fourth floor of Bloomingdale's. At the same time, fashion becomes a world unto itself, the abstract all-encompassing environment of the spectacle of circulation and consumption.

On the other hand, fashion accelerates time. From the style of a period to that of a generation, year, decade, season, or now from month to month in the volumes of *Vogue*, the cultivation of style is replaced by the obsessive, frantic search for style. As Guy Debord writes, "What the spectacle offers as eternal is based on change and must change with its base. The spectacle is absolutely dogmatic and at the same time cannot really achieve any solid dogma. Nothing stops for the spectacle; this condition is natural to it, yet completely opposed to its inclination."[34]

The fashion magazines of the '80s are yet another example of how this process of defining and redefining style has become extended to the whole of social life. No longer singularly preoccupied with the latest styles in clothing and hair, fashion magazines incessantly provide us with up-to-date reports on what, where, and with whom it is fashionable to be eating, working, living, travelling, etc. Readers of *Vogue*, for example, will find regular, monthly columns on "Beauty Style," "Food Style," "Health Style," "Travel Style," even "Driving Style,"[35] among others. But if these magazines still primarily target women, the proliferation of the "lifestyle" magazine (*Vanity Fair, Taxi*, etc.) now has as its mission the indiscriminate conversion of everyone to a fashion code.[36]

Even on television, fashion is establishing itself as a prime-time attraction. Huge budgets are set aside for the costuming of *Dallas, Dynasty*, and their competitors as each maintain whole design teams with a staff that often outnumbers the production crews. Fashion segments on the news, weekly programs on fashion (such as Toronto's *Fashion Television*) and fashion video shows now supplement as much as they simulate fashion advertising.

Fashion and abstraction

Yet I would argue that in the media, the more striking indication of a heightened "fashion consciousness" and pervasiveness is the increasing legibility of a formalized fashion code in programming and advertising in general. This is not quite fashion as spectacle, in the sense that feminist film theorists have used psychoanalysis to analyse the construction of woman as spectacle in the cinema. Rather, what can be observed is fashion's increasing influence as a subtle yet powerful process of stylized abstraction (one in which raw materials, the traces of production—including the production of subjectivity—are erased or smoothed over) that now seems to "overcode" other organizing thematics and narratives. In crime dramas such as *Miami Vice*, or films like *9 1/2 Weeks*, it is less the clothing or decor that is seductive than the perfected model-like postures and gestures, the capture of a glance that manages to distance the viewer in much the same way as does glamor photography. Here the cutting-out of transitional movements of the body and of details that produce the "reality effect" of time in the narrative allows the sense of speed to increase and transforms processes of "becoming" into a succession of instances, of frozen, discrete gestures. Where virtualities of meaning are erased in the rapid cross-cutting of images, each appears as an already completed, perfected moment that must fully signify on its own.[37]

In television (particularly television advertising) these formal tendencies implicit in the logic of fashion are those of the techno-logical medium converge, producing a kind of "hyper-space/time" of intensified fragmented surfaces. On the one hand, this produces the effect of "flatness or depthlessness, a new kind of superficiality in the most literal sense" that Fredric Jameson has described as "perhaps the supreme formal feature of postmod-ernism."[38] On the other hand, the sense of acceleration and distortion of time that the condensed/abstracted succession of images produces would seem to fit Baudrillard's (later) model of "ecstatic" communication, for which contact and speech are now too slow. "The look is much faster, it is the medium of the media, the quickest. Everything must occur instantaneously." Fashion itself is a form of ecstasy for Baudrillard:

> We have become completely absorbed by models,
> completely absorbed by fashion, completely absorbed by
> simulation. . . . Ecstasy is that quality specific to each body
> that spirals in on itself until it has lost all meaning, and
> thus radiates pure and empty form. Fashion is the ecstasy
> of the beautiful: the pure and empty form of a spiraling
> aesthetics. Simulation is the ecstasy of the real.[39]

While one might wonder how, in a fashion/simulation culture, such a distinction between aesthetics and "the real" could be upheld, Baudrillard's account of the formal tendencies in fash-ion as a spiraling code of abstraction would seem a not altogether inappropriate description of the trends that can be observed in fashion advertising and the popular, commercial media today.

Conclusion

Having previously elaborated on the ways in which fashion can be understood as a mode of consumption, we are now in a position to highlight at least three theoretically distinct moments inherent in its logical expansion. As we have observed, fashion develops 1) a totalizing dynamic of incorporation and systematic differentiation wherein those hitherto "uncoordinated" categories of commodity consumption find themselves increasingly subsumed under this or that fashion register; 2) a logic of accelerated obsolescence; and 3) a "specular logic" of abstraction in which the concrete dimensions of social life and the symbolic world are increasingly reduced, recoded, and smoothly reprocessed into the one-dimensional, glossy (or increasingly fluorescent) signifying surfaces of their photographic (or televisual) equivalent. To put this another way, social life has become displaced to the extent that its "display" value now supersedes it.

The fashion object then must be thought of as a very peculiar kind of commodity—one whose elaboration requires, as did the commodity itself for Marx, an understanding of how it functions as a system, a logic, and a code of abstraction. Fashion is thus a commodity whose form is at one and the same time its content, a commodity that is doubly abstract, both as exchange value *and* as use value.

Finally, a few words are needed to address the problem that the preceding analysis now poses for us in and of itself—namely, the frustration of what Jameson has referred to as a

> "winner loses" logic—which tends to surround any effort to describe a "system," a totalizing dynamic, as these are detected in the movement of contemporary society. What happens is that the more powerful the vision of some increasingly total system or logic . . . the more powerless the reader comes to feel. Insofar as the theorist wins . . . he loses, since the critical capacity of his work is thereby paralyzed, and the impulses of negation and revolt, not to speak of those of social transformation, are increasingly perceived as vain and trivial in the face of the model itself.[40]

Indeed, the conclusion that may be drawn from the foregoing model of consumption is that the late-capitalist marketplace has

developed ingenious strategies of expansion that allow it to remain as vigorous as ever in spite of the internal contradictions
on which it operates, and secondly, to be even more impervious
to outside challenges than it was before. This latter statement
appears true to the extent that fashion seems not only capable
of systematically diffusing any form of critical opposition, but
actually welcomes such authentic symbolic gestures as so much
more creative raw material for its storehouse of marketable signs.
Consider, for example, the current stampede of advertisers rac-
ing to appropriate this or that '60s rock classic for their latest
commercial jingle. Recently, the most famous of these is Nike
Incorporated's use of the Beatles' "Revolution" to market their
newest series of fitness shoes. Certainly there is a strange irony
in the fact that the very corporate America which was once so
threatened by the '60s generation of demonstrators that it called
out the National Guard is now fighting a legal battle with these
same people to use the music it once feared responsible for their
subversion.

While it is beyond the scope of this paper to evaluate the
contemporary critical force of specific counterhegemonic social
and cultural movements, I would like to insist on distancing
myself from the kinds of conclusions that Baudrillard may draw
in the face of the above model. I refer here specifically to Baudrillard's theory of the media as expressed in *Shadow of the Silent
Majorities*, where he excludes all such alternatives on the basis
that "the masses" can only, and will ever only, exert a "strategy
of indifference" toward their representation as "the social." Irre-
spective of the theoretical plausibility of this position, such a
"strategy" could only be viewed as ironic if one conceives of the
masses as strictly an *audience* of commercial culture. It makes
little sense for an analyses of consumption where ultimately it is
only the lines at the cash register that concern the executives of
capitalism, notwithstanding the executives of the media.

If the alibi for exchange value in postmodernity is no longer
the utility of a commodity but rather its "fashion value," this
indicates the degree to which the absence of the social has come
to be expressed as an unprecedented and ongoing search for
the social. While fashion represents the most conspicuous of all
forms of consumption, it is for that matter the most social in its
dependence on the eye of the other. It is the utopian longing for

some kind of authentic, socially symbolic participation in the collective that Benjamin grasped as the latent content of the phantasmagoria of fashion. Read in this way, the phantasmagoria of fashion can be found to embody not only the regressive tendencies of bourgeois culture but also the utopian desire to "overcome and transfigure the deficiencies of social reality."[41] As phantasmagoria, fashion produces the dream images of the collective, albeit only in the repressed and distorted form available in a commodity society; but like all dreams it thereby "strives toward the moment of awakening."[42]

NOTES

CHAPTER 1   BACK TO THE FUTURE

1 Maurice Blanchot, *Thomas the Obscure*, trans. Robert Lamberton (New York: David Lewis, 1973), p. 27 (henceforth, *TO*).

2 Jacques Derrida, "Différance," in *Margins of Philosophy*, trans. Alan Bass (Chicago: University of Chicago Press, 1982), p. 8.

3 Maurice Blanchot, *Le pas au-delà* (Paris: Gallimard, 1973), p. 34–5 (henceforth, *PA*). Unless otherwise indicated, translations throughout this paper are my own.

4 To deny *arche* and *telos* is to deny the Alpha and Omega that onto-theology names "God." Anarchy and ateleology meet in an atheology that declares the death of God.

5 The closely related images of the pit and the pyramid are important for Derrida as well as Blanchot. See, for example, "The Pit and the Pyramid: Introduction to Hegel's Semiology," in *Margins of Philosophy*, pp. 69–108. The cryptic figure of the pyramid is closely related to the problem of difference. Derrida compares the silent "A" in *différance* to a pyramid. See "Différance," p. 4.

6 Maurice Blanchot, *The Space of Literature*, trans. Anne Smock (Lincoln: University of Nebraska Press, 1982), p. 30 (henceforth, *SL*).

7 Blanchot distinguishes *la mort* and *mourir* from *l'être mort*. While being dead (or a dead being) remains an attribute of being, death and dying elude the polarity of being and non-being.

8 Elsewhere Blanchot associates death with the anonymity of the neuter. "*One dies*: he who dies is anonymous, and anonymity is the guise in which the ungraspable, the unlimited, the unsituated is most dangerously affirmed near us. Whoever experiences this suffers an anonymous, impersonal force, the force of an event which, being the dissolution of every event is starting over not only now, but was in its very beginning a beginning again" (*SL*, p. 241).

9 Inasmuch as death is never present, it cannot be thought. Death, in other words, is unthinkable. "Death," for Blanchot, "is only a

metaphor that helps us roughly to represent the idea of limit, while the limit excludes all representation all 'idea' of limit" (*PA*, p. 75).

10 Maurice Blanchot, *L'Entretien infini* (Paris: Gallimard, 1969), p. 310 (henceforth, *EI*).

11 "Impotent [*impotens*]" and "impossible [*impossibilis*]" are both related to the Latin stem *poti*: "Powerful; lord. 1. Latin *potis*, powerful, able: PODESTA. 2. Old Latin *poeter*, to be able or powerful (superseded by *posse*, to be able) POTENT, POWER, IMPOTENT, PREPOTENT. 3. Latin compound *posse*, to be able (contracted from *potis*, able + *esse*, to be): POSSESS, POSSIBLE, PUISSANT. 4. Variant of *pet-* in compound *ghost-pet-*, guest-master, host (see *ghosti*)" (*The American Heritage Dictionary of the English Language*).

12 Maurice Blanchot, "Discours sur la patience: en marges des livres d'Emmanuel Levinas," *Le Nouveau commerce*, no. 30–31 (1975), p. 25.

13 Maurice Blanchot, *Faux Pas* (Paris: Gallimard, 1971), p. 35.

14 "Thomas" in Aramic and Hebrew is not a proper name but an epithet meaning "twin" or "double."

15 At one point, Blanchot observes: "If it is true that there is (in the Chinese language) a written character signifying at once 'man' and 'two,' it is easy to recognize in man that which is always self and other, the fortunate duality of dialogue and the possibility of communication. But it is less easy, more important perhaps, to think that 'man' also means 'two' like the gap that lacks unity, the jump from '0' to duality, the '1' thus giving itself up as forbidden, the between" (*PA*, p. 57).

16 Maurice Blanchot, "Discours sur la patience," p. 22.

17 This strange humanism is, in a certain sense, inhuman, for it subverts the humanism characteristic for the ontotheological tradition. For Blanchot, the western humanism that ends in Hegel's divinization of man is not human enough.

18 Maurice Blanchot, *La part du feu* (Paris: Gallimard, 1949), pp. 314, 327.

19 Anne and Patrick Poirier, *Voyages . . . et caetera, 1969–1983* (Milan: Electra, 1983). This catalogue is for an exhibit in Paris at Chapelle de la Salpetriere from October 30 to December 5, 1983 and in Milan at Eglise de San Carpoforo in 1984 (henceforth, *V*).

20 Quoted by Claude Gintz in "Ruins and Rebellion," *Art in America* (April, 1984), pp. 149–50.

21 See, *inter alia*, Georges Bataille, *Visions of Excess: Selected Writings, 1927–1939*, trans. A. Stoekl, C. R. Lovitt, and D. M. Leslie (Minneapolis: University of Minnesota Press, 1985).

22 Maurice Blanchot, *The Writing of the Disaster*, trans. Anne Smock (Lincoln: University of Nebraska Press, 1986), p. 1.

CHAPTER 2   POSTMODERN LANGUAGE

1 Unless otherwise noted, references are to *Beyond Good and Evil: Prelude to a Philosophy of the Future*, trans. Walter Kaufmann (New York: Random House, 1966).

2 The directions of instincts are "valuations," i.e., *forces* of will; these are forces of life-preservation which are expressed as "estimates" (I.3). Estimates are interested in preserving our kind of creature. The kind of creature we are is a product of the conflicts, fears, punishments, successes, etc., that make up the creature's history. "Life-promotion" is the interest of a judgment, not particularly what it claims or sees. We live by judgments, by the "estimates" or "fictions" of cognition. We determine our lives by them. That they claim to be true or false, that they expect to reveal the connections among things just as the connections are, that they claim *a priori* or apodictic rightness: that is part of their own life-promoting efforts. That is part of their fiction, their insistence, their happy folly (I.4).

3 See, for example, I.6: "For every drive wants to be master—and it attempts to philosophize in *that spirit.*"

4 This project constitutes part of my *The Language of Difference* (Atlantic Highlands, N. J. Humanities Press, 1987).

CHAPTER 3   THE CONTRADICTORY CHARACTER OF POSTMODERNISM

1 Jochen Schulte-Sasse, "Modernity and Modernism, Postmodernity and Postmodernism: Framing The Issue," *Cultural Critique*, 5 (Winter, 1986–87), p. 6.

2 Charles Newman argues as much in *The Post-Modern Aura: The Act of Fiction in an Age of Inflation* (Evanston, Il.: Northwestern University Press, 1985). For Newman, "climax inflation" characterizes postmodernism, suggesting that the inflation of contradiction, resulting in irreparable social and personal fragmentation—apparent loss of even the possibility of cohesion—is another climax of bourgeois over-expansion.

3 I am suggesting that the feeling of impotence latent in bourgeois society has finally caught up with its critics, the intellectuals who have formulated the critical theory of postmodernism and who are themselves bourgeois. I would even go so far as to say that critical activism as such is an effort to fight off and overcome this feeling of impotence—at least of extreme vulnerability generated by the rationalized anonymity of the bourgeois system, among other factors inseparable from it. Especially does the general existence of seemingly unresolvable contradictions on every front of bourgeois activity

undermine the sensitive intellectual from within, generating that peculiar kind of despair called criticality. But the feeling of impotence is as unconscious as the critical activism is conscious. As Erich Fromm writes in "Zum Gefühl der Ohnmacht," *Zeitschrift für Sozialforschung* (Paris, 1937), p. 96, "Bourgeois man, in contrast to certain types of religious individual, is usually not conscious of the feeling of impotence." Later, Fromm modified his psychosocial theory by arguing that the feeling of impotence was less the response of the authoritarian character in search of symbiotic stability and submissive unity with a surrogate parent than a narcissistic response to an annihilative danger. This accords well with my interpretation of the rationale for postmodernism's conception of criticality, which in general follows Fromm's theory. In *Escape From Freedom* (New York: Farrar & Rinehart, 1941), p. 172, Fromm argues that the need for power is the expression of impotence, a "desperate attempt to gain secondary strength where genuine strength is lacking." Criticality is secondary strength at its best. But the climactic contradictions of bourgeois society sap everyone's genuine strength, so that critical activism in bourgeois society is as close to genuine strength as it is possible to come in bourgeois society. At the same time, postmodernist criticality inflates—re-empowers—an obsolete modernist idea of criticality in response to the climactic contradictions of bourgeois society, which make critical intellectuals feel irreparably impotent.

4 For a summary of the debate see Richard Rorty, "Habermas, Lyotard et le postmodernité," *Critique* 442 (1979; March 1984), pp. 181–97. Jean-François Lyotard's critique of Habermas appears in *The Postmodern Condition: A Report on Knowledge* (Minneapolis: University of Minnesota Press, 1984), pp. 71–82.

5 Lyotard, *The Postmodern Condition*, p. 77.

6 I am here mockingly following Lyotard, p. 81.

7 In *An Autobiographical Study* (1925; New York: W. W. Norton, 1963), p. 126, Sigmund Freud describes "the principle of 'the omnipotence of thoughts' " as "the overestimation of the importance of psychical reality." Karl Abraham pointed out that omnipotence of thought meant the unconscious belief that to think something was to make it happen, or that it was the case.

8 Sigmund Freud, *Totem and Taboo* (1913; New York, W. W. Norton, 1950), p. 190:

> In only a single field of our civilization has the omnipotence of thoughts been retained, and that is in the field of art. Only in art does it still happen that man who is consumed by desires performs something resembling the accomplishment of those

desires and that what he does in play produces emotional effects—thanks to artistic illusion—just as though it was something real. People speak with justice of the "magic of art" and compare artists to magicians. But the comparison is perhaps more significant than it claims to be. There can be no doubt that art did not begin as art for art's sake. It worked in the service of impulses which for the most part are extinct today. And among them we may suspect the presence of many magical purposes.

From this point of view, postmodernist criticality is a magical attempt to produce emancipatory emotional effects in its intellectual advocates.

9 In "primary narcissism" the libido of the child is completely self-directed, not yet extending to objects in the external world, which occurs with maturity. "Secondary narcissism" is a response to pathological conditions. The libido detaches itself from external objects and re-attaches itself exclusively to the self. See Sigmund Freud, "On Narcissism: An Introduction," *Standard Edition,* XIV. See also Freud, *Totem and Taboo,* pp. 88–90.

10 See Frederic Jameson, "Postmodernism and Consumer Society," *The Anti-Aesthetic,* ed. Hal Foster (Port Townsend, Wash.: Bay Press, 1983), pp. 113–4, for the distinction between pastiche and parody, and the argument for the dominance of the former in contemporary bourgeois culture. Jameson yearns for parody in what he takes to be a cultural situation of pastiche, but which others see as a special form of parody.

11 Lyotard, *The Postmodern Condition,* pp. 79–80, formulates the distinction as that between an avant-garde mode which shows "nostalgia for presence felt by the human subject, on the obscure and futile will which inhabits him in spite of everything" and the avant-garde mode which emphasizes "the power of the faculty [of presentation] to conceive, on its 'inhumanity,' so to speak . . . whether or not human sensibility or imagination can match what it conceives" (the mode of "invention of new rules of the game"). It is the difference between the mode of melancholy and the mode of deconstruction—between "the German Expressionists, and on the side of *novatio,* [the Cubism of] Braque and Picasso." Ever since Lyotard has made his distinction, it has been unthinkingly parroted, until the melancholy mode has been understood to be naively compensatory—a typical Marxist diminishment of psychologically oriented art—and the deconstructivist mode elevated as the only critically significant, genuinely activist one. Nonetheless, Schulte-Sasse, who accepts the valorization of the

polarity, has the courage to admit ("Modernity and Modernism . . .," p. 8) that even the "mode of deconstructive *novatio*" may fall victim to the nostalgia of melancholy, namely, "mesmerizing fascination with what already exists, viewing it as the only epistemologically relevant object." This is a prelude to institutionalization, and indeed, as Schulte-Sasse acknowledges, the mode of deconstructive *novatio* has become another institutionalized avant-garde discourse. What he fails to acknowledge is that in a situation of total administrative control of the avant-garde, correlate with a situation of bourgeois hypostatization of contradiction—which can be conceived in terms of T. W. Adorno's notion of "hyper-modernism" (*Aesthetic Theory* (London: Routledge & Kegan Paul, 1984), p. 22)— that is, a situation in which dissonance approximates to consonance or irreconcilability to reconciliation, the mode of melancholy may be more to the psychosocial point than the mode of deconstructive *novatio*. The latter mode plays into the hands of a bourgeois system which uses novelty to generate contradiction—which needs deconstruction to create the novelties that overthrow all that has hitherto been presented, thus establishing the convergence of permanent contradiction and permanent revolution. The psychosocial point made by the mode of melancholy is that of endurance in the face of an unendurable world— endurance, as Freud remarked, being the first obligation of the self to itself. (Under circumstances of extreme social contradiction, the melancholy (lonely) integration of the self, assuring its endurance, can be a revolutionary act in itself. Endurance is most revolutionary when the world has become most banal, that is, banally contradictory and self-contradictory—priding itself on its bourgeois administration of its contradictions.) No doubt this also turns into an obligation to the world. But so does the revolution-generating mode of deconstruction, with its endlessly artificial novelties, which serve the world without offering any integration—however melancholy—that can resist it. In line with this, psychoanalytically speaking the deconstructivist mode looks like a manic defense for the avoidance of melancholy (sense of death, tragedy, negativity, chaos) which the Germans articulate through their Expressionistic mode. See D. W. Winnicott, "The Manic Defence," *Collected Papers, Through Paediatrics to Psycho-analysis* (London: Tavistock, 1958), p. 132.

It is worth noting that Lyotard's view of German Expressionism ultimately derives from Georg Lukács's " 'Grösse und Verfall' des Expressionismus" (1934), which describes it as a "qualitative increase in the sense of loss and despair" in capitalistic society, resulting from the petit-bourgeois individual's "impatient submission" [*Unterordnung*] to capitalism. Ernst Bloch's response to Lukács, in

Bloch's "Diskussionen über Expressionismus" (1938), suggests an alternative conception, which I subscribe to: "But perhaps Lukács's reality . . . is not objective . . . perhaps genuine reality [totality] is also collapse [*Unterbrechung*]. Because Lukács has a closed objectivist conception of reality he turns against every artistic attempt, such as Expressionism, to articulate the world view of the broken (even if it is also the world view of capitalism)." Lukács, in other words, cannot give the subjective sense of vulnerability and impotence its full due because he has a narrow objectivist sense of the self as objectively determined and either mechanically reactionary or revolutionary in import. Thus, he cannot see the personal revolutionary potential in the feeling of impotence—cannot see that it may lead to a criticality that can transform society from within. Both quotations are from Paul Raabe, *Expressionismus: Der Kampf um eine literarische Bewegung* (Munich: DTV, 1965), pp. 264, 289.

12 Philip Rieff, *The Triumph of the Therapeutic* (New York: Harper & Row, 1966), makes this point decisively, if in psycho-philosophical terms.

13 Schulte-Sasse, "Modernity and Modernism . . .," p. 9, points out that modernist aesthetic practice involves an "institutionally always already achieved . . . defusion of . . . oppositional figurations, a transformation of their critical content into nostalgic, utopian images which reconcile the opposition in an imaginary mode." This holds as much for the deconstructive mode as the melancholy mode.

14 Linda Hutcheon, "The Politics of Postmodernism: Parody and History," *Cultural Critique*, 5 (Winter 1986–87), p. 184.

15 Lyotard, *The Postmodern Condition*, pp. 14–17, especially his assertion "that each of us knows that our *self* does not amount to much" (p. 15), which confirms the psychoanalytic view of diminished self-esteem—reflecting self-fragmentation—as the major pathology of the time. It may be true, as Lyotard says, that while the self does not amount to much, it "exists in a fabric of relations that is now more complex and mobile than ever before," and that it is "always located at 'nodal points' of specific communication circuits" (p. 15), but this itself seems to confirm the absence of primary relations and self-supportive communication. What Daniel Stern, *The Interpersonal World of the Child* (Cambridge, Mass.: Harvard University Press, 1983) calls the "sense of self" and what Heinz Kohut, in *The Analysis of the Self* (New York: International Universities Press, 1971) and *The Restoration of the Self* (New York: International Universities Press, 1977), calls the archaic narcissistic self—necessities of specifically human being—are not addressed by Lyotard's view of the self, which in fact confirms the diminished sense of self in administered bourgeois society.

16 In *The Philosophical Discourse of Modernity* (Cambridge, Mass.: MIT Press, 1987), pp. 3–5, Jürgen Habermas distinguishes between the *"neoconservative* leave-taking from modernity" and the "farewell to modernity" represented by the "aesthetically inspired anarchism"— a "revolt against it once again"—under whose sign postmodernity marches." Both modes of postmodernist critical activism are branches on the same tree of critical individualism from the bourgeois perspective, and as such confirm and reinforce the triumph of the bourgeois idea of "sameness with a difference." The question, of course, is whether Habermas's own advocacy of intersubjectivity in the name of communicative competence does not do the same.

17 Lyotard, *The Postmodern Condition,*

18 Kohut, *The Restoration of the Self,* passim. See especially chapter 2, "Does Psychoanalysis Need A Psychology of the Self?"

19 Schulte-Sasse, "Modernity and Modernism . . .," p. 13.

20 The argument for postmodernist schizophrenia is presented at its most concentrated in Jameson, "Postmodernism and Consumer Society," pp. 118–22, and even more succinctly in Jean Baudrillard, "The Ecstasy of Communication," *The Anti-Aesthetic,* pp. 132–3. It ultimately derives from Gilles Deleuze and Félix Guattari, *Anti-Oedipus: Capitalism and Schizophrenia* (1972; Minneapolis: University of Minnesota, 1983). From a psychiatric point of view, it involves a preposterous misunderstanding and misappropriation of the concept of schizophrenic pathology—a facile application of it to advanced capitalist society.

21 See Renato Poggioli, *The Theory of the Avant-Garde* (New York: Harper & Row, 1971), pp. 25–42 for an analysis of avant-gardism as a dialectic moving from activism to antagonism to nihilism to agonism.

22 Jürgen Habermas, "Modernity—an Incomplete Project," *The Anti-Aesthetic,* p. 5.

23 Lyotard, *The Postmodern Condition,* pp. 71, 81.

24 Peter Bürger, *Theory of the Avant-Garde* (Minneapolis: University of Minnesota Press, 1984).

25 Jameson, "Postmodernism and Consumer Society," pp. 111–2, discusses some of the details of this assimilation, showing how even the anti-authoritarian avant-garde acquires social authority and legitimacy, and becomes the preferred object of authoritarian desire— the basis of a new authoritarian character.

26 See Jay R. Greenberg and Stephen A. Mitchell, *Object Relations in Psychoanalytic Theory* (Cambridge, Mass.: Harvard University Press, 1983).

27 Hutcheon, "The Politics of Postmodernism," p. 180.

28 Ibid., p. 179.

NOTES TO CHAPTER 3

29 Ibid., p. 183. See also p. 185, n. 18 for Hutcheon's criticism of Jameson's concept of parody. "Contemporaneity," says Hutcheon, "need not signify wholesale implication without critical consciousness," as Jameson seems to think. Hutcheon in general points out the misguided nature of Jameson's characterization of postmodernism, which supposedly derived "from architectural debates," followed from Jameson's own [Marxist] odd angle.

30 Lyotard, *The Postmodern Condition*, pp. 10–16. Thus aggression is brought back in the sublimated form of contesting language games and the power of messages to "displace what traverses them." Roland Barthes also uses this supposedly post-Freudian view of aggression, but one which involves death-wishing and death-dealing as much as its Freudian source.

31 Hutcheon, "The Politics of Postmodernism," p. 185.

32 Ibid.

33 Ibid., p. 192.

34 Ibid., p. 193.

35 D. W. Winnicott, "Ego Distortion in Terms of True and False Self" (1960), *The Maturational Processes and The Facilitating Environment* (New York: International Universities Press, 1965), pp. 140–52. According to Winnicott the false self is compliant yet through its compliance protective of the true self, which may be unknown or incommunicado. From this point of view, postmodernist architecture seeks out the true self hidden in the false historical styles of past self. This incommunicado self becomes the core of the contemporary true self.

36 Winnicott, "Ego Distortion . . .," pp. 145–6 points out that the initial good-enough environment is the good-enough mother. However, the need for a good-enough, facilitating environment never diminishes throughout life, although one may become increasingly hardened to—superficially tolerant of—the variety of bad-enough environments, emotional and physical, which exist in the lifeworld. That is, one may develop a strong reality principle. From this point of view, the postmodernist pursuit of integrity through the past—a very indirect and on face value absurd, futile route—suggests the unconscious recognition that the present bourgeois environment will never be good-enough, that is, it will always subject one to new, increasingly inhuman, contradictions. The present is unconsciously perceived as totally inhuman because it is realized that it can never overcome its contradictions.

37 Kohut, *The Analysis of the Self*, chapters 2, 5, 6.

38 Heinrich Klotz, *Revision der Moderne: Postmoderne Architecture 1960–1980* (Munich: Prestel Verlag, 1984), p. 9. See also Klotz, *Moderne und Postmoderne, Architectur der Gegenwart, 1960–1980* (Braunschweig:

Vieweg, 1984); Paolo Portoghesi, *After Modern Architecture* (New York: Rizzoli, 1982); and Charles Jencks, *The Language of Postmodern Architecture* (New York: Rizzoli, 1985; 2nd ed.) for similar approaches to postmodern architecture.

39 Winnicot, "The Manic Defence," p. 185 sees play as an instrument of the realization of the creative impulse, that is, the impulse to integrate.

40 Klotz, *Revision der Moderne*, p. 9.

41 Heinz Kohut, *How Does Analysis Cure?* (Chicago: University of Chicago Press, 1984), p. 16 regards "disintegration anxiety" not as anxiety about "physical extinction but loss of humanness: psychological death." Psychological death is what Lyotard describes when he speaks of the self counting for nothing, and of what is behind the postmodernist account of the schizophrenia of contemporary existence. Lyotard and other postmodernist theorists almost seem to advocate such psychological death or loss of humanness. But postmodernist practice, at least as it exists in architecture, represents a refusal to accept it.

42 Ludwig von Bertalanffy, *General System Theory* (New York: George Braziller, 1968), pp. 190–1 describes the dominance of the robot model of behavior in contemporary society.

43 Sigmund Freud, "The 'Uncanny'," (1919), *Studies in Para-Psychology* (New York: Collier Books, 1963), p. 31. From this point of view, the sense of false self comes from the experience of oneself as an automaton (robot, machine). Modernist architecture presumably encourages this robotic sense of self, while postmodernist architecture repudiates it through the "poetry" of past selves it implicitly articulates. Yet it also subsumes—puts in its proper place—the robotic/technocratic self of modernism

44 See Ananda Coomaraswamy, "On Ornament," *Selected Papers*, vol. I (Princeton: Princeton University Press, 1977), p. 242 for an account of the "inner existential necessity" of ornament as a manifestation of humanness. For Coomaraswamy, it essentializes humanness into an attribute of a particular self—an attribute conferring personhood.

CHAPTER 4   POSTMODERNISM AND (POST)MARXISM

1 The theses owe something to Hal Foster, *Recodings: Art, Spectacle, Cultural Politics* (Port Townsend, Wash.: Bay Press, 1985). See also Ihab Hassan, "Making Sense: The Trials of Postmodern Discourse," *New Literary History*, 18:3 (1986–87), pp. 437–59.

2 John O'Neill, "Televideo Ergo Sum: Some Hypotheses on the Specular Functions of the Media." *Communication*, 7 (November 2, 1983), pp. 221–40.

3 Suzi Gablik, *Has Modernism Failed?* (New York: Thames and Hudson, 1985).

4 Hal Foster, "(Post) Modern Polemics," in his *Recodings*, pp. 121–37.

5 John O'Neill, *Five Bodies: The Human Shape of Modern Society* (Ithaca, N.Y.: Cornell University Press, 1985).

6 John O'Neill, "The Disciplinary Society: From Weber to Foucault." *The British Journal of Sociology*, 37:1 (March 1986), pp. 42–60; and "The Medicalization of Social Control," *The Canadian Review of Sociology and Anthropology*, 23:3 (August 1986), pp. 350–64.

7 Richard Bernstein, ed., *Habermas and Modernity* (New York: Basil Blackwell, 1985).

8 Alice A. Jardine, *Gynesis: Configurations of Women and Modernity* (Ithaca, N.Y.: Cornell University Press, 1985).

CHAPTER 5   *IN SITU*: BEYOND THE ARCHITECTONICS OF THE
                          MODERN

1 Michael Graves, "A Case for Figurative Architecture" in *Buildings and Projects* (New York: Rizzoli, 1982), pp. 11–2.

2 Ludwig Wittgenstein, *Philosophical Investigations,* trans. G. E. M. Anscombe (New York: Macmillan, 1953), pp. 8, 82.

3 Plato, *The Republic*, X (607b).

4 Homer, *The Odyssey* I;345, trans. Walter Shewring (Oxford: Oxford University Press, 1980), p. 9.

5 The dictionaries used for this information, in addition to the *Oxford English Dictionary*, are *Webster's Third International* and *The American Heritage Dictionary*.

6 Immanuel Kant, *Critique of Pure Reason,* trans. Norman Kemp Smith (New York: Macmillan, 1973), p. 576. In accordance with the standard practice for quoting this text, I will cite both the first and second editions (as A and B) and will provide these references within the text in this format.

7 Immanuel Kant, *The Critique of Judgement*, trans. J. H. Bernard (New York: Hafner, 1968), p. 38. The paginations for this text will henceforth be provided in parenthesis within the text.

8 Paul Guyer, *Kant and the Claims of Taste*, (Cambridge, Mass.: Harvard University Press, 1979), p. 254.

9 See Saint Augustine, "On Music" VI:13, trans. Catesby Taliaferro in *The Fathers of the Church* vol. 4 (New York: Christian Heritage, 1947), p. 364: "For there's not one of these sensibles doesn't please us from equality or likeness. But where equality and likeness, there numberliness [*numerositas*]. In fact, nothing is so equal or like as one and one. . . ." Compare this 'analogical' account based upon what

he calls the regular progression [*analogia*] or "rhythmicality" of the universe and our ability to participate within it by imagining [*figurae*] with Kant's account following the scientific revolution (below).

10 Still, Kant contends that "all stiff regularity (such as approximates to mathematical regularity) has something repugnant to taste" (80) and that the mere ascription of beauty "to geometrically regular features, such as a circle, a square, a cube . . . as mere presentations of a definite concept which prescribes the rule for the figure" (78) violates the aesthetic criteria (purposiveness without a concept). Nonetheless, while it may not be the case that beauty is merely the presentation of a mathematical concept, it by no means follows that it either challenges it, nor that its communicability may not cohere with it, as is evident from the following:

> mathematics, certainly does not play the least part in the charm and movement of the mind produced by music. Rather, it is only the indispensible condition (*conditio sine qua non*) of that proportion of the combining as well as changing impressions which makes it possible to grasp that all in one and prevents them from destroying one another, and to let them harmonize toward a continuous movement and quickening of the mind by affections that are consonant with it and thus (lead) to a comfortable self-enjoyment (173)

This *conditio sine qua non* which does not determine but "lets (impressions) harmonize toward a continuous movement and quickening of the mind by affections that are consonant with it" would then need to be referred to the unity and harmony of mathematical infrastructure of the first *Critique's Principles of Pure Understanding*—and contrasted with the failure of that experience in confrontation with the sublime, one which in fact the first *Critique* had already encountered in an event in which "all numbers (lose) their power to measure, our thoughts all definiteness, and . . . our judgment of the whole resolves itself into an amazement which is speechless, and only the more eloquent on that account" (A622/B650).

11 The experience of the Egyptian pyramids interested Kant throughout his major aesthetic writings. It appears as well in his *Observations on the Feeling of the Beautiful and Sublime*, trans. John Goldthwait (Berkeley: University of California Press, 1960), pp. 48–9.

12 Kant's description of the experience of the pyramid then violates the linear time sequence, "the rules of universal time determination" (A178/B228) that the *Principles of Pure Understanding* (regulatively in the Analogies) were to institute in bringing about the requisite

transcental unity of understanding. The failure of the sublime in this sense must be seen precisely as the instantiation of another *standpoint*, another horizon, and another world-order, and precisely itself the "counter-example" which verifies Kant's assertion at the outset of the *Critique's* treatment of the Analogies—which were to institute the strict determinism (and temporality) of Newtonian mechanism—that "existence cannot be constructed" (A179/B222):

> The effort, therefore, to receive in one single intuition a measure for magnitude that requires a considerable time to apprehend is a kind of representation which, subjectively considered, is contrary to purpose, but objectively, as requisite for the estimation of magnitude it is purposive. Thus the very violence which is done to the subject through the imagination is judged as purposive *in reference to the whole determination of the mind*. (98)

Note as well that while it is "the voice of reason" (93) that is in question, the faculty in question is the faculty of synthesis, the imagination, and that the feeling which arises precisely as an effect of this encounter with an event in which "violence is done to the subject" is precisely moral respect for what transcends (96).

13 See Charles Jencks, *Symbolic Architecture* (New York: Rizzoli, 1985), p. 21.

14 Compare Martin Heidegger, "Building Dwelling Thinking" in *Poetry, Language, Thought,* trans. Albert Hofstadter (New York: Harper & Row, 1971), p. 158.

> Because building produces locations, the joining of the spaces of these locations necessarily brings with it space, as *spatium* and as *extensio*, into the thingly structure of buildings. But building never shapes pure "space" as a single entity. Neither directly nor indirectly. Nevertheless, because it produces things as locations, building is closer to the nature of spaces and the origin of the nature of "space" than any geometry and mathematics.

For further discussion of Heidegger on architecture and the question of place, see Christian Norberg-Schultz, *Genius Loci: Towards a Phenomenology of Architecture* (New York: Rizzoli, 1980). Likewise, see Paolo Portughesi *Postmodern: The Architecture of the Postindustrial Society*, trans. Ellen Shapiro (New York: Rizzoli, 1983), pp. 59f.

15 Kenneth Frampton, "The Status of Man and the Status of His Objects:

A Reading of The Human Condition," in *Hannah Arendt: The Recovery of the Public World*, ed. Melvyn A. Hill (New York: St Martin's, 1979), p. 111.

16 Paolo Portoghesi, *After Modern Architecture* (New York: Rizzoli, 1982), p. 31.

17 Immanuel Kant, *First Introduction to the Critique of Judgement*, trans. James Haden (Indianapolis: Bobbs-Merrill, 1965), p. 18.

18 See for example, Mary Hesse, *The Structure of Scientific Inference* (Berkeley: University of California Press, 1974), and Ernan McMullin, "Fertility of Theory and the Unit of Appraisal in Science" in *Essays in Memory of Imre LaKatos*, Boston Studies in the Philosophy of Science, vol. 39, ed. R. S. Cohen, et. al. (Minneapolis: University of Minnesota Press, 1984).

19 Giulio C. Argan, *The Renaissance City* (New York: George Braziller, 1969), p. 26.

20 Maurice Merleau-Ponty, *Phenomenology of Perception*, trans. Colin Smith (New York: Humanities, 1962), p. 287. For further discussion of this point compare Michel de Certeau, "Practices of Space" in *On Signs*, ed. Marshall Blonsky (Baltimore: Johns Hopkins University Press, 1985). It is perhaps not accidental then that authors as diverse as Merleau-Ponty and Wittgenstein still understood architecture, like works of art generally, as 'gestures' and—notwithstanding the structural or syntactic constraints by which both had apparently limited the meaningful—in terms of the archive of expressivisim.

21 See Norberg-Schulz, *Genius Loci*.

22 Ludwig Wittgenstein, *The Blue and Brown Books* (New York: Barnes & Noble, 1969), p. 28.

23 Wittgenstein, *Philosophical Investigations*, p. 33.

24 Ibid., p. 48.

25 Norberg-Schulz, *Genius Loci*, p. 182.

26 Joseph Masheck, "Reflections in Onyx" *Art in America*, 74:4 (April 1986), p. 145.

27 Kant introduces the term in *Observations on the Feeling of the Beautiful and Sublime* as one which is "more peculiar to the glittering sublime; for this is properly a mixed feeling combining the beautiful and the sublime in which each taken by itself is colder. . . ," p. 98.

28 Ludwig Wittgenstein, *Culture and Value*, trans. Peter Winch, ed. G. H. von Wright (Chicago: University of Chicago Press, 1980), p. 3. As Jacques Bouveresse has rightly pointed out regarding Wittgenstein—and notwithstanding the ambivalence of his own architectural constructions (ones which he thought himself lacked 'health' in the Kierkegaardian sense[38])—Wittgenstein can hardly be classified as modernist, having in fact strongly dissociated himself from

the modern (see p. 7). See the article of Bouveresse, "Wittgenstein et L'Architecture" in *Vienne 1880–1938: L'apocalypse joyeuse* (Paris: Editions du Centre Pompidou, 1986).

29 This conjunction between *techne, arete,* and *prohairesis* must be carefully thought through. It cannot simply be true for the Greeks. Aristotle in fact contrasts the ethical and the technical here. See for example, *The Nichomachean Ethics,* trans. J. A. K. Thomson (New York: Penguin, 1979), p. 93.

30 Norberg-Schulz, *Genius Loci,* p. 54) points out that Vitruvius's canons retained a 'symbolic' meaning in architectural practices up until the eighteenth century. Further expansion of this issue would then need to take into account the complex and overdetermined relations between reason and taste during the Enlightenment, a contrast which had been valorized and hierarchialized precisely in terms of an opposition between the rational and the irrational, the intellect and imagination, and the beauty of the geometrical or the rational and that of the "corruptible faculties," as Perrault put it. See the detailed analyses of Joseph Rykwert in *The First Moderns: The Architects of the Eighteenth Century* (Cambridge, Mass.: MIT Press, 1980).

31 Erwin Panofsky, "Die Entwicklung der Poportionslehre als Abbild der Stilentwicklung," *Monatscheft fur Kunstwissenschaft,* IV (1921).

32 Nonetheless, no more than reason could deduce the figural from the formal could a canonical morality simply dictate or canonize the architectural, since the same figural extension, the same *lapsus judicii* (and resulting indeterminacy) arises in both. See in this regard the arguments of David Watkin in *Morality and Architecture* (Oxford: Clarendon Press, 1977), against such claims as Pugin's that Christian architecture just meant 'Gothic.' This denial however should not be taken to mean that the architectural and the moral have no relation at all to one another but rather, precisely that the relation is a figural or interpretative one which concerns the potential of the human. See in this sense Jencks's reply to Watkin in "Architecture and Morality," included in his *Late Modern Architecture* (New York: Rizzoli, 1980).

33 Ludwig Wittgenstein, *Culture and Value,* p. 16.

34 Vitruvius, *The Ten Books of Architecture,* trans. Mooris Hicky Morgan (New York: Dover Publications, 1960), p. 5.

35 Ibid., p. 73.

36 Ibid., p. 175.

37 Rykwert, *The First Moderns,* p. 10.

38 Ibid., p. 174.

39 Ibid., pp. 174–5.

40 Ibid., p. 6.

CHAPTER 6   A POSTMODERN LANGUAGE IN ART

1 Jacques Derrida, *La vérité en peinture* (Paris: Flammarion, 1978), p. 409 (henceforth, *VP*)

2 Octavio Paz, *Marcel Duchamp, Appearance Stripped Bare*, trans. Rachel Phillips and Donald Gardner (New York: Seaver Books, 1978), pp. 2, 7 (henceforth, *MD*).

3 Robert Hughes, *The Shock of the New* (New York: Knopf, 1981), p. 54.

4 Martin Heidegger, "The Origin of the Work of Art," in *Poetry, Language, Thought*, trans. Albert Hofstadter (New York: Harper and Row, 1971), p. 66 (henceforth, *OWA*).

5 Ortega Y Gasset, *The Dehumanization of Art and Other Essays on Art, Culture, Literature*, trans. Helene Weyl (Princeton: Princeton University Press, 1968), p. 10 (henceforth, *DHA*).

6 Julia Kristeva, *Desire in Language, A Semiotic Approach to Literature and Art*, ed. Leon S. Roudiez, trans. Thomas Gora, Alice Jardine, Leon S. Roudiez (New York: Columbia University Press, 1980), p. 247 (henceforth, *DIL*).

7 Roland Barthes, *Sade, Fourier, Loyola*, trans. Richard Miller (New York: Hill and Wang, 1982), p. 100.

8 Wendy Steiner, *The Colors of Rhetoric* (Chicago: University of Chicago Press, 1982), (henceforth, *TCR*).

9 Michel Foucault, *This is Not a Pipe*, trans. James Harkness (Berkeley: University of California Press, 1982), p. 35 (henceforth, *TNP*).

10 Michel Foucault, *The Order of Things* (New York: Vintage, 1973), p. 327 (henceforth, *OT*).

11 Thomas Lawson, "Generation in Vitro," *ArtForum* (September 1984), p. 99.

12 Donald Kuspit, "Philosophy and Art: Elective Affinities in an Arranged Marriage," *ArtForum* (April 1984), p. 94.

13 Kate Linker, "From Imitation, to Copy, to Just Effect: On Reading Jean Baudrillard," *ArtForum* (April 1984), p. 44 (henceforth, *JB*).

14 Mario Perniola, "Time and Time Again," trans. Meg Share, *ArtForum* (April 1983), pp. 54–5 (henceforth, *TTA*).

15 André Malraux, *The Voices of Silence*, trans. Stuart Gilbert (Princeton: Princeton University Press, 1978), pp. 31, 32, 36, 38, 42 (henceforth, *TVS*).

16 Jean-François Lyotard, "The Sublime and the Avant-Garde," trans. Lisa Liebmann, *ArtForum* (April 1984), p. 43 (henceforth, *SAG*).

17 Carter Ratcliff, "Stampede to the Figure," *ArtForum* (Summer 1984), 47–55, p. 50 (henceforth, *SF*).

18 Douglas Davis, "The Death of Semantics, the Corruption of Metaphors, the Birth of the *Punctum*," *ArtForum* (May 1984), 56–63, p. 62.

19 Harold Rosenberg, *The Anxious Object, Art Today and its Audience* (New York: Horizon, 1964), p. 111.

20 Gilles Deleuze, *Logique du sens* (Paris: Minuit, 1969), pp. 22–4 (henceforth, *LS*) (all translations are mine).

21 Michel Foucault, "Theatrum Philosophicum," in *Language, Counter-Memory and Practice*, ed. Donald F. Bouchard, trans. Donald F. Bouchard and Sherry Simon (Ithaca: Cornell University Press, 1977), p. 177 (henceforth, *TPH*).

22 Roland Barthes, *The Pleasure of the Text*, trans. Richard Miller (New York: Hill and Wang, 1975), p. 3.

23 Roland Barthes, *Camera Lucida*, trans. Richard Howard (New York: Hill and Wang, 1981), p. 4 (henceforth, *CL*).

CHAPTER 7   THE OTHERNESS OF WORDS: JOYCE, BAKHTIN, HEIDEGGER

1 Gerald Bruns, *Modern Poetry and the Idea of Language: A Critical and Historical Study* (New Haven: Yale Univ. Press, 1974), pp. 138–63.

2 Maurice Blanchot, "Literature and the Right to Death," in *The Gaze of Orpheus and Other Literary Essays*, trans. Lydia Davis (Barrytown, N.Y.: Station Hill Press, 1981), p. 43.

3 See Blanchot: "My hope lies in the materiality of language, in the fact that words are things, too, are a kind of nature—this is given to me and gives me more than I can understand. Just now the reality of words was an obstacle. Now, it is my only chance. A name ceases to be the ephemeral passing of nonexistence, and becomes a concrete ball, a solid mass of existence; language, abandoning the sense, the meaning which was all it wanted to be, tries to become senseless. Everything physical takes precedence: rhythm, weight, mass, shape, and then the paper on which one writes, the trail of the ink, the book" (*Gaze of Orpheus*, p. 46).

4 Clive Hart, "*Finnegans Wake* in Perspective," in *James Joyce Today: Essays on the Major Works* (Bloomington: Indiana University Press, 1966), pp. 152–3.

5 Jacques Lacan, *Écrits: A Selection*, trans. Alan Sheridan (New York: W. W. Norton, 1977), p. 154.

6 Umberto Eco, "The Semantics of Metaphor," in *Semiotics: An Introductory Anthology*, ed. Robert E. Innis (Bloomington: Indiana Univ. Press, 1985), p. 252. In an essay called "Ambiviolences: Notes for Reading Joyce," Stephen Heath writes: "*Ulysses*, definitive end of the realist novel . . . , is the negation of the daylight world of the natural attitude; in its urge for totality, in its perpetual process of fragmentation and hesitation of the multiplicity of fictions it assembles, *Ulysses* begins to unlimit that world, replacing it in the intertext of the fictions of its construction. *Finnegans Wake* opens onto a further level, fixing a totality not through an encyclopaedism . . . but

through an attention to the production of meaning." (*Post-structuralist Joyce*, ed. Derek Attridge and Daniel Ferrer (Cambridge: Cambridge University Press, 1984), p. 50).

7 Louis Althusser, *Reading Capital*, trans. Ben Brewster (London: NLB, 1970) p. 17.

8 Gilles Deleuze and Félix Guattari, *Anti-Oedipus: Capitalism and Schizophrenia*, trans. Robert Hurley, et al. (Minneapolis: University of Minnesota Press, 1983), p. 109.

9 Jean-Michel Rabaté, "Lapsus ex machina," in *Post-structuralist Joyce*, p. 81. See also, in this same volume, Jacques Aubert, on the first word of the *Wake*: " 'riverrun' seems to evoke the humming of a motor which is momentarily stuck or is building up tension; in order to free our reading, to transform this humming into an articulated sound, we must help the motor to get under way, and give it a throw; we will then be better able to see whether in fact something was locking, or whether there was only an excess of friction or a simple jamming of the cogs or components. We will then have to work out whether and how these images and others work coherently together, and what kind of mechanism this is" (p. 70).

10 John Bishop, *Joyce's Book of the Night* (Madison: University of Wisconsin Press, 1986), p. 307.

11 Julia Kristeva, "Within the Microcosm of 'The Talking Cure,' " trans. Thomas Gora and Margaret Waller, in *Reading Lacan*, ed. Joseph H. Smith and William Kerrigan (New Haven: Yale University Press, 1983), p. 40.

12 See John Gordon's *The Plot of Finnegans Wake*.

13 Where "restrictions of meaning" are to be understood according to Freud's analysis of the relation between meaning and repression. The motive of reading in this event is emancipatory on the model of the joke.

14 Jean-Jacques Lecercle, *Philosophy through the Looking-Glass: Language, Nonsense, Desire* (La Salle: Open Court, 1985), p. 6.

15 Jacques Lacan, *Encore: Le seminaire, livre xx* (Paris: Seuil, 1972), pp. 126–7.

16 Jacques Lacan, Preface to *The Four Fundamental Concepts of Psychoanalysis*, trans. Alan Sheridan (New York: W. W. Norton, 1981), p. ix.

17 See Paul de Man, "Shelley Disfigured," in *Deconstruction and Criticism*, ed. Harold Bloom, et al. (New York: Seabury Press, 1979), p. 68.

18 In Jacques Derrida's "Two Words for Joyce," *Post-structuralist Joyce*, p. 150. See Geoffrey Hartman, *Saving the Text: Literature/Derrida/Philosophy* (Baltimore: The Johns Hopkins University Press, 1981).

19 See Mikhail Bakhtin, *Problems of Dostoevsky's Poetics*, trans. Caryl Emerson (Minneapolis: University of Minnesota Press, 1984), pp. 122–37. For an excellent introduction to Bakhtin, see Dominick LaCapra, "Bakhtin, Marxism, and the Carnivalesque," in *Rethinking Intellectual History: Texts, Contexts, Language* (Ithaca: Cornell University Press, 1983), pp. 291–324.

20 See Mikhail Bakhtin, "Discourse in the Novel," in *The Dialogic Imagination: Four Essays by M. M. Bakhtin*, trans. Caryl Emerson and Michael Holquist (Austin: University of Texas Press, 1981), p. 270.

21 Susan Stewart, "Shouts in the Street: Bakhtin's Anti-Linguistics," in *Critical Inquiry*, 10:2 (December 1983), 276.

22 See Hans-Georg Gadamer, *Truth and Method* (New York: Seabury Press, 1975), p. 236.

23 Julia Kristeva, "Word, Dialogue, and the Novel," trans. Alice Jardine, Thomas Gora, and Leon S. Roudiez (New York: Columbia University Press, 1986), p. 44.

24 For a comprehensive taxonomy of intertextualities, see Laurent Jenny, "The Strategy of Form," in *French Literary Theory Today*, trans. R. Carter, ed. Tzvetan Todorov (Cambridge: Cambridge University Press, 1982), pp. 34–63.

25 Martin Heidegger, *Was heisst Denken?* (Tübingen: Max Niemeyer, 1961), p. 83; *What is Thinking?*, trans. J. Glenn Gray (New York: Harper & Row, 1968), p. 119 (hereafter, *WD*).

26 Samuel Beckett, *Watt* (New York: Grove Press, 1959), p. 83. It's remarkable how Watt's experience with language answers Heidegger's conception: "Not that Watt desired information, for he did not. But he desired words to be applied to his situation, to Mr Knott, to the house, to the grounds, to his duties, to the stairs, to his bedroom, to the kitchen, and in a general way to the conditions of being in which he found himself. For Watt now found himself in the midst of things which, if they consented to be named, did so as it were with great reluctance" (p. 81).

27 Heidegger, *Unterwegs zur Sprache* (Pfullingen: Günther Neske, 1959), p. 205; trans. Peter D. Hertz, *On the Way to Language* (New York: Harper & Row, 1971), p. 98.

28 US254/123: "It is the custom to put speaking and listening in opposition: one man speaks, the other listens. But listening accompanies and surrounds not only speaking such as takes place in conversation. The simultaneousness of speaking and listening has a larger meaning. Speaking is of itself a listening. Speaking is a listening to the language which we speak." Language speaks (*Die Sprache spricht*), but not in the structuralist's sense that we are constrained by its rules and can only say what it allows us to say. Language doesn't speak

through us, rather it calls or summons us, puts us under a claim, as
if we were answerable to what it says, as if it owned us. So there is
some connection between listening and belonging.

29 Heidegger's translators rewrite Heidegger's text in terms of Old
English rather than Old German: "The Old English *thencan*, to think,
and *thancian*, to thank, are closely related; the Old English noun for
thought is *thanc* or *thonc*—a thought, a grateful thought, and the
expression of such a thought; today it survives in the plural *thanks*"
(*What is Called Thinking?*, p. 139).

30 See Heidegger, *Gelassenheit* (Pfullingen: Günther Neske, 1985), esp.
pp. 23–24; trans. John M. Anderson and E. Hans Freund, *Discourse
on Thinking* (New York: Harper & Row, 1966), pp. 54–55.

31 See "Das Ding," in *Vorträge und Aufsätze* (Pfulligen: Günther Neske),
p. 170; trans. Albert Hofstader, *Poetry, Language, Thought*, p. 177:
"The thing things."

CHAPTER 8   POSTMODERNISM AND THEATER

1 Antonin Artaud, *The Theater and Its Double*, trans. Mary Caroline
Richards (New York: Grove Press, 1958), p. 13.

2 Ibid., p. 75.

3 Jacques Derrida, "The Theater of Cruelty and the Closure of Representation," *Writing and Difference*, (Chicago: University of Chicago
Press, 1978), p. 234.

4 Ibid., p. 239.

5 Ibid., p. 240.

6 Artaud, *The Theater and Its Double*, p. 75.

7 Julia Kristeva, "Modern Theater Does Not Take (A) Place," *Sub-
Stance*, 18/19 (1977), p. 131.

8 Artaud, *The Theater and Its Double*, p. 75.

9 See Jan Kott, "The Icon of the Absurd," and "After Grotowski: The
End of the Impossible Theater," *The Theater of Essence*, (Evanston:
Northwestern University Press, 1984), pp. 138, 149 for a discussion
of this problem of nudity in theater.

10 Jan Kott, "Witkiewicz, or The Dialectic of Anachronism," *The Theater
of Essence*, p. 73.

11 See Herbert Blau, *Take Up the Bodies: Theater at the Vanishing Point*
(Urbana: University of Illinois Press, 1982), pp. 272–5.

12 See Stefan Brecht, "Revolution at the Brooklyn Academy of Music,"
The Drama Review, 13:3 (Spring 1969), p. 64, and Stefan Brecht, "Review of *Dionysus in 69*," *The Drama Review*, 13:3 (Spring 1969), p. 162.

13 Nicolas Domenach, "Les Splendeurs et Decadences de la Creation
Collective," *Esprit*, 447 (June 1975), p. 967, cited by Leonora Cham-

pagne, *French Theatre Experiment Since 1968* (Ann Arbor: UMI Research Press, 1984), p. 40

14 Ibid., pp. 24–5.
15 Kristeva, "Modern Theater Does Not Take (A) Place," p. 131.
16 Champagne, *French Theater Experiment Since 1968*, p. 38.
17 Daniel Mesguich, "The Book to Come is a Theater," trans. Carl R. Lovitt, *Sub-Stance*, 18/19 (1977), p. 113.
18 Ibid., p. 114.
19 Ibid., p. 113.
20 Ibid., p. 119.
21 Blau, *Take Up the Bodies*, p. 19.
22 Derrida, "The Theater of Cruelty . . .", p. 247.
23 Blau, *Take Up the Bodies*, p. 90.
24 Ibid., pp. 93–4.
25 Ibid., pp. 106–7.
26 Herbert Blau, "Flights of Angels, Scattered Seeds," *Blooded Thought: Occasions of Theatre* (New York: Performing Arts Journal Publications, 1982), p. 149.

CHAPTER 9   LUCID INTERVALS:
POSTMODERNISM AND PHOTOGRAPHY

I wish to thank Therese Lichtenstein and Christopher Phillips for their extremely helpful suggestions in editing this article.

1 Michel Tournier, "Veronica's Shrouds," in *The Fetishist*, trans. Barbara Wright (New York: New American Library, 1983). On the relation between the Shroud of Turin and photography, see Patrick Maynard, "The Secular Icon: Photography and the Functions of Images," *The Journal of Aesthetics and Art Criticism*, 42:2 (Winter 1983), pp. 155–66.
2 Roland Barthes, *La chambre claire* (Paris: Gallimard/Seuil, 1980), p. 141.
3 Philippe Dubois, *L'Acte photographique* (Brussels: Éditions Labor, 1983), pp. 90–1. Dubois refers specifically in this discussion to the disquieting, ambiguous photographic index of death in Michelangelo Antonioni's film *Blow-Up*.
4 Pierre Klossowski, "On the Collaboration of Demons in the Work of Art," trans. Paul Foss and Allen S. Weiss, in *Art & Text*, 18: *Phantasm and Simulacra* (July 1985), ed. Paul Foss, Paul Taylor, and Allen S. Weiss, p. 9. This special issue on the works of Klossowski also contains related articles by Paul Foss, Alphonso Lingis, Chantal Thomas, and Allen S. Weiss.

5 Ibid., p. 9.

6 Pierre Klossowski, "Du tableau en tant que simulacre," in *La Ressemblance* (Marseille: Editions Ryôan-ji, 1984), p. 76.

7 Ibid., p. 77; cf. Nietzsche, "On Truth and Lie in an Extra-Moral Sense."

8 Ibid., p. 78.

9 Pierre Klossowski, "La décadence du nu," in *La Ressemblance*, p. 64. Indeed, Klossowski effected the presentation of his own phantasms in photography and film, both based on his fictional and critical works. See Pierre Zucca's photography for Klossowski's *La monnaie vivante* (Paris: Losfeld, 1970), and the special issue of *Obliques: Roberte au cinéma* (Paris: Editions Borderie, 1978) on Klossowski and Zucca's film, *Roberte Interdite*.

10 Walter Benjamin, "The Work of Art in the Age of Mechanical Reproduction," trans. Harry Zohn, in *Illuminations* (New York: Schocken, 1973), p. 221.

11 Ibid., p. 223. The main proponent of statistical theory as a critical mode is Jean Baudrillard, especially in *In the Shadow of the Silent Majorities*, trans. Paul Foss, Paul Patton, and John Johnston (New York: Semiotext(e), 1983); much earlier, in the 1950s, probability theory was utilized in artistic production, as in Iannis Xenakis's stochastic (probabilistic) music, such as his *Pithoprakta* (1955–56). On the relations between criminological photography and statistics in the nineteenth century, see Allan Sekula, "The Body and the Archive," *October*, 39 (Winter 1986).

12 Jean Baudrillard, *L'échange symbolique et la mort* (Paris: Gallimard, 1976), p. 115.

13 Jean Baudrillard, *Simulacres et simulation* (Paris: Galilée, 1981), p. 10.

14 Ibid., p. 17.

15 Baudrillard, *In the Shadow*, p. 36.

16 Ibid., p. 10.

17 Baudrillard, *L'échange symbolique*, p. 112.

18 The classic texts on narrative fascination and the ideological structure of the cinematic apparatus are: Laura Mulvey, "Visual Pleasure and Narrative Cinema" *Screen* (Autumn 1975), and Jean-Louis Baudry, "Effets idéologiques produits par l'appareil de base," *Cinétheque*, 7–8.

19 Andre Bazin, *What is Cinema?* vol. I, trans. Hugh Gray (Berkeley: University of California Press, 1967).

20 Craig Owens, "The Allegorical Impulse: Toward a Theory of Postmodernism (Part 2)" *October*, 13 (Summer 1980), p. 80.

21 Annette Michelson, "About *Snow*" *October*, 8 (Spring 1979), p. 123. On the importance of a theory of simulacra in the investigation of the transcendental subject, see Marc Richir, *Recherches phénoménolo-*

giques (I, II, III): Fondation pour la phénoménologie transcendantale (Brussels: Éditions Ousia, 1981). Briefly stated: the transcendental ego only appears as an illusion, ungraspable in itself, always masked by the psychological ego. This illusion—an *ontological simulacrum*—is investigated by transcendental phenomenology as a *poetics of origins*, an *art of simulation*. The field of originary ontological phantasma is revealed in the simulations produced by the transcendental phenomenological reduction, where the generation of variations accords with the figurative structure of the *as if*—the *simile.*

22 Roland Barthes, "Change the Object Itself," trans. Stephen Heath, in *Image, Music, Text* (New York: Hill & Wang, 1977), p. 167.

23 Charles Sanders Peirce, "Logic as Semiotic: The Theory of Signs," in *Philosophical Writings of Peirce*, ed. Justus Buchler (New York: Dover, 1955). On contemporary aesthetic theory of the sign, and especially its indexical aspect in photography, see Rosalind Krauss, "Notes on the Index, Parts I and II," in *The Originality of the Avant-Garde and Other Modernist Myths* (Cambridge, Mass.: MIT Press, 1985); and Dubois, *L'Acte photographique*: the first chapter of this work, "De la vérisimilitude à l'index" (co-authored with Geneviève van Cauwenberge) is an excellent history of the problematic, to which this section of my article is indebted.

24 Roland Barthes, "The Photographic Message," in *Image, Music, Text*, p. 17.

25 Dubois, *L'Acte photographique*, p. 49.

26 Barthes, *La chambre claire*, p. 165.

27 Dubois, *L'Acte photographique*, p. 80.

28 Douglas Crimp, "The Photographic Activity of Postmodernism," *October*, 15 (Winter, 1981), p. 98. On the postmodernist photographic practices of Sherrie Levine, Cindy Sherman, Barbara Kruger, and Martha Rosler, see also Craig Owens, "The Allegorical Impulse"; on the significance of the fact that these major postmodernist photographers are all women, see Craig Owens, "The Discourse of Others: Feminists and Postmodernism," in Hal Foster, *The Anti-Aesthetic* (Port Townsend, Wash.: Bay Press, 1983). On the use of text as icon, see Allen S. Weiss, "Cartesian Simulacra," in *Persistence of Vision* (Spring, 1987).

29 On the narrative structure of Muybridge's *Studies in Human Locomotion*, see Hollis Frampton, "Eadweard Muybridge: Fragments of a Tesseract," in *Circles of Confusion* (Rochester: Visual Studies Workshop Press, 1983), and Marta Braun, "Muybridge's Scientific Fictions," *Studies in Visual Communication*, 10:3 (Summer 1984). We should note here the influence of Marey's chronophotography on both Marcel Duchamp and the Italian Futurists, Duchamp's work

especially having had great repercussions on the transition from modernism to postmodernism. On Duchamp's use of photography, see Jean Clair, *Duchamp et la photographie* (Paris: Chêne, 1977).

30 We might remember that the antihumanism of post-structuralist thought—transformed from Heideggerian phenomenology to Derridian deconstructionism—founds the "death of the subject" and the "death of the author" on the Nietzschean "death of God." This, in fact, is the central theme of Klossowski's entire oeuvre. We might also remember that post-structuralism and postmodernism are not homologous terms: in fact, the object of most post-structuralist research and criticism, especially at its height in the *Tel Quel* group, is modernist art: postmodernist works are noticably neglected.

The key texts on postmodernism as an epochal shift are those of Jean-François Lyotard, Fredric Jameson, and Jürgen Habermas. See especially the entire issue of *New German Critique*, 33: *Modernity and Postmodernity* (Fall 1984).

CHAPTER 10 FILMING: INSCRIPTIONS OF *DENKEN*

1 Susan Sontag, *On Photography* (New York: Penguin, 1977), p. 153.
2 Martin Heidegger, "The Age of the World Picture," in *The Question Concerning Technology*, trans. William Lovitt (New York: Harper and Row, 1977), p. 115. The original German title was "Die Begrundung des neuzeitlichen Weltbildes durch die Metaphysik."
3 Martin Heidegger, "Die Zeit des Weltbildes," in *Holzwege* (Frankfurt: Vittorio Klostermann, 1977), p. 94.
4 Heidegger, "Age of the World Picture," p. 136.
5 Ibid., p. 132.
6 Ibid., p. 128.
7 Ibid., p. 136.
8 Cf. Vincent B. Leitch, *Deconstructive Criticism* (New York: Columbia University Press, 1983), p. 34.
9 Heidegger, "Age of the World Picture," p. 183.
10 Cf. Gilles Deleuze, *Cinema 1: L'Image-Mouvement* (Paris: Minuit, 1983). Deleuze's reading of "movement-images" does not seem to reflect upon the crisis of imagination as it is disclosed in the genealogical play of images from the time of Kant's third critique to that of commodity aesthetics.
11 Immanuel Kant, *Critique of Pure Reason*, trans. N. K. Smith (New York: St. Martin's Press, 1965), p. 183.
12 Immanuel Kant, *Kritik der Urteilskraft* (Stuttgart: Philipp Reclam, 1976), p. 146.

13 Ibid., p. 147.

14 Is the whole therefore really false, or can imagination still attain pleasure from its transcendental disintegration and the continual discontinuity of the play of the manifold? The former position has become that of Adorno's negative dislectics, the latter has developed into "positions" of deconstruction.

15 John Sallis, *The Gathering of Reason* (Athens, Ohio: Ohio University Press, 1980). Regarding the phenomenon of occlusion Sallis writes: "Nietzsche called it the advent of nihilism. I would prefer to allude to it with the word 'occlusion'—to speak of the occlusion of the distinction between the intelligible and sensible, and correspondingly, of the occlusion, hence crisis, of metaphysics. Central to this phenomenon is the recurrent emptying of every refuge in which a pure intelligibility would be secure—that is, the recurrent appropriation of every alleged intelligible to the sphere of the sensible" (p. 5).

16 Heidegger, "Age of the World-Picture," p. 140.

17 Cf. Derrida's "The Pit and the Pyramid: Introduction to Hegel's Semiology," in *Margins of Philosophy*, trans. Alan R. Bass (Chicago: University of Chicago Press, 1982), p. 80.

18 Friedrich Nietzsche, *The Birth of Tragedy and The Case of Wagner*, trans. Walter Kaufmann (New York: Vintage Books, 1967), p. 52.

19 Heidegger, "Age of the World Picture," p. 136.

20 Ibid., p. 135.

21 Martin Heidegger, "What Calls For Thinking?" in *Basic Writings*, trans. David F. Krell (New York: Harper and Row, 1977), p. 350.

22 Kant, *Kritik der Urteilskraft*, p. 135.

23 Cf. Appendix 1 in Heidegger's *The Question Concerning Technology*.

24 Ibid., p. 147.

25 Ibid., p. 136.

26 Ibid., p. 28.

27 Ibid., p. 153.

28 Cf. Timothy Corrigan's *The Displaced Image* (Austin: University of Texas Press, 1983) for a fine deconstructive reading of the New German Cinema.

29 Cf. Kant, *Critique of Pure Reason*, p. 204, A170: "Such magnitudes may also be called *flowing*, since the synthesis of productive imagination involved in their production is a progression in time, and the continuity of time is ordinarily designated by the term flowing or flowing away."

30 Michel Foucault, *The Order of Things* (New York: Vintage, 1973), p. 341.

31 Ibid., p. 342.

32 Ibid., pp. 342–3.

33 Heidegger, "Age of the World Picture," p. 132.
34 Ibid., p. 128.

CHAPTER 11   THE TELEVISED AND THE UNTELEVISED:
KEEPING ON EYE ON/OFF THE TUBE

1 Jean Baudrillard and Sylvère Lotringer, "Forget Baudrillard," trans. Phil Beitchman, Lee Hildreth, and Mark Polizzotti, in Jean Baudrillard, *Forget Foucault* (New York: Semiotext(e), 1987), p. 134 (henceforth, *FF*).

2 Given the diversity of forms of television production (programming, "sponsorship" (funding, control), etc.) in the world, *this article intersects American television specifically,* and it is necessary to keep this specificity in mind (an insistence that might conflict with the white image of generalized television offered by Baudrillard). In other words, these remarks are clearly not to be read as philosophical observations about television as a universal; one of our points here is that even while the hardware and the play between the televised and the untelevised relate the networks to each other, there is no universal television. On the one hand, it might also be a mistake to identify any particular instance of television as absolutely unique; state-"sponsored" and "non-commercial" television, for example, are not entirely unrelated to "commercial" television. On the other hand, though, the different television networks ("networks" in the broadest sense) are not equivalent to each other, just as the televised and the untelevised are not interchangeable.

3 Among other ruptures, and in conjunction with other technocultural developments, another opposition reformulated if not effaced by "postmodern" culture is the former complex of lines drawn between the public and the private (cf. Joshua Meyrowitz, *No Sense of Place: The Impact of Electronic Media on Social Behavior* (New York: Oxford University Press, 1985)).

4 "The mass media . . . fabricate non-communication . . . if one agrees to define communication as an exchange. . . . The media founds itself on this latter definition: *they are what always prevents response,* making all processes of exchange impossible (except in various forms of response *simulation,* themselves integrated in the transmission process, thus leaving the unilateral nature of the communication intact)," Jean Baudrillard, "Requiem for the Media," in *For a Critique of the Political Economy of the Sign,* trans. Charles Levin (St. Louis, Mo.: Telos Press, 1981), pp. 169–70. See also Baudrillard's reference to this earlier piece and extension of its point in "Implosion of Meaning in the Media," in *In the Shadow of the Silent Majorities,* trans.

Paul Foss, Paul Patton, and John Johnston (New York: Semiotext(e), 1983), p. 105.

5 For a compelling criticism of the pervasive, general idea that technology is monolithic, or has uniform, universalizing, or universal (possibly universally "bad") characteristics or effects, I refer the reader to Peter Kulchyski, "Technology and Community: Northern Natives and a Deconstruction of Development" (delivered at the Strategies of Critique Symposium, York University, Toronto, March, 1987). The paper's effectiveness in addressing and criticizing that conception of technology is derived from its specificity. It focuses on the Inuit Broadcasting Corporation in Canada's far north, which programs and broadcasts television in the Inuktitut language, and which, Kulchyski argues, marks the incorporation of television into Inuit culture more than the other way around (the Inuit are still primarily a hunting culture, and the content of their television reflects that).

6 While there would be no serious analysis of phenomena such as television without the various strategies employed by, e.g., economics, psychology, semiotics, sociology, anthropology, feminist criticism, film criticism, literary criticism, communications studies, etc., not to mention *engineering*, we must insist that none of these can be *the* fundamental line, the final story about television (the programming continues, there is no "final story").

7 John Fiske and John Hartley, *Reading Television* (New York: Methuen, 1978), e.g., pp. 15, 86, 116 ff., the straining pair of columns on 124–5, and ch. 11, "Television Realism" (henceforth, *RT*).

8 It is worth considering the curious possibility that "information" and "data" may have anthropological, sociological, and, indeed ($$$) economic, but *no epistemological* dimensions (they may have little to do with "knowledge"), even if the discourse of "information" is central to what Foucault might have called our current episteme.

In connection with issues raised by Jean-François Lyotard in *The Postmodern Condition*, trans. Geoff Bennington and Brian Massumi (Minneapolis: University of Minnesota Press, 1984), philosophy cannot help but wonder about its own possible future roles and functions in the operations of data management in an "information age" or a "communications society."

9 "Markmaking"—a word used to describe art processes, practices, and products—is a happily or hopelessly general term that could be applied with equal imprecision to a Paleolithic pictograph, a glob of glistening oil paint on canvas, a track in the sand, the depression made in a rock by the motion of grinding meal, and even to a slab of reinforced concrete, or any graphic marking—shaping, tracing—or system of marking, not necessarily "art" or artifact, not even

necessarily human (wolves, for example, mark their territory by urinating on trees, and toothmarks (carvings) on a tree mark the beaver's building and food acquisition habits; the gesture of linemaking or the trace of creation cannot be reserved for human creatures).

The linkage may not sound direct, but what I have in mind here with "markmaking" is connected to Castoriadis's conception of "absolute creations," and his insightful articulation of the difference between what is natural and what is made (cf. Cornelius Castoriadis, "Technique," in *Crossroads in the Labyrinth*, trans. Kate Soper and Martin H. Ryle (Cambridge, Mass.: MIT Press, 1984), e.g., pp. 239, 241).

10 cf. Stanley Karnow, *Vietnam* (New York: Viking Press, 1983), p. 529.

11 For an interesting discussion of Dad and Mrs. Dad in the Golden Age of Television, see Mark Crispin Miller, "Deride and Conquer," in *Watching Television*, ed. Todd Gitlin (New York: Pantheon Books, 1986), pp. 196ff. (henceforth, *WT*).

12 Gloria Steinem published the lead article in a February, 1988 issue of *TV Guide*, arguing the importance of *Cagney and Lacey*.

13 *To Tell the Truth*, was a popular, long-running, American quiz show in which the contestants questioned a panel of three individuals who all claimed to be the same person. The aim, of course, was to eliminate the two imposters, and to find the one real identity.

14 This is part of the force of the symbolic order that Fiske and Hartley describe as "bardic."

15 "Anti-saga," because, almost paradoxically, television is both so fragmented (e.g., the programs are all competing with each other) and so repetitive (there really is no master program, and the competitive programmings produce remarkable similarities in their attempts to snag the audience, attempts that in prime time often seem to shoot for the lowest common denominator).

16 For an interesting discussion of the technologies of speed, I refer the reader to Paul Virilio and Sylvère Lotringer, *Pure War*, trans. Mark Polizotti (New York: Semiotext(e), 1983) (henceforth, *P.O.W.*), and Paul Virilio, *Speed and Politics*, trans. Mark Polizotti (New York: Semiotext(e), 1986) (and see n. 19). And for some philosophical remarks on the speed of technology and its empty telos (the name of nothing), I refer the reader to Jacques Derrida, "No Apocalypse, Not Now," trans. Catherine Porter and Philip Lewis, *Diacritics*, 14 (Summer 1984), pp. 20–31.

17 Foucault points out that war may be a better point of reference than "the great model of language and signs." As he puts it, history is warlike, not signlike, "relations of power, not relations of meaning" (Michel Foucault, "Truth and Power," in *Power/Knowledge*, ed. Colin Gordon (New York: Pantheon Books, 1980), p. 114).

18 ". . . 'The news'—a euphemism for ideological images of the world that determine political reality for a vast majority of the world's population . . .," Edward Said, "Opponents, Audiences, Constituencies and Community," in, *The Anti-Aesthetic*, ed. Hal Foster (Port Townsend, Wash.: Bay Press, 1983), p. 157.

19 From Virilio's standpoint, the essence of technology is speed, and the priority of the contestation for space (geography) has been surpassed and displaced by the struggle for control of time, a struggle whose effect is the overcoming of distance. Television is a good example of this displacement, as is the (not just random) question, "whose missiles move faster?," which means, "whose have the shortest gap or difference between launch and impact?"

As Virilio acknowledges (e.g., *P.O.W.*, p. 40), his insight is derived from the ancient Chinese militarist Sun Tzu's observation in *The Art of War* that, "Speed is the essence of war" (Sun Tzu, *The Art of War*, trans. Samuel B. Griffith, (New York: Oxford University Press, 1971), p. 134 (henceforth, *AW*). However, Sun Tzu makes this particular observation in Chapter XI, "The Nine Varieties of Ground" (". . . ground may be classified as dispersive, frontier, key, communicating, focal, serious, difficult, encircled, and death," *AW*, p. 130), which follows a chapter entitled, "Terrain" (". . . may be classified according to its nature as accessible, entrapping, indecisive, constricted, precipitous, and distant," *AW*, p. 124). Both chapters follow the assertion that the first element of war is "the measurement of space," and that "Measurements of space are derived from the ground" (*AW*, p. 88).

Twenty-four or so centuries have passed since Sun Tzu, and things have changed; for one thing, communications and transportation technologies have actually mobilized territory itself in some important ways. However, the point is that we must not let ourselves believe that technology and its "essence" (speed) have surpassed their intimate ties to territory. Territory—space—necessarily continues to have an inescapable, geographically specific aspect, which may be complicated and even transformed by the technologies of speed, but never surpassed by them.

It may be true that the technological war is a war over speed (an ideal of the instant, perfect time control), and that the one who "wins" will be the one who is fastest (assuming that the missile's speed is augmented by, among others, guidance systems, for *placing* the weapon, and devices for evading and deceiving radar, which do not depend upon its speed (e.g., radar-invisible materials, decoy warheads, etc.)). However, 1) the main categories of numbers used in ballistics measure not only velocity but energy (the most interesting figure here would be the energy transferred at impact), and 2) what is most important with any weapon is control of the projectile's point of impact, its *placement*. So accuracy is a crucial factor; a missile's velocity is only as meaningful as its ability to reach its target. The point of impact of the warheads, and the ability to predict and control that point—the ability to control *where* the warhead lands—is what really matters, what the warheads are really for, really about. Along with speed (control of time), territory (control of space) remains the critical factor.

20 The extremely widespread use of satellite communications technology has brought more than "entertainment" to rural America, as demonstrated dramatically by the development of video cattle auctions, which ranchers and other interested parties watch at home on their satellite dish-equipped TVs, and in which they participate by means of telephone bidding.

" 'This has lifted ranchers out of the past,' Jim Wingate, the auctioneer, said today. 'It has put them in as close contact with the world as downtown Houston, put them on Main Street' " (Robert Reinhold, "Video Cattle Auctions," *The New York Times* (June 29, 1987), p. A10).

However, and to keep open the question of the televised and the untelevised (to avoid being too mesmerized by the giddiness of commutations), it may be important to remember that while those cattle are brought into the network or are made to intersect the tube—while they are mark(et)ed via this abstract or nonlocalized "medium" (a medium that directly and instantaneously connects Colorado with Kansas, Texas, Utah, Montana, New Mexico, etc.)— the creatures continue to be grazing somewhere specific and definite (somewhere where the smell of the breeze is unlike that anywhere else), chewing their cuds, as usual, each one marked also for a civilized ("humane") death in a slaughterhouse, each one potential plastic-wrapped, supermarket meat, food for consumers, death effaced.

21 "The heartbeat of America" (". . . today's Chevrolet") is the jewel at the heart of a massive, ongoing General Motors Corporation advertising campaign.

22 ". . . you can do it, in the Army," a good place *to be*, because, "We're not a company. We're your country; the Air Force, the Marines, the Army, the Navy. We're the Armed Forces."

23 Jane Brody, "Personal Health," *The New York Times* (January 21, 1987), p. C8.

24 "In any case, number is a first-class pointer. It provides an index of success and failure," Fernand Braudel, *The Structures of Everyday Life*, trans. Sian Reynolds (New York: Harper & Row, 1981), p. 31. Clearly,

television has become a very successful aspect of everday, "postmodern" life.

25 Just to mention two important analyses of MTV, see Pat Aufderheide, "The Look of the Sound," in *WT*, and E. Ann Kaplan, *Rocking around the Clock* (New York: Methuen, 1987), particularly the chapter, "Gender Address and the Gaze in MTV."

But then, on a different side of the tube, there is another, alternative story, which is CBS's polymorphous-subverse *Pee-wee's Playhouse*, a manic Saturday morning children's program. Pee-wee routinely slams the door in the face of a pushy salesman, a gleeful, televised blow against the culture of consumption. For a lucid discussion of "Pee-wee's Playhouse" see, Glenn O'Brien, "Pee-wee Hermeneutics," *ArtForum* (Summer 1987), pp. 90–3.

26 This is a wholly Cartesian subject, since it is founded on the certainty of the axiom, "I am deceived, therefore, I exist." Nowdays, of course, we may be forced to buy pomo artist Barbara Kruger's updated version of the formula—"I shop, therefore I am"—which offers a different identity for the subject, one perhaps more appropriate for the subject of a TV culture.

27 This suggestion was aired by Kevin MacDonald at the G. S. L. Lecture Center, Stony Brook, New York, Spring, 1987.

28 Again, this seems to be something like what Fiske and Hartley are getting at in describing TV as "bardic." Also, we may write this through Derrida's bind, the doubled aspect here being comprised of that which unites a culture or holds it together and that which keeps the members of a tribe locked in to place.

29 For an excellent discussion of this issue, see Tim Luke, "Televisual Democracy and the Politics of Charisma," *Telos*, 70 (Winter 1986–87), pp. 59–79.

30 Ralph Nader, "Candidates Avoid the Public," *New York Times*, November 4, 1986, p. A31. While his point is clear, Nader's title is somewhat inappropriate, since it seems to be based upon a pretelevision articulation of the difference between public and private.

31 Reagan made this statement (6/16/87) in response to congressional investigations of the role of the White House in the Iran-Contra scandal. At the same time, he said that most Americans were getting bored with the investigation and had returned to "watching their favorite television shows." The simulcast Oliver North Special had not been aired yet; it became the summer's instantaneous favorite, although, like most other TV shows, it was soon forgotten.

32 Vladimir Volkoff's espionage novel, *The Set-up*, trans. Alan Sheridan (New York: Arbor House, 1985), elaborates a convincing version of this type of paranoic scenario, in which leftist Parisian intellectuals

are used by a veiled political/martial apparatus (the K.G.B.), whose outstanding characteristic is patience, since time is on its side, time even to contemplate Sun Tzu.

33 cf. Jean Baudrillard, "The Orders of Simulacra," trans. Philip Beitchman, in *Simulations* (New York: Semiotext(e), 1983), p. 138: "We should compare this kind of control with the traditional repressive space, the police-space that still corresponded to a *signifying* violence. . . . All of that no longer has any meaning."

"Repressive space" provides an apparent point of contact with Foucault (who would have been disinclined to follow Baudrillard's reliance on the discourse of "signification" (see n. 17)). However, one obvious difference between Baudrillard and Foucault here is that Foucault would not simply associate "police-space" with the past, but would more likely and with a more specific eye be interested in the ways that past, predominantly coercive formations of police-space have been displaced by or incorporated into other, newer police-spaces, including the "totalitarian, bureaucratic concentration" that Baudrillard seems to suggest (p. 138ff.) has displaced the police. Having developed into *agencies of intelligence*, the police have not disappeared. They have simply developed "more sophisticated" techniques of regulation and control, which produce less need for coercion. Not that coercion has disappeared, either. Perhaps Baudrillard has never been arrested by the police, who are not equivalent to or interchangeable with *Miami Vice* officers Crockett and Tubbs.

34 Derrida points to what Baudrillard has forgotten when he asks, "What is South Africa? . . . If we could forget about the suffering, the humiliation, the torture and the deaths, we might be tempted to look at this region of the world as a giant tableau or painting, the screen for some geopolitical computer" ("Racism's Last Word," trans. Peggy Kamuf, *Critical Inquiry*, 12 (Autumn 1985), p. 297–8).

35 "The truth." To say that it is between the televised and the untelevised is not to locate it in some mystical void, but, more simply, to admit the necessity of the connection between them.

36 In *The Archaeology of Knowledge*, trans. A. M. Sheridan Smith (New York: Pantheon, 1972), p. 130, Michel Foucault states that, "It is not possible for us to describe our own archive, since it is from within these rules that we speak, since it is that which gives to what we can say . . . its modes of appearance. . . ." In short, the problem with an "archaeology of the present" is the impossible position of independence it implies, an independence from any specific discursive (/subject) position which, as usual, would transform the philosopher into a discourse-neutral divinity (what a tired and pathetic delusion), or at least into a thoroughgoing metaphysician (most likely someone

claiming to be unaffected by TV, methodologically or epistemologically independent of this information age).

However—and this is a crucial philosophical point—given that Foucault also states that no archive is exhaustible anyway, it seems that his observation should be taken as a note of precaution regarding invisible, inarticulable, "silent," determinative and constitutive limitations (marginalia) rather than as a hard and fast rule, which would have to be and would necessarily remain metaphysical. Foucault's archaeology, which analyzes rules, cannot itself set up new rules too seriously. If this particular precaution were read as a (necessarily metaphysical) rule—if we let the power of Foucault rule our discourse—we would all just have to shut up about television, since TV belongs to no archive other than the current one(s), the American site of which might be dubbed the eternal rerun of *Death Valley Days*.

CHAPTER 12   POSTMODERNISM AND DANCE: DANCE, DISCOURSE, DEMOCRACY

1 Herbert Marcuse, *The Aesthetic Dimension: Toward a Critique of Marxist Aesthetics* (Boston: Beacon Press, 1978), p. 73. Also see Theodor Adorno, *Aesthetic Theory* (New York and London: Routledge & Kegan Paul, 1983).

2 Walter Benjamin, "Surrealism: The Last Snapshot of the European Intelligentsia," in *Reflections: Essays, Aphorisms, Autobiographical Writings* (New York: Harcourt, Brace, Jovanovich, 1978), pp. 189, 192. Also see his study on "The Artwork in the Age of Technical Reproduction," in *Illuminations* (New York: Schocken, 1969).

3 Richard Wolin, *Walter Benjamin: An Aesthetic of Redemption* (New York: Columbia University Press, 1982), p. 31.

4 Herbert Marcuse, *Counter-revolution and Revolt* (Boston: Beacon Press, 1972), p. 99.

5 John Dewey, *Art as Experience* (New York: G. P. Putnam's Sons, 1958), p. 39.

6 John Dewey, *Democracy and Education* (New York: Macmillan, 1966), p. 123.

7 Ibid., p. 22.

8 Maurice Merleau-Ponty, "The Philosopher and Sociology," in *Signs* (Evanston, Ill.: Northwestern University Press, 1964), p. 110.

9 See my essay on "Balanchine's Formalism," in *Dance Perspectives*, 55 (Autumn 1973), pp. 123–45, reprinted in M. Cohen and R. Copeland, eds., *What Is Dance? Readings in Theory and Criticism* (New York: Oxford University Press, 1983). Also see Lincoln Kirstein, *Movement and Metaphor* (New York: Praeger, 1974) and Marcia Siegel, *The Shapes*

of Change: Images of American Dance (New York: Houghton Mifflin, 1979).

10 See Clement Greenberg, *Art and Culture: Critical Essays* (Boston: Beacon Press, 1961); Michael Fried, *Three American Painters: Stella, Olitski, Noland* (Cambridge: Fogg Museum of Art, Harvard University, 1965); Fried, "Art and Objecthood," *Artforum* (June 1967); Fried, *Absorption and Theatricality: Painting and the Beholder in the Age of Diderot* (Berkeley: University of California Press, 1980); and Rosalind Krauss, *Terminal Iron Works: The Sculpture of David Smith* (Cambridge: MIT Press, 1971).

11 See Krauss, *Terminal Iron Works*.

12 See my study, "The Novelhood of the Novel: The Limits of Representation and the Modernist Discovery of Presence," *The Chicago Review*, 48:4 (Spring 1977), pp. 87–108. Also see my "Foreword" to the English translation of Roman Ingarden, *The Literary Work of Art* (Evanston, Il.: Northwestern University Press, 1973). In preparing the present essay, I consulted Richard Ellman and Charles Feidelson, eds., *The Modern Tradition: Backgrounds of Modern Literature* (New York: Oxford University Press, 1965) and Irving Howe, ed., *The Idea of the Modern in Literature and the Arts* (New York: Horizon, 1977).

13 Suzi Gablik, *Has Modernism Failed?* (London and New York: Thames and Hudson, 1984), p. 11. Also see Andreas Huyssen, "Mapping the Postmodern," *New German Critique*, 33, (Fall 1984); Charles Jencks, *The Language of Post-Modern Architecture* (London: London Academy, 1977); Jencks, *Post-Modern Classicism: The New Synthesis* (New York: Rizzoli International, 1981); R. Lane Kauffmann, "The Limits of Avant-Garde Theory," *Telos*, 64 (Spring 1986); Manfredi Tafuri, *Architecture and Utopia* (Cambridge, Mass.: MIT Press, 1976); Stanley Trachtenberg, *The Postmodern Movement* (Westport, Conn.: Greenwood Press, 1985); Gregory Ulmer, "The Object of Postmodern Criticism," in Hal Foster, ed., *The Anti-Aesthetics: Essays on Postmodern Culture* (Port Townsend, Wash.: Bay Press, 1983); Jean-François Lyotard, "Qu'est-ce que le Post-moderne?" in *Critique* (April 1982); and John Brenkman, *Culture and Domination* (Ithaca, N.Y.: Cornell University Press, 1987).

14 Wolin, *Walter Benjamin*, p. 227.

15 Ibid., pp. 230–1. On the Frankfurt School aesthetic, see Adorno, *Aesthetic Theory*; Peter Bürger, *Theory of the Avant Garde* (Minneapolis: Minnesota University Press, 1984); Benjamin, "The Artwork in the Age of Mechanical Reproduction"; Max Horkheimer and Theodor Adorno, *Dialectic of Enlightenment* (New York: Continuum, 1972); Herbert Marcuse, *Eros and Civilization: A Philosophical Inquiry into Freud* (Boston: Beacon Press, 1955); and Marcuse, *The Aesthetic Dimension*.

16 See, for example, Jürgen Habermas, "Modernity versus Post-modernity," *New German Critique*, 22, (Winter 1981) and "Neoconservative Culture Criticism in the United States and West Germany," in Richard Bernstein, ed., *Habermas and Modernity* (Cambridge: MIT Press, 1985). See Martin Jay, "Habermas and Modernism," and Richard Rorty, "Habermas and Lyotard on Postmodernity," in the same volume; also John Brenkman, *Culture and Domination* (Ithaca, N.Y.: Cornell University Press, 1987); and David Kolb, *The Critique of Pure Modernity* (Chicago: University of Chicago Press, 1986).

17 Sally Banes, *Terpsichore in Sneakers: Postmodern Dance* (Middletown, Conn.: Wesleyan University, 1986). The Preface from which I am quoting appears for the first time in the revised edition of 1987. I am grateful to Sally Banes for letting me read the typescript prior to publication. My interpolation in brackets. Also see Banes, *Democracy's Body: Judson Dance Theatre, 1962–1964* (Ann Arbor, Mich.: University Microfilms, 1983) and "After Postmodern Dance: Pointe of Departure," *Boston Review*, 11:5 (October 1986).

18 See Banes, *Terpsichore in Sneakers*. My interpolations in brackets. Also see Noel Carroll, "Post-Modern Dance and Expression," in Gordon Fancher and Gerald Myers, eds., *Philosophical Essays on Dance* (New York: Dance Horizons, 1981), and Carroll and Banes, "Working and Dancing: A Response to Monroe Beardsley's Question, What is going on in a dance?" in *Dance Research Journal*, 15:1 (Fall 1982).

19 Banes, Preface to *Terpsichore in Sneakers*. My interpolation.

20 Ibid. My interpolations in brackets.

21 Ibid. Also see my study, "The Embodiment of Performance," *Salmagundi*, 31/32 (Fall 1975–Winter 1976); Susan Foster, *Reading Dancing: Bodies and Subjects in Contemporary Dance* (Berkeley: University of California Press, 1986); Jill Johnston, "The New American Modern Dance," *Salmagundi*, 33/34 (Spring–Summer 1976); and Deborah Jowett, *The Dance in Mind* (Boston: David Godine, 1985).

22 Banes, *Terpsichore in Sneakers*. My interpolations in brackets.

23 See Stephen Toulmin, "The Construal of Reality: Criticism in Modern and Postmodern Science," *Critical Inquiry*, 9:1 (September 1982). Also see Seyla Benhabib, "Epistemologies of Postmodernity," *New German Critique*, 33 (Fall 1984) and Jean-François Lyotard, *The Postmodern Condition: A Report on Knowledge* (Minneapolis: University of Minnesota Press, 1984).

24 See Nelson George, with Sally Banes, Susan Flinker, and Patty Romanowski, *Fresh, hip hop don't stop* (New York: Random House, Sarah Lazin Books, 1985).

25 Fredric Jameson, "Postmodernism, or The Cultural Logic of Late Capitalism," *New Left Review*, 146 (July–August 1984), p. 57.

26 See Hal Foster, *Recodings: Art, Spectacle, Cultural Politics* (Port Townsend, Wash.: Bay Press, 1985).

27 See Jürgen Habermas, "Modernity versus Postmodernity," *New German Critique*, 22 (Winter 1981). Also see *The Theory of Communicative Action*, vol. 1 (Boston: Beacon Press, 1983) and *The Philosophical Discourse of Modernity* (Cambridge, Mass.: MIT Press, 1987).

28 Jürgen Habermas, "Neoconservative Culture Criticism in the United States and West Germany," in Bernstein, *Habermas and Modernity*.

29 Jürgen Habermas, "Questions and Counterquestions," in Bernstein, *Habermas and Modernity*.

30 Wolin, *Walter Benjamin*, p. 134.

31 Ibid.

32 See Bürger, *The Theory of the Avant Garde*.

33 See Jürgen Habermas, *Legitimation Crisis* (Boston: Beacon Press, 1975).

34 In this regard, see Albrecht Betz, "Commodity and Modernity," *New German Critique*, 33 (Fall 1984). Also note Wolin's reflections on "postauratic" art in his *Walter Benjamin*.

35 See Jürgen Habermas, *Knowledge and Human Interests* (Boston: Beacon Press, 1971), p. 284. But of course, in the text from which I have abstracted them, his sentences do not refer to dance.

36 Michel Foucault, "Nietzsche, Genealogy, History," in *Language Countermemory, Practice* (Ithaca, N.Y.: Cornell University Press, 1977), p. 148. Foucault's conception of the body is critically examined in more detail in my trilogy: *The Body's Recollection of Being* (London & New York: Routledge & Kegan Paul, 1985); *The Opening of Vision* (London & New York: Routledge, 1988); and *The Listening Self* (London and New York: Routledge, 1989).

37 Foucault, "Nietzsche, Genealogy, History."

38 Dewey, *Democracy and Education*, p. 141.

39 Ibid., p. 153.

40 Ibid., p. 198.

41 Maurice Merleau-Ponty, "The Indirect Language," *The Prose of the World* (Evanston, Ill.: Northwestern University Press, 1973), p. 94.

42 Benjamin, "Surrealism," p. 192.

43 Merleau-Ponty, "The Indirect Language," p. 83.

44 See my essay, "Hermeneutics as Gesture," *Tulane Studies in Philosophy*, 32 (1984), pp. 69–77, together with an essay "On Heidegger: The Gathering Dance of Mortals," *Research in Phenomenology*, 10 (1981), pp. 251–76. Also see Jerome Rothenberg, "New Models, New Visions: Some Notes Toward a Poetics of Performance," in Michael Benamon and Charles Caramello, eds., *Performance in Postmodern Culture* (Madison, Wis.: Coda Press, 1977).

CHAPTER 13   OBSOLESCENCE AND DESIRE:
FASHION AND THE COMMODITY FORM

1 Guy Debord, *The Society of the Spectacle*, (Detroit: Black and Red, 1983), #6. Henceforth cited as *SS*.

2 Fredric Jameson, "Postmodernism and The Cultural Logic of Late Capitalism," *New Left Review* (Fall 1985), p. 66. Henceforth cited as *PL*.

3 While Baudrillard moves to distance himself from this early work by the time of his *Mirror of Production*, he never actually gives up this notion of symbolic exchange which he refers to as late as his "Forget Baudrillard" interview in *Forget Foucault*, (New York: Semiotext(e), 1987), p. 89. Nevertheless, it is certainly the case that this concept, along with many others, undergoes some odd twists in Baudrillard's later writings, where at times it is difficult to distinguish between his social theory and science fiction.

4 Jean Baudrillard, *For a Critique of the Political Economy of the Sign*, trans. Charles Levin, (St. Louis, Mo.: Telos Press, 1981), p. 64.

5 It is possible perhaps to fetishize these quantitative values (prices) in and of themselves, that is to say, desire something only because it costs such and such, but this alone would not account for the innumerable and intense advertising strategies that usher consumer goods into the modern marketplace.

6 Marx's concept of use value should not be reduced to the bourgeois notion of utility, as Baudrillard unfortunately does in *The Mirror of Production*. Rather, use value includes *any* socially determined value other than quantified exchange value (units of abstract labor), the discovery of which, Marx states, is "the work of history." See p. 1 of *Capital*, vol. I.

7 Because labor is also a commodity, these 'individuals,' or rather propertied classes, are from the outset actually locked into an antagonistic and inherently unequal struggle. Of course, for Marx, as earlier for Hegel, and later Lukács and the Frankfurt School, the critique of surplus value necessitated also a critique of the alienation of labor as a commodity, insofar as labor and production, inseparable from exchange, held for them an ontological status.

8 As Debord writes, "In all its specific forms, as information or propaganda, as advertisement or direct entertainment consumption, the spectacle is the present model of socially dominant life. It is the omnipresent affirmation of the choice already made in production and its corollary consumption." *SS*, #5–6.

9 Advertising, of course, has become the multi-million dollar industry built on denying this contradiction. We see this most obviously in corporate image commercials that repeat such tiresome slogans as,

"We do it all for you," "We care," or "We are committed to excellence," to the "future," to "America," etc.—phrases that clutter political speeches as much as our television screens.

10 It might be interesting to look at the proliferation of the souvenir as consumerism's weak attempt to associate itself with a special, unique, or "once in a lifetime" symbolic event (for example, the Pope's visit to Toronto a few years ago, which spawned everything from Pope ashtrays to umbrellas). The degradation of the symbol into the souvenir parallels the degradation of such events themselves.

11 Jean Baudrillard, *Le Système des objets*, trans. Jacques Morain, *Baudrillard: Selected Writings*, (London: Polity Press, forthcoming 1988), ch. 2, p. 22. Henceforth cited as *SW* (all pages cited are from the manuscript). ch. 2, p. 22.

12 Baudrillard, *SW*, ch. 2, p. 25.

13 Baudrillard, *SW*, ch. 3, p. 4.

14 Baudrillard, *SW*, ch. 3, p. 21.

15 Earlier we saw that it was not enough to say that signs (as they have been defined here) are simply substituted for symbols without elaborating how it is really the sign of a relationship that is substituted for a symbolic relationship. Likewise a symbolic relationship cannot be understood in isolation from, and indeed presupposes the idea of a symbolic unity of which it is both an expressive and constitutive moment.

16 Baudrillard, *SW*, ch. 3, p. 35.

17 Baudrillard, *SW*, ch. 3, p. 10.

18 Baudrillard, *PS*, p. 78–9.

19 Baudrillard, *PS*, p. 201.

20 Witold Rybezynski, *Home: The Short History of an Idea* (New York: Viking, 1986), p. 5. Henceforth cited as *HS*.

21 Baudrillard, *SW*, ch. 3, p. 8.

22 Rybczynski, *HS*, p. 6.

23 Rybczynski, *HS*, p. 7.

24 Baudrillard, *SW*, ch. 3., pp. 24, 25.

25 *Vogue* (October 1984), p. 611.

26 Ibid., p. 685.

27 Ibid., p. 686.

28 Ibid., p. 684.

29 Michel Foucault, *The History of Sexuality*, vol. 1 (New York: Vintage Books, 1980), p. 46.

30 *Vogue* (October 1984), p. 685.

31 Walter Benjamin, *Das Passagen-Werk* vol. 2, ed. Rolf Tiedemann (Frankfurt-am-Main: Suhrkamp Verlag, 1982), p. 1246: quoted in Susan Buck-Morss, "Benjamin's *Passagen-Werk*: Redeeming Mass Culture for the Revolution," *New German Critique*, 29 (1983), p. 232.

32 Henri Lefebvre, *Everyday Life in the Modern World*, trans. Sacha Rabinovitch, (Hammondsworth: Penguin, 1971), p. 76.

33 Walter Benjamin, "The Work of Art in the Age of Mechanical Reproduction," *Illuminations* (New York: Schocken Books, 1968), p. 221.

34 Debord, *SS*, #71.

35 If one is curious as to what might appear in a column on driving style, *Vogue* (March 1987) has this to say: "In springtime, a driver's thoughts turn to images of Grace Kelly in *To Catch a Thief* cruising lush roads of the Riviera in a convertible. . . . New coupes to make such dreams come true: Toyota's '87 convertible with increased horsepower and Chevy's '87 Cavalier RS convertible. . . . Trend in cars showing up at Los Angeles' hottest see and be seen restaurant Spago: . . . anything in black or dark gray—in particular, Mercedes-Benzes (like Raquel Welch's and Linda Blair's), Porsches (like Tatum O'Neal's). . . ."

36 It is interesting to note in this regard a new genre of fashion magazines currently being launched in Toronto which have made it their explicit intention to capitalize on what they see as a fashion advertising-as-entertainment trend. Magalogues, as they are called, are retailer-generated publications that combine "the promotional aspects of a catalogue with the editorial content of a high-fashion magazine." According to one retailer, the strategy is to have visually stunning advertising that will be thematically related to "tell a story" while at the same time produce direct sales: *The Globe and Mail*, Toronto (August 14, 1987), p. B2.

37 It may be interesting to compare this with what Jameson has described in E. L. Doctorow's narratives as use of the 'perfective' tense that "serves to separate events from the present of enunciation and to transform the stream of time and action into so many finished, complete, and isolated punctual event-objects which find themselves sundered from any present situation . . ." (*PL*, p. 70).

38 Jameson, *PL*, p. 60.

39 Baudrillard, *Fatal Strategies*, *BW*, ch. 2, p. 4.

40 Jameson, *PL*, p. 60.

41 Walter Benjamin, *Das Passagen-Werk*, translated in John McCole, "Benjamin's *Passagen-Werk*," *Theory and Society*, 14 (1985), p. 507.

42 Benjamin, cited in McCole, "Benjamin's *Passagen-Werk*," p. 501.

I would like to thank Erno Lazlo and Ralph Lauren (Chicago) for the permission to reproduce their respective advertisements.

I would also like to thank Richard Dienst and Sourayan Mookerjea for their many helpful comments and suggestions on earlier versions of this essay.

Bibliography

POSTMODERNISM

Hélène Volat-Shapiro

BOOKS

Allen, Donald, and Georges F. Butterick. *The Postmoderns: The New American Poetry Revised*. New York: Grove Press, 1982.

Arac, Jonathan. *Critical Genealogies: Historical Situations for Postmodern Literary Studies*. New York: Columbia University Press, 1987.

———, ed. *Postmodernism and Politics*. Minneapolis: University of Minnesota Press, 1986.

Banes, Sally. *Democracy's Body: Judson Dance Theatre, 1962–1964*. Ann Arbor, Mich.: University Microfilms, 1983.

———. *Terpsichore in Sneakers: Postmodern Dance*. Middletown, Conn.: Wesleyan University Press, 1986.

Barthes, Roland. *The Rustle of Language*. Trans. Richard Howard. New York: Hill and Wang, 1986.

Baudrillard, Jean. *The Mirror of Production*. Trans. Mark Poster. St. Louis, Mo.: Telos, 1975.

———. *For a Critique of the Political Economy of the Sign*. Trans. Charles Levin. St. Louis, Mo.: Telos, 1981.

———. *In the Shadow of the Silent Majorities*. Trans. Paul Foss, Paul Patton, John Johnston. New York: Semiotext(e), 1983.

———. *Simulations*. Trans. Paul Foss, Paul Patton, P. Beitchman. New York: Semiotext(e), 1983.

———. *Forget Foucault*. New York: Semiotext(e), 1987.

———. *The Ecstacy of Communication*. Trans. by Bernard and Caroline Schutze. New York: Semiotext(e), 1988.

Benamou, Michel, and Charles Caramello, eds. *Performance in Postmodern Culture*. Madison, Wis.: Coda Press, 1977.

Bernstein, Richard J., ed. *Habermas and Modernity*. Cambridge, Mass.: MIT Press, 1985.

Blanchot, Maurice. *The Space of Literature*. Trans. Anne Smock. Lincoln: University of Nebraska Press, 1982.

——. *The Gaze of Orpheus and other Literary Essays*. Ed. P. Adams Sitney. Trans. Lydia Davis. New York: Station Hill Press, 1981.

——. *The Writing of the Disaster*. Trans. Anne Smock. Lincoln: University of Nebraska Press, 1982.

Blau, Herbert. *Blooded Thought: Occasions of Theatre*. New York: Performing Arts Journal Publications, 1982.

——. *The Eye of the Prey: Subversions of the Postmodern*. Bloomington: Indiana University Press, 1987.

——. *Take Up the Bodies: Theater at the Vanishing Point*. Urbana: University of Illinois Press, 1982.

Bradbury, Malcolm, and James McFarlane, eds. *Modernism: 1890–1930*. London: Penguin Books, 1976.

Burgin, Victor. *The End of Art Theory: Criticism and Post-Modernity*. Atlantic Highlands, N.J. Humanities Press, 1986.

Butler, Christopher. *After the Wake: An Essay on the Contemporary Avant-Garde*. New York: Oxford University Press, 1980.

Calinescu, Matei. *Faces of Modernity: Avant-Garde, Decadence, Kitsch*. Durham: Duke University Press, 1987.

Champagne, Leonora. *French Theatre Experiment since 1968*. Ann Arbor, Mich.: UMI Research Press, 1984.

Chefdor, Monique, Ricardo Quinones, and Albert Wachtel, eds. *Modernism: Challenges and Perspectives*. Urbana: University of Illinois Press, 1986.

Cixous, Hélène, and Catherine Clement. *Newly Born Woman*. Trans. Betsy Wing. Minneapolis: University of Minnesota Press, 1986.

Couturier, Maurice, ed. *Representation and Performance in Postmodern Fiction*. Montpellier: Delta, Université Paul Valéry, 1983.

De Man, Paul. *Allegories of Reading*. New Haven: Yale University Press, 1979.

——. *Blindness and Insight*. Minneapolis: University of Minnesota Press, 1983.

——. *Resistance to Theory*. Minneapolis: University of Minnesota Press, 1986.

——. *The Rhetoric of Romanticism*. New York: Columbia University Press, 1984.

Dews, Peter. *Logics of Disintegration*. London: Verso, 1987.

Duchen, Claire. *Feminism in France: From May '68 to Mitterand*. London: Routledge and Kegan Paul, 1986.

Ellmann, Richard, and Charles Feidelson, eds. *The Modern Tradition: Backgrounds of Modern Literature*. New York: Oxford University Press, 1964.

Faulkner, Peter. *Modernism*. London: Methuen, 1977.

Federman, Raymond, ed. *Surfiction: Fiction Now and Tomorrow*. Chicago: Swallow Press, 1975. Repr. 1981.

Fokkema, Douwe. *Literary History, Modernism and Postmodernism*. Amsterdam: John Benjamins, 1984.

Fokkema, Douwe, and Hans Bertens, eds. *Approaching Postmodernism*. Papers presented at a Workshop on Postmodernism, September 21–23 1984, University of Utrecht. Amsterdam/Philadelphia: John Benjamins, 1986.

Fokkema, Douwe, and Matei Calinescu, eds. *Exploring Postmodernism*. Amsterdam: John Benjamins, 1988.

Foster, Hal, ed. *The Anti-Aesthetic: Essays on Postmodern Culture*. Port Townsend, Wash.: Bay Press, 1983.

———, ed. *Recodings: Art, Spectacle, Cultural Politics*. Port Townsend, Wash.: Bay Press, 1985.

Foster, Susan. *Reading Dancing: Bodies and Subjects in Contemporary Dance*. Berkeley: University of California Press, 1986.

Frankovits, Andre, ed. *Seduced and Abandoned: The Baudrillard Scene*. Glebe, Australia: Stonemoss Services, 1984.

Gablik, Suzi. *Has Modernism Failed?* London and New York: Thames and Hudson, 1984.

Garvin, Harry R., ed. Romanticism, Modernism, Postmodernism. Bucknell Review, 25. Lewisburg, Oh.: Bucknell University Press, 1980.

George, Nelson, with Sally Banes, Susan Flinker, and Patty Romanowski, *Fresh, hip hop don't stop*. New York: Random House, Sarah Lazin Books, 1985.

Graff, Gerald. *Literature Against Itself: Literary Ideas in Modern Society*. Chicago: Chicago University Press, 1979.

Habermas, Jügen. *Legitimation Crisis*. Trans. Thomas McCarthy. Boston: Beacon Press, 1975.

———. *The Philosophical Discourse of Modernity*. Cambridge, Mass.: MIT Press, 1987.

Harari, Josué V., ed. *Textual Strategies: Perspectives in Post-Structuralist Criticism*. Ithaca, N.Y.: Cornell University Press, 1979.

Hassan, Ihab. *The Dismemberment of Orpheus: Toward a Postmodern Literature*. Madison: University of Wisconsin Press, 1982.

———. *Paracriticisms: Seven Speculations of the Times*. Urbana: University of Illinois Press, 1975.

———. *The Postmodern Turn: Essays in Postmodern Theory and Culture*. Columbus: Ohio State University Press, 1987.

———, and Sally Hassan, eds. *Innovations/Renovation: New Perspectives on the Humanities*. Madison: University of Wisconsin Press, 1983.

Heller, Agnes, ed. *Deconstructing Aesthetics*. Oxford: Blackwell, 1986.

Hertz, Richard. *Theories of Contemporary Art*. Englewood Cliffs, N.J.: Prentice-Hall, 1985.

302

Higgins, Dick. *Horizons: The Poetics and Theory of the Intermedia*. Carbondale: Southern Illinois University Press, 1984.

Hughes, Robert. *The Shock of the New: Art and the Century of Change*. New York: Knopf, 1981.

Hutcheon, Linda. *Narcissic Narrative: The Metafictional Paradox*. Waterloo, Canada: Wilfrid Laurier University Press, 1980.

———. *A Poetics of Postmodernism*. New York: Methuen, 1987.

Jameson, Fredric. *The Political Unconscious: Narrative as a Socially Symbolic Act*. Ithaca, N.Y.: Cornell University Press, 1981.

Jardine, Alice, and Hester Eisenstein, eds. *The Future of Difference*. Boston: Barnard College Women's Center, 1980.

Jardine, Alice. *Gynesis: Configurations of Women and Modernity*. Ithaca, N.Y.: Cornell University Press, 1985.

Jauss, Hans Robert. *Toward an Aesthetics of Reception*. Trans. Timothy Bahti. Intr. Paul de Man. Minneapolis: University of Minnesota Press, 1985.

Jefferson, Ann. *The Nouveau Roman and the Poetics of Fiction*. Cambridge: Cambridge University Press, 1980.

Jencks, Charles. *The Language of Post-Modern Architecture*. London: Academy Editions, 1981.

———. *Post-Modern Classicism: The New Synthesis*. London: Architectural Design 5/6, 1980.

Jowett, Deborah. *The Dance in Mind*. Boston: David R. Godine, 1985.

Kaplan, E. Anne. *Rocking Round the Clock: Music Television, Post-Modernism and Consumer Culture*. New York: Methuen, 1987.

Kearney, Richard. *Dialogues with Contemporary Continental Thinkers: The Phenomenological Heritage: Paul Ricoeur, Emmanuel Levinas, Herbert Marcuse, Stanislas Breton, Jacques Derrida*. Manchester: Manchester University Press, 1984.

Kenner, Hugh. *A Homemade World: The American Modernist Writers*. London: Marion Boyars, 1977.

Kirby, Michael. *The Art of Time: Essays on the Avant-Garde*. New York: E. P. Dutton, 1969.

Klinkowitz, Jerome. *Literary Disruptions: The Making of a Post-Contemporary American Fiction*. Urbana: University of Illinois Press, 1980.

Kostelanetz, Richard, ed. *Avant-Garde Tradition in Literature*. Buffalo, N.Y.: Prometheus Books, 1982.

Kott, Jan. *The Theater of Essence*. (Evanston, Ill.: Northwestern University Press, 1984.

Kramer, Hilton. *The Age of the Avant-Garde: An Art Chronicle of 1956–1972*. New York: Farrar, Strauss, and Giroux, 1973.

———. *The Revenge of the Philistines: Art and Culture, 1972–1984*. New York: Free Press, 1985.

Krauss, Rosalind E. *Originality of the Avant-Garde and other Modernist Myths*. Cambridge, Mass.: MIT Press, 1985.

Kristeva, Julia. *Desire in Langurage: A Semiotic Approach to Literature and Art*. Trans. Thomas Gora, Alice Jardine and Leon S. Roudiez. New York: Columbia University Press, 1980.

———. *Powers of Horror: An Essay on Abjection*. Trans. Leon S. Roudiez. New York: Columbia University Press, 1982.

Kroker, Arthur, and David Cook. *The Postmodern Scene: Excremental Culture and Hyper-Aesthetics*. New York: St. Martin, 1986.

Lawson, Hilary. *Reflexivity: The Post-Modern Predicament*. La Salle, Ind.: Open Court, 1985.

Lecercle, Jean-Jacques. *Philosophy through the Looking-glass: Language, Nonsense, Desire*. La Salle, Ind.: Open Court, 1985.

Lentricchia, Frank. *After the New Criticism*. Chicago: University of Chicago Press, 1983.

Levin, David M. *The Opening of Vision: Nihilism and the Post-Modern Situation*. London: Routledge and Kegan Paul, 1987.

Lodge, David. *Working with Structuralism: Essays and Reviews on Nineteenth and Twentieth-Century Literature*. London: Arnold, 1981.

Lucie-Smith, Edward. *Art Today: From Abstract Expressionism to Superrealism*. Oxford: Phaidon, 1977.

Lunn, Eugene. *Marxism and Modernism: An Historical Study of Lukács, Brecht, Benjamin, and Adorno*. Berkeley: University of California Press, 1982.

Lyotard, Jean-François. *Driftworks*. Ed. Roger McKeon. New York: Semiotext(e), 1984.

———. *Just Gaming*. Trans. Wlad Godzich and Brian Massumi. Minneapolis: University of Minnesota Press, 1985.

———. *The Postmodern Condition: A Report on Knowledge*. Trans. Geoff Bennington and Brian Massumi. Minneapolis: University of Minnesota Press, 1984.

———. *Le Postmoderne expliqué aux enfants*. Paris: Galilée, 1986.

Malmgrem, Carl Darryl. *Fictional Space in the Modernist and Postmodernist American Novel*. Lewisburg, Oh.: Bucknell University Press, 1985.

Marks, Elaine, and Isabelle de Courtivron, eds. *New French Feminisms*. New York: Shocken Books, 1981.

Mazzaro, Jerome. *Postmodern American Poetry*. Urbana: University of Illinois Press, 1980.

McCaffery, Lawrence, ed. *Post-Modern Fiction: A Biobibliographical Guide*. Westport, Conn.: Greenwood Press, 1986.

McHale, Brian. *Postmodernist Fiction*. New York: Methuen, 1987.

Megill, Allan. *Prophets of Extremity: Nietzsche, Heidegger, Foucault, Derrida*. Berkeley: University of California Press, 1985.

Mellard, James M. *The Exploded Form: The Modernist Novel in America.* Urbana: University of Illinois Press, 1980.

Mendez-Egle, Beatrice, ed. *John Gardner: True Art, Moral Art.* Edinburgh: Pan American University School of Humanities, 1983.

Meyrowitz, Joshua. *No Sense of Place.* New York: Oxford University Press, 1985.

Moi, Toril. *Sexual/Textual Politics: Feminist Literary Theory.* London: Methuen, 1985.

Mitchell, W. J. T., ed. *Against Theory: Literary Studies and the New Pragmatism.* Chicago: University of Chicago Press, 1985.

Mukarovsky, Jan. *Structure, Sign and Function.* Ed. Karl Schlechta and Peter Steiner. New Haven: Yale University Press, 1978.

Newman, Charles. *The Post-Modern Aura: The Act of Fiction in an Age of Inflation.* Evanston, Ill.: Northwestern University Press, 1985.

O'Connor, William Van. *The New University Wits and the End of Modernism.* Carbondale: Southern Illinois University Press, 1963.

Perkins, David. *A History of Modern Poetry: From the 1890s to the High Modernist Mode.* Cambridge, Mass.: Harvard University Press, 1976.

Poggioli, Renato. *The Theory of the Avant-Garde.* Trans. Gerald Fitzgerald. Cambridge, Mass.: Harvard University Press, 1968.

Portoghesi, Paolo. *After Modern Architecture.* Trans. Meg Shore. New York: Rizzoli, 1982.

———. *Postmodern.* Trans. Ellen Shapiro. New York: Rizzoli, 1983.

Pratt, Mary Louise. *Toward a Speech Act Theory of Literary Discourse.* Bloomington: Indiana University Press, 1977.

Ricoeur, Paul. *The Rule of Metaphor: Multi-disciplinary Studies of the Creation of Meaning in Language.* Trans. R. Czerny with K. McLaughlin and J. Costello. Toronto: University of Toronto Press, 1977.

Rose, Margaret. *Parody/Meta-Fiction: An Analysis of Parody as a Critical Mirror to the Writing and Reception of Fiction.* London: Croom Helm, 1979.

Russell, Charles. *The Avant-Garde Today: An International Anthology.* Urbana: University of Illinois Press, 1981.

———. *Poets, Prophets, and Revolutionaries: The Literary Avant-garde from Rimbaud through Postmodernism.* New York: Oxford University Press, 1985.

Said, Edward. *The World, the Text, and the Critic.* Cambridge, Mass.: Harvard University Press, 1983.

Scholes, Robert. *Fabulation and Metafiction.* Urbana: University of Illinois Press, 1980.

———. *Semiotics and Interpretation.* New Haven: Yale University Press, 1982.

Schwartz, Sanford. *The Matrix of Modernism: Pound, Eliot and Early 20th Century Thought*. Princeton: Princeton University Press, 1985.

Shattuck, Roger. *The Banquet Years: The Origins of the Avant-Garde in France, 1885 to World War I: Alfred Jarry, Henri Rousseau, Erik Satie, Guillaume Apollinaire*. Rev. ed. New York: Random House, 1968.

Silverman, Hugh J., and Donn Welton, eds. *Postmodernism and Continental Philosophy*. Albany: State University of New York Press, 1988.

Simard, Rodney. *Postmodern Drama: Contemporary Playwrights in America and Britain*. Landham: University Press of America, 1984.

Singer, Alan. *A Metaphorics of Fiction: Discontinuity and Discourse in the Modern Novel*. Tallahassee: Florida State University Press, 1984.

Spanos, William. *Repetitions: The Postmodern Occasion in Literature and Culture*. Baton Rouge: Louisiana State, 1987.

––––––, ed. *Martin Heidegger and the Question of Literature: Towards a Postmodern Literary Hermeneutics*. Bloomington: Indiana University Press, 1982.

Steiner, Wendy. *The Colors of Rhetoric: Problems in the Relation between Modern Literature and Painting*. Chicago: University of Chicago Press, 1982.

Suleiman, Susan, and Inge Crosman, eds. *The Reader in the Text: Essays on Audience and Interpretation*. Princeton: Princeton University Press, 1980.

Tani, Stefano. *The Doomed Detective: The Contribution of the Detective Novel to Postmodern American and Italian Fiction*. Carbondale: Southern Illinois University Press, 1984.

Taylor, Brandon. *Modernism, Postmodernism, Realism: A Critical Pespective for Art*. Winchester, Hampshire: Winchester School of Art Press, 1987.

Thiher, Allen. *Words in Reflection: Modern Language Theory and Postmodern Fiction*. Chicago: University of Chicago Press, 1984.

Thompson, John B. *Critical Hermeneutics: A Study in the Thought of Paul Ricoeur and Jürgen Habermas*. Cambridge: Cambridge University Press, 1981.

Tomkins, Calvin. *The Scene: Reports on Post-Modern Art*. New York: Viking Press, 1976.

Tompkins, Jane P., ed. *Reader-Response Criticism: From Formalism to Post-Structuralism*. Baltimore: Johns Hopkins University Press, 1980.

Trachtenberg, Stanley, ed. *The Postmodern Moment*. Westport, Conn.: Greenwood Press, 1985.

Tyler, Stephen. *The Unspeakable*. Madison: Wisconsin University Press, 1987.

Ullmer, Gregory. *Applied Grammatology: Post(e)-Pedagogy from Jacques Derrida to Joseph Beuys*. Baltimore: Johns Hopkins University Press, 1984.

Virilio, Paulo. *Speed and Politics* Trans. Mark Polizzotti. New York: Semiotext(e), 1986.

———. *Pure War*. New York: Semiotext(e), 1983.

Weightman, John. *The Concept of the Avant-Garde: Explorations in Modernism*. London: Alcove Press, 1973.

Wilde, Alan. *Horizons of Assent: Modernism, Postmodernism, and the Ironic Imagination*. Baltimore: Johns Hopkins University Press, 1981.

ARTICLES IN BOOKS

Bertens, Hans. "Change of Dominance from Modernist to Postmodernist Writing," in: *Approaching Postmodernism*. Ed. Douwe Fokkema and Hans Bertens. Amsterdam: John Benjamins 1986. Pp. 9–53.

Bigsby, Christopher. "Art, Theater and the Real," in: *Representation and Performance in Postmodern Fiction*. Montpellier: Delta, 1983. Pp. 134–47.

Bradbury, Malcolm. "Modernism/Postmodernism," in: *Innovation/Renovation: New Perspectives on the Humanities*. Ed. Ihab and Sally Hassan. Madison: University of Wisconsin Press, 1983. Pp. 311–27.

Butler, Christopher. "The Pleasures of the Experimental Text," in: *Criticism and Critical Theory*. Ed. Jeremy Hawthorn. London: E. Arnold, 1984.

Calinescu, Matei. "From the One to the Many: Pluralism in Today's Thought," in: *Innovation/Renovation: New Perspectives on the Humanities*. Pp. 263–288.

Carroll, Noel. "Post-Modern Dance and Expression," in: *Philosophical Essays on Dance*. Ed. Gordon Fancher and Gerald Myers. New York: Dance Horizons, 1981.

Cixous, Hélène. "Where is she?" and "The Laugh of Medusa," in: *New French Feminisms: An Anthology*. Ed. and trans. E. Marks and I. de Courtivron. Amherst: University of Massachusetts Press, 1980.

D'Haen, Theo. "Modernism Cut in Half: The Exclusion of the Avant-garde and the Debate on Postmodernism," in: *Approaching Postmodernism*. Pp. 211–33.

Derrida, Jacques. "Structure, Sign, and Play," in: *The Languages of Criticism and the Sciences of Man*. Ed. Richard Macksey and Eugenio Donato. Baltimore: Johns Hopkins University Press, 1970.

———. "The Theater of Cruelty and the Closure of Representation," in: Jacques Derrida, *Writing and Difference*. Chicago: University of Chicago Press, 1978.

Eco, Umberto. "Lector in Fabula: Pragmatic Strategy in a Metanarrative Text," in: Umberto Eco, *The Role of the Reader: Explorations in Semiotics of Texts*. Bloomington: Indiana University Press, 1979. Pp. 220–266.

Fiedler, Leslie. "Cross the Border—Close that Gap: Postmodernism," in: *American Literature since 1900*, ed. Marcus Cunliffe. London, Sphere Books, 1975. Pp. 344–66.

———. "The Death and Rebirths of the Novel: The View from '82," in: *Innovation/Renovation: New Perspectives on the Humanities*. Pp. 225–42.

Fokkema, Douwe. "The Presence of Postmodernism in British Fiction: Aspects of Style and Selfhood," in: *Approaching Postmodernism*. Pp. 81–99.

Graff, Gerald. "The Myth of the Postmodernist Breakthrough," in: *The Novel Today: Contemporary Writers on Modern Fiction*, ed. Malcolm Bradbury. Glasgow: Fontana, 1977. Pp. 217–49.

Hartman, Geoffrey H. "The New Wilderness: Critics as Connoisseurs of Chaos," in: *Innovation/Renovation: New Perspectives on the Humanities*. Pp. 87–110.

Hassan, Ihab. "Ideas of Cultural Change," in: *Bucknell Review: Romanticism, Modernism, Post-modernism*, ed. Harry R. Garvin. Lewisburg, Oh.: Bucknell University Press, 1980. Pp. 117–26.

Hoffman, Gerhard. "Frames of Reference: Native American Art in the Context of Modern and Postmodern Art," in: *The Arts of the North American Indian: Traditions in Evolution*.

———. "Postmodernism in American Fiction and Art," in: *Approaching Postmodernism*. Pp. 185–211.

Holland, Norman N. "Postmodern Psychoanalysis," in: *Innovation/Renovation: New Perspectives on the Humanities*. Pp. 291–309.

Ibsch, Elrud. "Duplication and Multiplication: Postmodernist Devices in the Novels of Italo Calvino," in: *Approaching Postmodernism*. Pp. 119–35.

Jameson, Fredric. Postmodernism and Consumer Society," in: *The Anti-Aesthetic: Essays on Postmodern Culture*, ed. Hal Foster. Port Townsend, Wash.: Bay Press, 1983. Pp. 111–26.

Lethen, Helmut. "Postmodernism and Some Paradoxes of Periodization," in: *Approaching Postmodernism*. Pp. 233–9.

Levin, Harry. "What was Modernism?" in: *Harry Levin, Refractions: Essays in Comparative Literature*. New York: Oxford University Press, 1966. Pp. 271–95.

Lodge, David. "Mimesis and Diegesis in Modern Fiction," in: *Contemporary Approaches to Narrative*, ed. Anthony Mortimer. Tubingen: Narr, 1984. Pp. 89–108.

Lyotard, Jean-François. "Answering the Question: What is Postmodernism?" in: *Innovation/Renovation: New Perspectives on the Humanities*. Pp. 329–41.

McHale, Brian. "The Semantic and Syntactic Organization of Postmoderist Texts," in: *Approaching Postmodernism*. Pp. 53–81.

Martin, Wallace. "Postmodernism: Ultima Thule or Seim Anew? " in: *Bucknell Review: Romaticism, Modernism, Postmodernism*. Pp. 142–54.

Musarra, Ulla. "Postmodernism in Russian Drama: Vampilov, Almarik, Aksenov," in: *Approaching Postmodernism*. Pp. 135–57.

BIBLIOGRAPHY

Palmer, Richard E. "Towards a Postmodern Hermeneutics of Performance," in: *Performance in Postmodern Culture,* eds. Michel Benamou and Charles Caramello. Madison, Wisc.: Coda Press, 1977. Pp. 19–32.

Pladott, Dinnah. "The Semiotics of Post-Modern Theater: Gertrude Stein," in: *Approches de l'opéra/Approaches of the Opera.* Paris: Didier, 1986. Pp. 303–14.

Rorty, Richard. "Habermas and Lyotard on Postmodernity," in: *Habermas and Modernity,* ed. Richard Bernstein. Cambridge: MIT Press, 1985. Pp. 174–5.

Schmid, Herta. "The Absurd and its Forms of Reduction in Postmodern Amercan Fiction," in: *Approaching Postmodernism.* Pp. 157–85.

Suleiman, Susan Rubin. "Naming and Difference: Reflections on Modernism versus Postmodernism' in Literature," in: *Approaching Postmodernism.* Pp. 256–68.

Tatham, Campbell. "Mythotherapy and Postmodern Fictions: Magic is Afoot," in: *Performance in Postmodern Culture.* Pp. 137–57.

Todd, Richard. "From Hypothesis to Korrektur: Refutation as a Component of Postmodernist Discourse," in: *Approaching Postmodernism.* Pp. 99–119.

JOURNAL ARTICLES

Altieri, Charles. "From Symbolist Thought to Immanence: The Ground of Postmodern American Poetics," *Boundary 2,* (1973):605–41.

———. "Postmodernism: A Question of Definition," *Par Rapport,* 2 (1979):87–100.

Banes, Sally. "After Postmodern Dance: Pointe of Departure," *Boston Review,* 11:5 (1986).

Barth, John. "The Literature of Replenishment: Postmodernist Fiction," *Atlantic Monthly,* 245:1 (1980):65–71.

Beebe, Maurice. "What Modernism Was," *Journal of Modern Literature,* 3 (1974):1065–84.

Benhabib, Seyla. "Epistemologies of Postmodernity," *New German Critique,* 33 (Fall 1984).

Boisvert, Raymond. "Avant-Garde or Arriere-Garde: Turn-of-the Century Art and the History of Ideas," *International Philosophy Quarterly,* 24 (1984):79–80.

Bové, Carol. "The Politics of Desire in Julia Kristeva," *Boundary 2,* 12 (1984).

Butterick, George F. "Editing Postmodern Texts," *Sulfur,* 11 (1984):113–40.

Calinescu, Matei. "Avant-Garde, Neo-Avant-Garde Post-Modernism: The Culture of Crisis," *Clio,* 4 (1975):317–40.

———. "Postmodernist Criticism," *Contemporary Literature*, 21:632–8.

Carroll, Noel and Sally Banes. "Working and Dancing: A Response to Monroe Beardsley's Question, 'What is Going On in a Dance?'," *Dance Research Journal*, 15:1 (Fall 1982).

Cixous, Hélène. "Castration or decapitation?" *Signs*, 7 (1981).

Colvile, Georgiana. "Labor Delivered Is Love Regained: Women's Writing and Art in Postmodern America," *Revue Française d'Etudes Americaines*, 8:225–42.

Davidson, Michael. "Languages of Post-Modernism," *Chicago Review*, 27 (1975):11–22.

Davis, Douglas. "The Death of Semantics, the Corruption of Metaphors, the Birth of the *Punctum*," *ArtForum* (May 1984).

Ebert, Teresa. "The Convergence of Postmodern Innovative Fiction and Science Fiction," *Poetics Today*, 1 (1980):91–104.

Fokkema, Douwe. "A Semiotic Definition of Aesthetic Experience and the Period Code of Modernism," *Poetics Today*, 3 (1982):61–79.

Galloway, David. "Postmodernism," *Contemporary Literature*, 14 (1973):398–405.

Graff, Gerald. "Some Doubts About Postmodernism," *Par Rapport*, 2 (1979):101–6.

Greenberg, Clement. "Modern and Postmodern," *Arts Magazine*, 54 (1980):64–66.

Guattari, Félix. "The Post-Modern Impasse (Art, Philosophy, Linguistics, Architecture)." *Quinzaine Littéraire*, 456 (1986):1–21.

Habermas, Jürgen. "The French Path to Postmodernity: Bataille between Eroticism and General Economics," *New German Critique*, 33 (1984):79–102.

———. "Modernity versus Postmodernity," *New German Critique*, 22 (1981):3–14.

Hafrey, Leigh. "The Gilded Cage: Postmodernism and Beyond," *TriQuarterly*, 56 (1983):126–36.

Hassan, Ihab. "Culture, Indeterminacy, and Immanence: On the Margins of the (Post-modern) Age," *Humanities in Society*, 1 (1978):51–85.

———. "Desire and Dissent in the Postmodern Age," *Kenyon Review*, 5 (1983): 1–18.

———. "Making Sense: The Trials of Postmodern Discourse," *New Literary History*, 18 (1986–87):437–59.

———. "POSTmodernISM: A Paracritical Bibliography," *New Literary History*, 3:1 (Autumn 1971):5–30.

———. "Prometheus as Performer: Toward a Posthumanist Culture," *Georgia Review*, 31 (1977):830–50.

Hayman, David. "Double-Distancing: An Attribute of the 'Post-Modern' Avant-Garde," *Novel*, 12 (1978):33- 47.

Hoffman, Gerhard, Alfred Horning and Rudiger Kunow. " 'Modern,' 'Postmodern,' and 'Contemporary' as Criteria for the Analysis of 20th Century Literature," *Amerikastudien*, 28 (1977):19–46.

Hutcheon, Linda. "The Politics of Postmodernism: Parody and History," *Cultural Critique*, 5 (Winter 1986/87).

Huyssens, Andreas. "Mapping Postmodernism," *New German Critique*, 33 (1984):5–52.

———. "The Search for Tradition: Avant-Garde and Postmodernism in the 1970s," *New German Critique*, 22 (1981):23–40.

Jameson, Fredric. "Postmodernism, or the Cultural Logic of Late Capitalism," *New Left Review*, 146 (July–August 1984):53–92.

Jay, Martin. "Habermas and Modernism," *Praxis International*, 4:1 (1984):1–14.

Kafalenos, Emma. "Fragments of a Partial Discourse on Roland Barthes and the Postmodern Mind," *Chicago Review*, 35 (1985):72–94.

Kauffmann, R. Lane. "The Limits of Avant-Garde Theory," *Telos*, 64 (Spring 1986).

Kirby, Michael. "Post-Modern Dance Issue: An Introduction," *Drama Review*, 19 (1975):3–4.

Kramer, Hilton. "Postmodern Art and Cultrue in the 1980s," *The New Criterion*, 1 (1982):36–42.

Kristeva, Julia. "Postmodernism?" *Bucknell Review*, 25 (1980):136–41.

———. "Modern Theater Does Not Take (A) Place," *Sub-Stance*, 18/19 (1977).

Linker, Kate. "From Imitation to Copy to Just Effect: Reading Jean Baudrillard," *ArtForum* (April 1984).

McHale, Brian. "Modernist Reading, Postmodernist Text: The Case of *Gravity's Rainbow*," *Poetics Today*, 1 (1982):85–110.

———. "Writing About Postmodern Writing," *Poetics Today*, 3 (1982):211–27.

Mesguich, Daniel. "The Book to Come is a Theater," *Sub-Stance*, 18/19 (1977).

Morrissette, Bruce. "Post-Modern Generative Fiction: Novel and Film," *Critical Inquiry*, 2 (1975):253–62.

Murray, Timothy. "What's Happening," *Diacritics*, 14:3 (Fall 1984):100–110.

Nägele, Rainer. "Modernism and Postmodernism: The Margins of Articulation," *Studies in Twentieth Century Literature*, 5 (1980):5–25.

Norris, Christopher. "Philosophy as a Kind of Narrative: Rorty on Postmodern Liberal Culture," *Enclitic*, 7 (1983):144–59.

O'Doherty, Brian. "What is Postmodernism?" *Art in America*, 59 (1971):19.

Oliva, Achille Bonito. "The International Trans-Avant-Garde," *Flash*, 104 (1982):36–43.

Olson, Alan. "On Primordialism versus Postmodernism: A Response to Thomas Dean," *Philosophy East West*, 35 (1985).

O'Neill, John. "Televideo Ergo Sum: Some Hypotheses on the Specular Functions of the Media." *Communications*, 7 (November 2, 1983).

Owens, Craig. "The Allegorical Impulse: Toward a Theory of Postmodernism," Part 1: *October*, 12 (1980):67–86; Part 2: *October*, 13 (1980):59–80.

Palmer, Richard. "Postmodernity and Hermeneutics," *Boundary 2*, 5 (1977):363–93.

———. "The Postmodernity of Heidegger," *Boundary 2*, 4 (1976):411–32.

———. "Toward a Postmodern Interpretive Self-awareness *Journal of Religion*, 55:313–26.

Pavis, Patrice. "The Classical Heritage of Modern Drama: The Case of Postmodern Theatre," *Modern Drama*, 29 (March 1986):1–22.

Peper, Jürgen. "Postmodernismus: Unitary Sensibility," *Amerikastudien*, 22 (1977):65–89.

Peters, Steven. "Modern to Postmodern Acting and Directing: An Historical Perspective," *Dissertation Abstracts International*, 47:4 (October 1986):1120A.

Peters, Ted. "David Bohm, Postmodernism, and the Divine," *Zygon*, 20 (1985):193–218.

Pippin, Robert. "Nietzsche and the Origin of the Idea of Modernism," *Inquiry*, 26 (June 1983):151–80.

Putz, Manfred. "The Struggle of the Postmodern: Books on a New Concept in Criticism," *Kritikon Litterarum*, 2 (1973):225–37.

Radhakrishnan, R. "The Post-Modern Event and the End of Logocentrism," *Boundary 2*, 12 (1983):33–60.

Richardson, John Adkins. "Assault of the Petulant: Postmodernism and Other Fancies," *Journal of Aesthetic Education*, 18 (Spring 1984):94–108.

Rorty, Richard. "Habermas and Lyotárd on Post-Modernity," *Critique*, 442 (1984):181–97.

Said, Edward. "An Ideology of Difference," *Critical Inquiry*, 12:1 (1985):41–67.

Sandler, Irving. "Modernism, Revisionism, Pluralism, and Post-Modernism," *Art Journal*, 40 (1980):345–7.

Schulte-Sasse, Jochen. "Modernity and Modernism, Postmodernity and Postmodernism: Framing the Issue," *Cultural Critique*, 5 (Winter 1986–87):6.

Spanos, William. "Breaking the Circle," *Boundary 2*, 5 (1977):421–57.

———. "De-Struction and the Question of Postmodernist Literature: Towards a Definition," *Par Rapport*, 2:107–22.

——. "The Detective and the Boundary: Some Notes on the Postmodern Literary Imagination," *Boundary 2*, 1 (1972):147–68.

——. "Heidegger, Kierkegaard, and the Hermeneutic Circle: Towards a Post-modern Theory of Interpretation as Dis-closure," *Boundary 2*, 4 (1976):455–88.

Suleiman, Susan Rubin. "The Question of Readability in Avant-Garde Fiction," *Studies in 20th Century Literature*, 6:1–2 (1981–82):17–35.

Szabolcsi, Miklos. "Avant-Garde, Neo-Avant-Garde, Modernism: Some Questions and Suggestions," *New Literary History*, 3 (1971):49–70.

Tatham, Campbell. "Critical Investigations: Language Games: (Post) Modern(Isms)," *Substance*, 10 (1974):67–80.

Toulmin, Stephen. "The Construal of Reality: Criticism in Modern and Postmodern Science," *Critical Inquiry*, 9 (September 1982).

Turner, Frederick. "Escape from Modernism: Technology and the Future of the Imagination," *Harper's Magazine*, (November 1984):47–55.

Updike, John. "Modernist, Postmodernist, What Will They Think of Next?" *New Yorker*, 10 September 1984, 136–42.

Wasson, Richard. "From Priest to Prometheus: Culture and Criticism in the Postmodern Period," *Journal of Modern Literature*, 3 (1974):1188–1202.

Watson, Stephen. "Criticism and the Closure of 'Modernism,'" *Substance*, 13 (1984):15–30.

——. "Jürgen Habermas and Jean-François Lyotard: Postmodernism and the Crisis of Rationality," *Philosophy and Social Criticism*, 10 (1984):1–24.

Wellmer, Albrecht. "On the Dialectic of Modernism and Postmodernism," *Praxis International*, 4 (1985):337–62.

Wilde, Alan. "Modernism and the Aesthetics of Crisis," *Contemporary Literature*, 20 (1979):13–50.

Wilder, Amos. "Post-modern Reality and the Problem of Meaning," *Man and World*, 13 (1980):303–24.

Ziolkowski, Theodore. "Toward a Post-Modern Aesthetics?" *Mosaic*, 2:4 (1969):112–9.

SPECIAL ISSUES ON POSTMODERNISM

Amerikastudien, 22:1 (1977).

Caliban, 12 (1975).

Chicago Review, 33:2–3 (1983).

Cultural Critique, 5 (Winter, 1986/87). Issue on "Modernity and Modernism, Postmodernity and Postmodernism."

The Drama Review, 19:1 (1975).

ICA Documents: *Postmodernism*.

Desire.

Ideas from France.

Journal of Modern Literature, 3:5 (1974). Issue on "From Modernism to Postmodernism."

Krisis, 2 (1984). Issue on "Negative Thinking, Crisis, Postmodernism."

Krisis, 3–4 (1985). Issue on "Postmodernism: Search for Criteria." Articles and papers from the Cérisy-la-Salle Conference on Postmodernism.

Minnesota Review, 23 (Fall 1984). Issue on "The Politics of Postmodernism."

New German Critique, 22 (1981). Issue on "Habermas and Postmodernism."

New German Critique, 33 (1984).

New Literary History, 3:1 (1971). Issue on "Modernism and Postmodernism: Inquiries, Reflections and Speculations."

New Literary History, 7:1 (1975). Issue on "Critical Challenges: The Bellagio Symposium."

Par Rapport, 2:2 (1979).

Poetics Journal, 7 (1987). Issue on "Postmodernism?"

Salmagundi, 67 (1985):163–97. Responses to Charles Newman's *The Post-Modern Aura* by various critics.

Semiotext(e). Issue on "Autonomia: Post-Political Politics."

Theory Culture and Society, 2:3 (1985). Issue on "The Fate of Modernity."

TriQuarterly, 26 (1973); 30 (1974); 32 (1975); 33 (1975). Issues on Postmodern Art, Literature and Criticism.

Wallace Stevens Journal, 7 (1983). Issue on "Stevens and Postmodern Criticism."

Yale French Studies, 36–37 (1966). Issue on Structuralism.

Zone, 1/2.

NOTES ON CONTRIBUTORS

GERALD L. BRUNS

Gerald L. Bruns holds the William White Chair in English at the University of Notre Dame. He taught previously at the University of Iowa and is author of *Modern Poetry and the Idea of Language: A Critical and Historical Study* (Yale, 1974), *Inventions: Writing, Textuality, and Understanding in Literary History* (Yale, 1982), and a new book entitled *Heidegger's Estrangements* (Yale, 1989).

GAIL FAURSCHOU

Gail Faurschou is completing a doctorate in Sociology at York University, Toronto on the topic of *Fashion, Reproduction, and Publicity Culture*. She has published a paper entitled "Fashion and the Cultural Logic of Postmodernity" in the *Canadian Journal of Political and Social Thought*. She is also writing on the subject of Andy Warhol.

DONALD KUSPIT

Donald Kuspit is Professor of Art History and Philosophy at the State University of New York at Stony Brook. He is a Contributing Editor of *Art in America*, a staff member of *Artforum*, and editor of *Art Criticism*. In 1983, the College Art Association awarded him the Frank Jewett Mather Prize for Distinction in Art Criticism. His most recent books are *The New Subjectivism: Art of the Eighties* (UMI Research Press) and *Louise Bourgeois* (Random House).

DAVID MICHAEL LEVIN

David Michael Levin is Professor of Philosophy at Northwestern University. His books include *Reason and Evidence in Husserl's Phenomenology* (Northwestern, 1970), *The Body's Recollection of Being* (Routledge and Kegan Paul, 1985), and *The Opening of Vision: Nihilism and the Postmodern Situation* (Routledge, 1988). He has also edited an anthology entitled *Pathologies of the Modern Self: Postmodern Studies on Narcissism, Schizophrenia and Depression* (New York University Press, 1987).

FRED MCGLYNN

Fred McGlynn is Associate Professor of Philosophy at the University of Montana. He studied acting in New York in the late fifties before turning to philosophy. He is particularly interested in the theater of Samuel Beckett.

DOROTHEA OLKOWSKI-LAETZ

Dorothea Olkowski-Laetz is Assistant Professor of Philosophy at the College of Charleston (South Carolina). She taught previously at the University of San Diego and the University of Nevada. Her publications include essays on Heidegger, Merleau-Ponty, Derrida, Freudianism, and theories of art and language. She is currently working on a book to be entitled *The Limits of Representation*.

JOHN O'NEILL

John O'Neill is Distinguished Professor of Sociology at York University, Toronto. He is author of many books, including *Perception, Expression and History* (Northwestern 1970), *Sociology as a Skin Trade* (Harper & Row, 1972), *Making Sense Together: An Introduction to Wild Sociology* (Harper & Row, 1974), *Essaying Montaigne* (Routledge and Kegan Paul, 1982), and *Five Bodies: The Human Shape of Modern Society* (Cornell, 1985).

CHARLES E. SCOTT

Charles E. Scott is Professor and Chair of the Department of Philosophy at Vanderbilt University. His books include most recently *The Language of Difference* (Humanities Press, 1987) and previously *Boundaries in Mind* (AAR Studies in Religion, 1982). He is currently Executive Co-Director of the Society for Phenomenology and Existential Philosophy.

BRIAN SEITZ

Brian Seitz recently completed a doctorate in philosophy at the State University of New York at Stony Brook. His dissertation, *The Production of Political Representations*, is an analysis of the political subject constituted by the discourse, practices, and processes of modern, democratic political representation. He has taught at Stony Brook, Parsons School of Design, and Queens College of the City University of New York, and is an Assistant Editor of *Continental Philosophy*.

MARK C. TAYLOR

Mark C. Taylor is William R. Kenan, Jr., Professor of Religion and Director of the Center for the Humanities and Social Sciences at Williams College. He is author or editor of numerous books, including *Journeys to Selfhood: Hegel and Kierkegaard* (1980), *Erring: A Postmodern A/theology* (1984), *Deconstruction in Context: Literature and Philosophy* (1986), and *Altarity* (1987).

STEPHEN H. WATSON

Stephen H. Watson is Associate Professor of Philosophy at the University of Notre Dame. He is a member of the Executive Committee of the Society for Phenomenology and Existential Philosophy and author of many essays in continental philosophy, including "The Closure of Modernism," "Merleau-Ponty's Involvement with Saussure," "The Philosopher's Text," and "The Adventures of the Narrative: Lyotard and the Passage of the Phantasm." He is also an Associate Editor of *Continental Philosophy*.

ALLEN S. WEISS

Allen S. Weiss has published in the fields of philosophy, cinema studies, art history, comparative literature and psychoanalytic theory in such journals as *Art & Text*, *Dada/Surrealism*, *Enclitic*, *October*, *Persistence of Vision*, *Philosophy Today*, *Substance*, etc.. He has edited two special issues of *Art & Text* and has coedited *Psychosis and Sexual Identity* (SUNY Press, 1988).

WILHELM S. WURZER

Wilhelm S. Wurzer is Associate Professor of Philosophy at Duquesne University. His publications include *Nietzsche und Spinoza* (Anton Hain, 1975) and articles in the *Journal of the British Society for Phenomenology*, *Postmodernism and Continental Philosophy* (SUNY Press, 1988), and *The Horizons of Continental Philosophy: Essays on Husserl, Heidegger, and Merleau-Ponty* (Nijhoff/Kluwer, 1988). He is currently completing a book entitled *Heidegger in the Age of Filming*.

About the Editor
HUGH J. SILVERMAN

Hugh J. Silverman is Professor of Philosophy and Comparative Literature at the State University of New York at Stony Brook. He has held visiting teaching posts at the Universities of Warwick and Leeds in England, at the University of Nice in France, and at Stanford University, Duquesne University, and New York University in the United States. Author of *Inscriptions: Between Phenomenology and Structuralism* (Routledge & Kegan Paul, 1987) and more than fifty articles in continental philosophy, philosophical psychology, aesthetics, literary theory, and cultural studies, he is also editor of *Piaget, Philosophy and the Human Sciences* (Humanities/Harvester, 1980), coeditor of *Jean-Paul Sartre: Contemporary Approaches to his Philosophy (Duquesne/Harvester, 1980), Continental Philosophy in America* (Duquesne, 1983) *Descriptions* (SUNY Press, 1985), *Hermeneutics and Deconstruction* (SUNY Press, 1985), *Critical Dialectical Phenomenology* (SUNY Press, 1987), *The Horizons of Continental Philosophy: Essays on Husserl, Heidegger, and Merleau-Ponty* (Nijhoff/Kluwer, 1988), *Postmodernism and Continental Philosophy* (SUNY Press, 1988), and *The Textual Sublime: Deconstruction and its Differences* (SUNY Press, 1989).